Understand Your Brain:
On Its Own @ Work -
A Field Guide

Phil Dixon, MSc
Scott Fitzgerald, MBA

OBI Press

OBI Press
Oxford, North Carolina, USA

ISBN-13: 978-1-7338307-3-7
ISBN-10: 1-7338307-3-1

Understand Your Brain:
Your Brain on its Own @ Work - A Field Guide

This book, *Understand Your Brain: On its Own @ Work – A Field Guide* is the second volume in the *Understand Your Brain* series. If you are new to the brain, or new to understanding the brain, or the understanding of yourself, we strongly suggest that you read the first volume – before reading this book. It is called *Understand Your Brain: For a Change* or, as you will see it referenced through this book, *UYBFAC*. The series of books all go together. Like strawberries and cream, but less tasty.

UYBFAC addressed the fundamentals of the brain, how it works, and how it relates to the self.

This, the second volume in the series, is the first of four volumes which deal with your brain in the workplace. The following sequence lays out the order in which these four books will be offered:

1. Your brain when it is working on its own
2. Your brain when it is working with one other person
3. Your brain when it is leading a team
4. Your brain when it is leading an organization.

The titles of the four volumes will be:

- *Understand Your Brain: On its Own @ Work – A Field Guide*
- *Understand Your Brain: With Another Person @ Work – A Field Guide*
- *Understand Your Brain: With a Team @ Work – A Field Guide*
- *Understand Your Brain: Leading an Organization – A Field Guide*

The contents of this book are shown in the Table of Contents on page 5

Heads up! Warning! Watch out! Do not try this at home!

This book is based on a mixture of lots of research and the opinions of the authors, Phil Dixon and Scott Fitzgerald. It is intended to provide interesting and helpful information about our brains as they relate to working on one's own, working with another person, leading a team and leading an organization.

To the best of our abilities, the information is accurate at the time of publication.

The information provided is NOT, however, intended to give medical, health, psychological, psychiatric, therapeutic, or any other professional advice whether related to those fields or otherwise.

The reader should NOT use the information provided as a substitute for the guidance of specialized health care and/or other providers.

Table of Contents

A Few Notes Up Front to Set the Stage

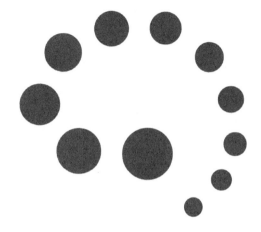

Introduction

We would like to thank those of you that have given us comments about our first book, *Understand Your Brain: For a Change* or *UYBFAC*; henceforth, we will use this abbreviation rather than write the title out in full each time. It has been wonderful hearing how so many people have already put the concepts from the book to use.

<u>Questions you have asked, comments you have made and some comments we want to make.</u>

After many presentations, book signings and questions, there have been several themes that have become clear, so we thought that, up front, we would respond to a few:

1. One of the treasures that is available on the Internet to do research for these types of books is Google Scholar. It is invaluable, yet so many people don't seem to know about it. If you are wanting to follow up some of our thoughts in more detail, then Google "Google Scholar" and you will find a whole new world at your fingertips. The world of scientific papers, journals and articles. The results from Google Scholar explicitly exclude the results from all of the commercial and private websites that clutter up a regular Google search. It gives you just the facts. Just the facts, Ma'am. Just the facts.

2. Another theme to the questions was how does one go about reading scientific papers? Once you get over the initial shock concerning how complex some of them seem to be, then they are actually OK. Or at least, not as bad as they first seem. Hang in there. Here's a few tips. First, they will almost always start with an *abstract*. It's a summary of the main body of the paper itself. Read that first. The abstract is very similar to a book summary, in that most of the time, they give you the characters, the plot, and what happens at the end. No need for spoiler alerts! The abstract will typically give you what the author's hypothesis is, what they did to prove it and what the result was. Start there. The result - it's usually in the last couple of sentences of the abstract. If it intrigues you, read the rest of the abstract. If you are still hooked, then take a look at the paper. You may not understand it all to start with. That's OK. Go with what you do understand. Ignore the fancy words that are there to impress you with how smart the authors are!

3. Many people have asked us to recommend other books about the brain. Book recommendations are clearly a very subjective activity – but we have bitten the bullet and included some of our favorites in Appendix B. We have 'ranked' them with one to five stars. But this is just our opinion. If you get a chance, let us know your thoughts.

4. Talking of papers and books, we have received several comments with regard to the amount of research and support material that we included in *UYBFAC*. We

reviewed your comments and our approach, and decided to maintain that relatively detailed level; we want those of you that like the detail and have a desire to investigate these topics further, to be able to do so – but, as Richard Graves [1] so eloquently puts it, we have kept this detailed material "in the decent obscurity of reference notes" which are included at the very end of the book.

5. The 5 P Model has resonated with many people and is being applied in many directions. One of the first was when Scott and his wife, Stephanie, were doing some relationship work with a couple. They, the couple, decided to use the phrase "You have stepped on my P" as one of the bases of their communication protocol – to indicate that one of them had caused a threat state in the other's brain.

6. We have received the following question many times: Who are these books intended for? As we stated in UYBFAC, it was written primarily for leaders or potential leaders. Like the previous book, this book is written mostly for leaders. But, as most of us have some leadership role within our lives, this book is written for everyone who has a brain. ☺

Literacies.

Moving on from the questions, let's talk literacies for a moment. Now we suspect that's probably not a sentence that you have read very often ☺. Bob Johansen, who has written [2, 3] on the topics of the future and the leadership skills required as we move into the future, introduces the term "literacies" meaning "competence or knowledge in a specified area". We prefer it to just the term "competencies" as it implies something which is deeper, more engrained and more practiced. If you read, or even glanced at, the list of contents of this book, you will have seen that we have selected several "literacies" to be addressed.

So, how and why did we pick the literacies that we did? In some ways it was quite simple. We reviewed the many leadership models that are out there, and there are plenty of them believe us! General models for leadership, the future, global thinking, human interaction - the list goes on. We elected to focus on those literacies that appeared to have the greatest impact, and would, having a knowledge of how the brain works, be most valuable to being able to effectively embrace, develop and master that literacy.

Let's take one of the literacies that Bob offers, by way of example. He calls it "Voluntary Fear Engagement." Now, if you have read UYBFAC you will recall that, for many reasons, the brain severely dislikes the thought of "engaging with our fears." It has evolved to do the exact opposite! You will recall that we all have different things that cause us to be fearful, or that put us into a threat state. These are the, approximately, 60 facets of the 5 P's. So, in order for someone to be able to "Voluntarily Engage Fear" it will be easier if they understand their own fears, which they can do by taking their *Personal Threat Profile*.

The Personal Threat Profile is explained in great detail in *UYBFAC*. If you haven't read this, we recommend that you do so, as it will greatly enhance your understanding of this book. Regardless of whether or not we have convinced you to read the prior book, for your convenience we have included a brief recap in the next few pages.

New discoveries about the brain.

Our knowledge and understanding of neuroscience is constantly changing. There are new discoveries every week. Like all science, some of these discoveries confirm and expand upon our understanding, while others adjust or refute it. In many ways, the more we find out the more that we realize how much more there is to find out!

"New discoveries" is a deliberately loose term. ☺ What we have looked for is new information that is useful for us to include in this book to help further our understanding and application of brain-based neuroscience; by this we mean a couple of things:

1. The information is new to us; we didn't know about it when we wrote *UYBFAC*.
2. The information is new to the world in general - new publications, books and journal articles etc. that have been issued since the publication of *UYBFAC*
3. The information is a new interpretation of existing data

We have, therefore, included in Appendix A, new information about the brain.

A Field Guide? What's a Field Guide?

Some of the words that best describe a Field Guide are "application", "hands-on" and "practical." We received a lot of wonderful feedback about *UYBFAC*, but some of it came with a couple of additions. What can we do about the knowledge of the brain on a day-to-day basis? How can we put it into practice? To answer these questions, we have structured this book in such a manner that, although we introduce a number of new topics and concepts, the focus is on "What to do." As you will have learned from *UYBFAC*, all of our brains are different. Hence any advice on what to do needs to recognize that. What will work for one brain profile, may not work for the next.

We have included, therefore, many lists of approaches that we know have worked. In any given list, however, there are many more items than any one person is likely to need. Pick and choose which of them you feel will work for you, in your situation. And try them out for size!

Book structure

The purpose of this book, as the title suggests, is to examine the aspects of the brain that impact you when you are on your own at work. You may be contemplating who to promote, or planning for your next meeting, or simply taking some time for yourself.

In determining the sequence of topics for this book, we wanted to take two approaches into account. First, we wanted to present the topics in a logical progression - it is easier, for example, to go about making decisions if you understand yourself. In turn, it is difficult to understand yourself, if you are not self-aware. Hence the starting point: Self-Awareness.

In addition, on the chance that reading this book may cause you to change something in your own life, we wanted to remain faithful to our understanding of the way that we all deal with personal change. So, we arranged the topics in the way change frequently occurs.

Furthermore, all of the topics covered by this book interact with each other. It may not, for instance, be possible to pursue your Purpose without having a high degree of Self-Awareness .... and Courage .... and good Decision-Making skills ... and Innovation.

We have structured each chapter as follows:

- ➢ General comments
- ➢ What works
- ➢ Brief examples or case studies
- ➢ Discussion
- ➢ Bottom line summary
- ➢ A call to action

We introduce each topic with some **general comments** to set the lay of the land and to frame the topic.

The next part is **what works**; this portion is intended for those readers who want to get straight to the suggestions about brain-friendly tools and tips, as well as their application. There's no explanation – but a lot of suggestions. It's the direct, results-oriented, bullet-point driven, functional part of the field guide, summarizing everything we have learned that integrates brain-based and many other principles into a no-frills list.

The third part of each chapter is to give some **real-life examples** where a brain-based approach to the topic has worked.

For those who want more detail, theory and explanation: the **discussion** section is next. This is where we add extra layers of information. We refer back to the brain aspects of the topic and add in any new and relevant research. It is for those of you that like to dig in a little deeper and know what is going on in the science behind the scenes. In many instances, this section contains explanations of some of the recommended "what works" bullet points.

The fifth portion is, as it says: **the bottom-line**. If you, as the reader want to get a **summary** of the chapter, this is where you should look.

Finally, the last section, **a call to action,** is a place for you to determine and record what you are going to do with the knowledge you have just gained.

<u>Writing style</u>

Finally, we wanted to make a comment about our writing style, but then we came across a paragraph written by Robert L Solso, [4] which summarized the intent of our style so well, that we quote it here".

> *"The writing style is designed to be interesting while informative. Occasionally, I have incorporated a pun or humorous read in the middle of an otherwise cheerless topic; sometimes the prose turns slightly purple when my enthusiasm gets out of hand, and, at times, the language vacillates from the technical to the whimsical. Many ideas in the book are drawn from highly complicated sources. I have tried to make complex ideas understandable without making them simplistic."*

Other than changing the pronouns from "I" to "we" - what he said ☺

Dedication

We dedicated our previous book to a number of people (and other, four-legged, animals) that had been important in our lives, but who are no longer with us. Unfortunately, that is an ever-growing list. At this time, we would like to honor these people who had major impact on us, but have since moved on:

Frank Fitzgerald III

Jake

Fred Lowder

Pablo Riera

Al Scalise

Rich Stiller

Larry Tesler

Recap of Understand Your Brain: For a Change

In this section, we cover the salient points from *UYBFAC*. We strongly recommend, as we have already said, if you haven't read it, that you do so before embarking on this book. That suggestion is not just so that we can sell you another book, although that would be nice – rather it would give you so much more of an understanding of the brain than this summary.

Here, in summary, is what we learned:

- 99% of the activity of the brain is occurring at a nonconscious level.
- We are all subject to a large number of biases, and even when we learn about our biases it is tough do anything about them.
- We often behave irrationally – for a whole variety of reasons.
- Social pain or emotional pain is handled in the brain in a very similar way to physical pain
- There are many untruths and myths circulating about the brain.
- Chronic stress is really bad for us - both for our bodies and our brains.
- There are a large number of things that can act as triggers to put us under stress.
- There are a large number of things that influence our brains (and hence our thinking) that we are not consciously aware of - anchoring numbers in our brains, for example.
- There are complex interactions between the brain and other parts of our bodies
- Taste is not a simple sense – it is the result of interactions between all our other senses.

Here's what we learned about the brain in slightly more detail:

- That the brain:
  - weighs about 3 pounds and is an energy hog
  - uses oxygen and glucose for energy
  - is made up of 86 billion highly networked neurons
  - has many glial cells which outnumber the neurons
  - is wrinkly
  - is primarily driven by visual cues
  - is plastic i.e. it can change
  - has dozens, if not hundreds, of chemicals running around
  - handles about 11 million bits of information per second – all but 40 of them nonconsciously

- There are Five Brain Principles:
  1. has <u>One</u> purpose – your survival
  2. operates in <u>Two</u> modes – conscious mode and a nonconscious mode
  3. has <u>Three</u> physical layers which have different functions

4. has <u>Four</u> processes going on – cue recognition, thinking, feeling and self-control
5. has <u>Five</u> driving forces

➢ There are Five Brain Dynamics, which operate mostly in nonconscious mode. These are:
1. we are biased
2. we are irrational
3. we are stress-driven
4. most of us naturally resist change
5. we are driven by internal rhythms

➢ There are Five Driving Forces
1. Protection   – we want to feel safe
2. Participation   – we are social and want to engage with others
3. Prediction   – if we can predict what is going to happen, we can feel even safer
4. Purpose   – we want to have meaning in our lives
5. Pleasure   – we seek to have some pleasure (and reward) in our lives

And here's what we covered about the "Self," i.e., YOU!

➢ That you can take a deeper look at yourself, what you are driven by, and how you might react and behave by using some simple profiles.
➢ You can identify some of your tendencies by looking at your habits, biases, patterns, triggers, and your worldview.
➢ You can examine how the general influences that we all have, as well as your specific influences and influencers affect you.
➢ Looking at your context, you can help explain why you are driven (or not) to do certain things and resist others, i.e., what has happened in your past, where you want to be in the future, and what is going on in your world right now.

Finally, in order to pull all of this together and apply it to the various challenges and changes that you will inevitably face, you will need a healthy brain. Research suggests that you can best maintain your brain health by:

➢ Identifying what your stress drivers are, using the Personal Threat Profile.
➢ Identifying your current Personal Threat Context.
➢ Ensuring that you have a good, healthy diet.
➢ Exercising appropriately.
➢ Using deep breathing as a way of ameliorating your reaction to stress.
➢ Getting an appropriate amount of sleep.
➢ Associating with the right people.
➢ Having a healthy relationship with a significant other.
➢ Having a spiritual life which works for you.

- ➤ Holding a future-oriented, positive attitude that encourages, supports and facilitates growth.
- ➤ Creating a positive and supportive social life, i.e., family and friends.
- ➤ Being mindful and practicing a meditation regime that works for you.
- ➤ Listening to music or playing an instrument.
- ➤ Using brain training exercises.
- ➤ Being careful about your use of technology.
- ➤ Increasing your education and engaging in intellectual pursuits.
- ➤ Being ethical and moral, surrounding yourself with similar people, and engaging in business and political practices that support your values.

---

[1] Robert Graves: The Assault Heroic. (1990
[2] Johansen, B. (2012). Leaders Make the Future: (2nd ed.). Berrett-Koehler Publishers.
[3] Johansen, B. (2017). The New Leadership Literacies (1st ed.). Berrett-Koehler.
[4] Solso, R. E. (2003). The Psychology of Art and the Evolution of the Conscious Brain. MIT Press.

Chapter 1:

Self-awareness

1. Self-Awareness

General comments

We thought that becoming increasingly self-aware would be a good starting point for any of us, whether we are leaders or not. We certainly thought it would be a great place to start this book. BUT. An apparently simple phrase can have so many different interpretations. At the most detailed level it could mean we are aware of what is going on in our bodies and our brains at any given moment. At the other end of the timescale, it could mean we are aware of our patterns over time. Or it could mean are we actually conscious - as in the famous "cogito ergo sum" – I think, therefore, I am.

Peter Drucker, arguably one of the most influential leadership and management gurus in recent times, published a paper in Harvard Business Review. [5] The sub-title of the article was this:

> *"Success in the knowledge economy comes to those who know themselves - their strengths, their values, and how they best perform."*

Our focus in this chapter is to follow Drucker's advice and help you become aware, not only of what is going on within yourself, but also to understand how you are impacting others – and both of these are in the moment and over time.

What works [a]

> ➤ Identify what fears you are driven by
> ➤ Drop your "personal internal armor"
> ➤ Identify your values and the principles that guide you
> ➤ Identify your passions and what you love to do
> ➤ Identify your aspirations and what you want to experience and achieve
> ➤ Identify the environment you require to be happy and energized
> ➤ Identify your biases, habits, patterns and triggers
> ➤ Identify your reactions i.e. the thoughts, feelings, and behaviors that reveal who you are (your strengths and weaknesses)
> ➤ Identify your impact and the effect you have on others
> ➤ Use new life events, such as a new job, or role, or project to gain a new insight into yourself
> ➤ Use significant emotional or life events to gain a new insight into yourself
> ➤ Identify small victories – gain insights from everyday situations
> ➤ Assess your performance based upon reality rather than beliefs or assumptions
> ➤ Recognize and be able to label your own emotions
> ➤ Recognize how you are going about making the next decision

---

[a] Taken from a variety of sources, each of which is cited at some point in the rest of the chapter

- ➤ Ask for feedback on how you are coming across to others and on your abilities and behaviors
- ➤ Identify and confront your assumptions
- ➤ Keep learning – a commitment to learning and growing is key to self-awareness
- ➤ Practice asking deep questions
- ➤ Practice listening to the answers and notice the feelings and thoughts that they bring up in you
- ➤ Be fully present when you are in conversations
- ➤ Notice what you notice
- ➤ Cultivate humility
- ➤ Be willing to give up on a viewpoint
- ➤ Admit when you are wrong or don't have the answer
- ➤ Practice self-acceptance
- ➤ Keep a multi-year self-awareness journal based on your assumptions, decisions and expected outcomes

Just as a heads up, if you decide to investigate these areas, many of them are written up in *UYBFAC*.

Brief examples or case studies

Some years back, Phil who was the Acting Director of Information Technology for a large well-known company, received a call from the Executive Assistant to the CEO. Could Phil come up and see the CEO immediately? Talk about scary! His brain went straight into threat mode. As he was walking over to the CEO's office, Phil found himself shaking. Literally shaking. Phil stopped and analyzed what was going on in his head. This was way before he knew anything about what goes on in our brains and he realized that he felt like a thirteen or fourteen year-old boy who had done something wrong, and was being called to the Headmaster's (Principal's) office in order to find out what his punishment was to be. This brings up certain clues about mental models that we all hold, but let's leave that be for the time being. ☺ Phil took a deep breath, told himself that the request could be anything and there was no point in prejudging the purpose of the visit and confidently knocked on the CEO's office door. As it turned out, the CEO was just inquiring as to whether an idea he had was feasible and the conversation was as pleasant as it could have possibly been.

In 2019, Scott was working for a well-known utility firm on the west coast when he was asked to meet for dinner with one of the senior executives running a critical arm of the operation. As the conversation progressed, it became clear that this executive, who we will call John, was struggling with his role in the company. He revealed that he had come across some information that indicated he was no longer being invited to a senior meeting held every Thursday. As the discussion continued, John reflected that he had been disenchanted by the usefulness of the meeting in the past and was glad in some ways that he was not required to go anymore. It was, however, bothering him that he was not invited anymore. Scott pointed out this apparent contradiction and incongruency and John revealed that it was like he had been "thrown out of the tribe". While he hated the time spent in this "useless" meeting, he loved the inclusion and status that came with being on this list of invitees. As the conversation continued, John took note of the conversation he was having internally and related it to having been cut from his high school football team. "All I remember was I was no longer on the team". He laughed and said that he hated football but loved wearing the uniform. In a rather stark moment of reflection he slowly raised his glass and said, "I have been joining tribes all my life and contributing as little as possible to stay in them. It might be time for me to examine what tribe I can contribute to vs simply join". He is now the CEO of a company that serves the same industry but whose services are aligned with his passion and expertise.

Recently Scott become a grandfather thanks to the good work of his daughter and her husband. As part of this new chapter in his life he and his wife chose to move from his home which was 45 minutes from his daughter to 4 minutes from his daughter and her family in order to be involved with the new-born grandchild. During this transition Scott noticed a significant level of angst internally as he made this move which should have been one of the most exciting times in his life. He noticed that he was easily irritated or worn out at the end of each day during the move process. When he examined why he noted that nearly every pattern that he had established in his previous home, such as wake up schedule, eating schedule, favorite restaurants, dry cleaning and even gym visits had to be rewritten and established. "This was surprisingly hard. It seems that with age, each new habit seemed to take so much energy to change or establish." His wife noted, "Almost daily he would talk about why he was feeling so anxious. I appreciated that he was not ignoring his feelings and actions. He was willing to notice it and take steps to manage the negative impact to himself and those around him". Scott later reflected that the new patterns created a tremendous amount of stress and he had to remain mindful that while it was normal to be "Out of sorts" he had to pay close attention to the signs of irritation he still had to ask himself probing questions which allowed him to become more aware of what was naturally happening. By doing this, he was able to figure out a way to work with his brain to create a more productive, positive experience in his daily life.

Discussion

As we did many times in *UYBFAC*, we thought it would be good to start this chapter with a definition. As in the past, this proved somewhat difficult until Tasha Eurich came to our rescue with a recent, highly readable, book [6] and an article published in Harvard Business Review. [7] But before we go there, she gives us some interesting data:

> *"We've found that even though most people believe they are self-aware, self-awareness is a truly rare quality: We estimate that only 10%-15% of the people studied fit the criteria."*

She and her team propose a two-part definition:

> *"Internal self-awareness represents how clearly we see our own values, passions, aspirations, fit with our environment, reactions (including thoughts, feelings, behaviors, strengths and weaknesses) and impact on others.*

> *"External self-awareness means understanding how others view us in terms of the same factors."*

They found that:

> *" … internal self-awarenes is associated with higher job and relationship satisfaction, personal and social control, and happiness."*

and that lack of it related to anxiety, stress and depression.

So that indicates that self-awareness is an activity or state that is worthy of some attention. Self-awareness is not a passive activity. We find in our coaching practices and our seminars that the process of becoming self-aware requires some rather deep self-discovery and inventory. This cannot be done in a vacuum. Often times it requires an accountability partner or coach. Take a moment and think about your own internal inventory based on Eurich's definition. Have you taken the time to truly script out the elements she described? You will find that the more active and prescriptive you are in identifying your values, passions, aspirations etc., your brain will start to seek the things that support those well-defined elements and discount those things that do not support your well-defined outcomes. The brain knows how to filter distractions; however, it needs help by actively, consciously, and in a calm state, defining the things most important to us in the context of the various criteria we have discussed so far in this chapter.

In addition, Eurich and her team found that:

> *" … people who know how others see them are more skilled at showing empathy and taking others' perspectives. For leaders who see themselves as their employees do, their employees tend to have a better relationship with them, feel more satisfied with them, and see them as more effective in general."*

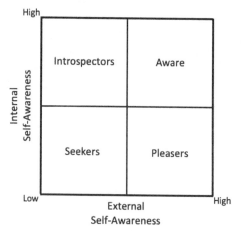

In their words:

Introspectors	Are clear on who they are, but don't challenge their own views or search for blind spots by getting feedback from others. This can harm their relationships and limit their success.
Seekers	Do not yet know who they are, what they stand for, or how their team sees them. As a result, they might feel stuck, or frustrated with their performance or relationships.
Pleasers	Can be so focused on appearing a certain way to others that they could be overlooking what matters to them. Over time, they tend to make choices that aren't in service to their own success and fulfillment.
Aware	Know who they are and what they want to accomplish and seek out and value others' opinion. This is where leaders begin to fully realize the true benefits of self-awareness.

They found a couple of other interesting and somewhat unexpected results. Once again, in their words:

Experience and power hinder self-awareness.

- People do not always learn from experience
- Expertise can get in the way of rooting out more information
- Seeing ourselves as experienced can prevent us from doing our homework, seeking disconfirming evidence, and questioning our assumptions
- More experienced managers were less accurate in assessing their leadership effectiveness
- More experienced managers more significantly overvalued their skills in 19 out of 20 competencies

Introspection doesn't always help to increase self-awareness. People who introspect:

- are less self-aware
- report worse job-satisfaction and well-being

When doing any introspection, "what" questions are more productive than "why" questions. In more detail, asking yourself "What may have caused you to react a certain way" will lead to richer results than asking yourself "Why did you react the way you did."

- "Why" questions tend to result in rationalizing and denying
- "What" questions tend to lead to being open to new information and learning from it.

Bottom line? Research shows that people who are self-aware:

- ➤ are more confident
- ➤ are more creative
- ➤ are apt to make more sound decisions
- ➤ build stronger relationships
- ➤ communicate more effectively
- ➤ are less likely to lie, cheat and steal
- ➤ are better workers
- ➤ get more promotions
- ➤ are more effective leaders
- ➤ have more satisfied employees
- ➤ produce more profitable companies

What's not to like?

On the other hand, research about people who are not self-aware is pretty scary; here's a few examples from Euric:

In one very large study (n = 13,000):

> " ... researchers found almost no relationship between self-assessed performance and objective performance ratings."

In another:

> " ... more than 33 percent of engineers rated their performance in the top 5% relative to their peers."

In yet another:

> " ... a full 94% of college professors thought they were above average at their jobs."

Empirical research shows that employees who lack self-awareness:

> " ... reduce decision quality by an average of 36 percent, hurt coordination by 46 percent, and increase conflict by 30%."

One study with hundreds of publicly traded companies found:

> " ... that those with poor financial returns were 79 percent more likely to employ large numbers of un-self-aware employees."

and

> "When leaders are out of touch with reality, they're six times more likely to derail."

You have to love the next piece of research! In a study of prisoners in England, Sedikides et al. [8] compared two groups – prisoners, most of whom had committed violent crimes, and average non-incarcerated members of the community. They compared nine personality traits, namely: moral, kind to others, trustworthy, honest, dependable, compassionate, generous, self-controlled and law-abiding. It's worth reading that list again.

Wait. Now it gets really good. Here's how Eurich describes it:

> " ... not only did they (the prisoners) rate themselves as superior to their fellow inmates, on no fewer than eight of the nine traits, they even thought they were superior to average non-incarcerated community members. The one exception .... inexplicably, they rated themselves as equally law-abiding compared to community members."

When we came to write this part of the book, we realized that there is a lot of overlap between "becoming self-aware" and "peeling the layers off your own personal onion" so it's not an accident that the Personal Onion chapter comes next. In a way, both chapters are about examining yourself – but if you are not self-aware, then it is almost impossible to go about peeling back the layers of the onion. There are some fundamental principles that need to be in place first.

Some people have stated that the opposite of self-awareness is self-delusion. The word "delusion" however implies some level of conscious intent. Some sort of deliberate action. "Self-unawareness" is not a deliberate act. It is the absence or void of intent or deliberation. We'll try to illustrate by way of an example. This is a real-life case of a woman with almost no self-awareness. The names and circumstances have been changed in order to protect the people involved. Let's call her Mary.

Mary was a very senior software engineer and was often the smartest person in the room. At least she would always tell people she was. Again and again! When she wasn't satisfied with the way that one of her colleagues was doing their job, she would tell them, in no uncertain terms, directly and brutally. In one case, Mary was dissatisfied with the marketing plan that the marketing team had developed so she developed one of her own. Needless to say, it was not that good and was not well-received. In meeting after meeting, she would berate the other people in the room, and would be downright rude to the rest. She would fly off the handle at the slightest provocation. She belittled her boss, and his boss, saying that they clearly did not know how to manage.

Yet, when she was taken to one side to discuss her behavior, she couldn't see anything wrong with it. When it was pointed out to her that her behavior and emotional outbursts were harming her career in the company, she assured everyone in the room that she was in total control of her emotions at all times. This type of conversation took place several times over as many weeks. At one point the Chief Technology Officer of the company, together with a supporter and mentor of hers, got involved in order to counsel her. Even after that "intervention" her behavior did not change and she was terminated as she was becoming very toxic to the whole team.

As part of her severance package, she was assigned an executive coach to help her address the behavioral issues that she exhibited. After meeting with her coach, a couple of times, she independently decided to write a letter to the CEO, describing what was wrong with everyone else, that there were many people in the company who loved her, and that if everyone else changed, she would be willing to come back to the company.

As we said, this is a real story. Not one whit of it made up. That behavior illustrates having low "self-awareness." Whether it becomes from being unaware or self-delusional, the result can be the same.

On a different, but related note, Eurich describes the relationship between self-absorption, narcissism and social media. She cites a 2015 study by Utz: [9]

> *"Even though social media is supposed to be social ... maintaining relationships can often be the last reason we use these platforms. At the top of the list is sharing information about ourselves, which is often called self-presentation."*

She notes that since the year 2000, when the use of social media sites exploded people started becoming less empathetic and more self-centered. She then asks a crucial question. Is social media causing our self-absorption? One study had participants spend just 35 minutes online; one half spent time on a social media site and the other half on a mapping site. Those that were on the social media site showed significantly higher narcissism levels, suggesting that not only does social media activity increase these levels, but has a virtually immediate impact. (It is amusing to see the social media sites that were the basis of some of these studies ... MySpace, Friendster, etc.)

She then translates this to the workplace:

> *" ... while narcissistic leaders can be confident setting a clear vision, they tend to overrate their performance, dominate decision processes, seek excessive recognition, and are more likely to behave unethically."*

So how do we become more self-aware? One of the first things we need to do, is, as we have suggested earlier, to identify the fears by which we are driven. We can do this by answering the questions in the Personal Threat Profile. Then we need to drop our "personal internal armor." That's part of the process of becoming honest with ourselves.

Once again, Tasha Euric [10] comes to our aid. She suggests a number of attributes that self-aware people have and some specific actions that we can take to become more self-aware, all of which are well researched:

Self-aware people *"understand their:*

- *values (the principles that guide them)*
- *passions (what they love to do)*
- *aspirations (what they want to experience and achieve)*
- *fit (the environment they require to be happy and energized)*
- *patterns (consistent ways of thinking, feeling and behaving)*
- *reactions (the thoughts, feelings, and behaviors that reveal their strengths and weaknesses)*
- *impact (the effect they have on others)"*

Most of these topics are covered in the next chapter on Your Personal Onion, so we won't go into all of them now. But let's dig in a little deeper to the last one – impact! Again, from Euric:

"So far, each pillar of insight has been about us – what we value, what we're passionate about, what we aspire to do, what environment we need, how we behave, how we respond to the world. But to be truly self-aware, we must build on that to understand our impact: that is, how our behavior affects others."

Euric adds:

" … and remember, not only is there little to no relationship between internal and external self-awareness, having one without the other can often do more harm than good."

She goes on to say:

"The key skill we must develop to read our impact is perspective-taking, or the ability to imagine what others are thinking and feeling."

She suggests that people who have a highly developed sense of self-awareness, use their life experiences to constantly enhance their skills, during three types of event:

➢ When they get a new role, a new set of rules, or a change of job or project
➢ Earthquake events – an event of significant life or emotional impact
➢ Everyday insights – gaining insight from otherwise mundane situations

Euric suggests that our errors in, or absence of, self-awareness are due to three blind-spots:

➢ Knowledge blindness – we base our assessments on our beliefs rather than how we actually perform
➢ Emotion blindness – we drive our assessments and decisions based on emotion without realizing it
➢ Behavior blindness – we aren't very good at understanding how we are coming across to others

She continues by suggesting three steps to ameliorate the situation:

➢ Identify and confront our assumptions
➢ Keep learning – a commitment to learning and growing is key to self-awareness
➢ Seek feedback on our abilities and behaviors

Sassenrath [11], however, offers us a word of caution, in particular with regard to perspective taking:

"Threat can emerge from the very act of perspective taking if the target of perspective taking is perceived as too different from the self or if adopting another's perspective creates the potential for negative self-evaluation."

This clearly ties back into the concept of the Personal Threat Profile. If you know your Personal Threat Profile, and can anticipate how another's perspective might impact you, and potentially put you into a threat state, then you can at least be prepared.

Back to the question of becoming more self-aware, Eurich suggests three specific strategies:

> Become an informer

> *"Instead of logging on and posting a selfie, an update about their upcoming vacation, or their latest professional achievement, they (people with high self-awareness) used social media as a way to truly engage and stay connected with others."*

> Cultivate humility

> *"Focus on other people. Admit when you don't have the answers. Be willing to learn from others. Be willing to give up your viewpoint. As a result, people on teams with humble leaders are more engaged, more satisfied with their jobs, and less likely to leave."*

> Practice self-acceptance

> *"Understand your objective reality and choose to like yourself anyway. Monitor your own inner monologue. Not only be aware of yourself but love the person you find out you are."*

In 2002, Timothy Wilson an American social psychologist, writer and Professor of Psychology at the University of Virginia is well-known for his research on self-knowledge and the influence of the nonconscious mind. In 2002, he published a book entitled *Strangers to Ourselves* [(12)]. The title gives us a strong clue as to Wilson's view about how easy it is to become self-aware. He expands this viewpoint throughout the book, saying that since so much of what we do is driven by our nonconscious, we are, in essence, on a futile journey trying to become self-aware by introspection. In his book, Burton [(13)] summarizes:

> *"Wilson suggests that we are better off by combining introspection with observing how others react to us and deducing the otherwise inaccessible nature of our minds from their responses. If others see us differently than we see ourselves, we need to incorporate this alternative view of ourselves into our personal narrative."*

This combination of approaches, i.e. self-review and feedback from others, has been combined into a well-known tool in the Leadership Development field which is known as the JoHari window. [(14)] Once again, like many things in this field, it is a 2 x 2 grid, and we show it on the next page.

The principle of this grid, as with all similar 2 x 2 grids, is that it combines two dimensions; in this case they are whether you are aware of something about yourself and whether other people are aware of that thing about you. If a personal attribute is known to you, and known by everyone else, as indicated by the top left quadrant, then it is something which is out in the open for all to see.

	Known to Self	Unknown to Self
Known to Others	**OPEN** Public knowledge; what I show you	**BLIND** Feedback - your gift to me
Unknown to Others	**HIDDEN** Private; mine to share if I trust you	**UNCONSCIOUS** Unknown; new awareness can emerge

If, on the other hand, you know something about yourself and you do not show it to other people, that is a secret or is private. You are only likely to share it with someone who has earned your trust.

Now let's look at attributes that you are not aware of. If other people see them, and you don't, then this is a blind spot that you have. You can become more self-aware by having other people give you feedback – and making you aware of those attributes. Whether you register the feedback and act upon it is another matter entirely. ☺

Finally, there may be attributes that you are not aware of, and other people are not aware of them in you either. They may show up over time, but, for right now, we are not concerned with them.

A final element of an analysis of self-awareness, in addition to all of the factors described above, is that we are not very good at looking at ourselves, even when we intend to do our very best. Our brains, both the conscious and nonconscious modes, send us dubious "messages." On the one hand, those messages can be based on feelings of inadequacy or self-doubt. On the other hand, feelings of over-confidence and narcissism could be coming to the fore. If and when you decide to explore and become more self-aware, keep these "messages" in mind.

Speaking of being self-aware, and on a humorous note, Scott was running a workshop in 2019 on self-awareness. A member of the audience said, "I am often skeptical of other's opinions of me when I ask for feedback". This piqued Scott's interest, so he asked, "Why do you ask for feedback then?" the audience member said, "Because my annual review indicated that I never solicit feedback, so I recently tried to get some from eight of my colleagues." Scott asked him if the recent feedback had any common themes and what did he learn? The response was "The common theme is that no one likes to give me feedback because I appear to be skeptical." Scott commented that, ironically, he had done a good job of increasing his self-awareness. When Scott asked him if he would be taking action on that feedback, he smiled and replied, "I am not sure it's possible."

Finally, we would like to add in some additional comments about your "worldview." In *UYBFAC*, we spent some time talking about the facets that might lead to your overall worldview. Since then, we have discovered a gold-mine of a paper by Mark E. Koltko-Rivera. [b] In it, Koltko-Rivera summarizes much of the work done on worldviews over the past hundred years and develops a "comprehensive model of the dimensions of world-view." En route, he gives us a working definition of worldview which, although somewhat lengthy, we reproduce here:

> *"A worldview is a way of describing the universe and life within it, both in terms of what is and what ought to be. A given worldview is a set of beliefs that includes limiting statements and assumptions regarding what exists and what does not (either in actuality, or in principle), what objects or experiences are good or bad, and what objectives, behaviors, and relationships are desirable or undesirable. A worldview defines what can be known or done in the world, and how it can be known or done. In addition to defining what goals can be sought in life, a worldview defines what goals should be pursued. Worldviews include assumptions that may be unproven, and even unprovable, but these assumptions are superordinate, in that they provide the epistemic and ontological foundations for other beliefs within a belief system."*

In other words, your worldview is that package which defines all of your positions, beliefs and stances on almost every issue – whether they are realistic and provable, or fictitious and simply work for you.

In order to become self-aware, understanding your own worldview is imperative. As a means to that end, in Appendix C, we provide an extract from Koltko-Rivera's model which outlines a comprehensive set of dimensions for a describing or establishing one's worldview. We encourage you to take a look. In the next book we will be exploring the use of these dimensions as a way of predicting harmony and agreement, or confusion and conflict, between individuals.

In *UYBFAC* we emphasized the need to get help when you are trying to understand yourself. As unfortunate as it may be, each of us is ill-equipped when it comes to understanding ourselves fully without help. We are biased in that we tend not to be able to look at ourselves in the mirror. So, in becoming self-aware, getting help from others is important. This bias not only affects us when we reflect upon who we are but influences us moment-to-moment.

"Most of us think well of ourselves, often unrealistically so" report Field and Kuperberg [15] before going on to give many examples of this self-positivity bias. They then question some of the research techniques that have been used to support this self-positivity bias, suggesting that there may be better ways of measuring whether it really is true or not. Guess what? They reaffirmed that it is true but did so, not by questionnaire as is typically the case, but by taking objective electrical measurements inside the brain.

---

[b] We would like to thank Dr. Larry Kuznar for bringing this gem of a paper to our attention.

"Event-related potentials (ERPs), a direct measure of neural activity with excellent temporal resolution, are an ideal technique for this purpose"

What they found was that their test subjects did, indeed, have a built-in bias:

" … making them more likely to expect positive information when a scenario referred to themselves. This finding indicates that the self-positivity bias is available online, acting as a general schema that directly influences real-time."

On a slightly different note, at the end of 2019, Phil was working with one of our partners, doing some coaching specifically designed to help a senior executive increase his self-awareness. Our partner uses a video camera to help people become more self-aware of how they come across to others. Before the video session began, the executive was asked to complete a series of questions about himself. His answers were then used as a basis to have him act, on video, in accordance with his answers. We include the list of questions in Appendix C, so that you too might have the chance to determine your own answers – and how you would use those answers to improve how you came across on video.

We opened this chapter with a reference to Peter Drucker, and we propose to close it with some advice from him with regard to developing self-awareness. He refers to it as feedback analysis, and he has used it to become aware of his strengths. His summary of what it is and how useful it can be, perfectly rounds out our review of self-awareness, and we cite extracts from the article:

"Whenever you make a key decision or take a key action, write down what you expect will happen. Nine or 12 months later, compare the actual results with your expectations…. Practiced consistently, this simple method will show you within a fairly short period of time, maybe two or three years, where your strengths lie - and this is the most important thing to know. The method will show you what you are doing or failing to do that deprives you of the full benefits of your strengths. It will show you where you are not particularly competent. And finally, it will show you where you have no strengths and cannot perform.

Several implications for action follow from feedback analysis. First and foremost, concentrate on your strengths. Put yourself where your strengths can produce results. Second, work on improving your strengths. Analysis will rapidly show where you need to improve skills or acquire new ones. It will also show the gaps in your knowledge - and those can usually be filled. Third, discover where your intellectual arrogance is causing disabling ignorance and overcome it. Far too many people - especially people with great expertise in one area - are contemptuous of knowledge in other areas or believe that being bright is a substitute for knowledge…. It is equally essential to remedy your bad habits - the things you do or fail to do that inhibit your effectiveness and performance. Such habits will quickly show up in the feedback.

At the same time, feedback will also reveal when the problem is a lack of manners. Manners are the lubricating oil of an organization. It is a law of nature that two moving bodies in contact with each other [to] create friction. This is as true for human beings as it is for inanimate objects. Manners – simple things like saying 'please' and 'thank you' and knowing a person's name or asking after her family - enable two people to work together whether they like each other or not. Bright people, especially bright young people, often do not understand this. If analysis shows that someone's brilliant work fails again and again as soon as cooperation from others is required, it probably indicates a lack of courtesy - that is, a lack of manners.

Comparing your expectations with your results also indicates what not to do. We all have a vast number of areas in which we have no talent or skill and little chance of becoming even mediocre.

In those areas a person and especially a knowledge worker should not take on work, jobs, and assignments.

For knowledge workers 'How do I perform' may be an even more important question than 'What are my strengths?' This leads to the following questions:

Am I a listener or a reader?
How do I best learn?
Do I act on this knowledge?
Do I work well with people or am I a loner?
If you do work well with people, you then must ask "In what relationship?"
Do I produce results as a decision maker or as an adviser?
Do I perform well under stress or do I need a highly structured and predictable environment?
Do I work best in a big organization or a small one?"

While not strictly part of "Your Brain on its Own" Drucker continues with advice on relationships at work.

"Managing yourself requires taking responsibility for relationships."

"The first step is to accept the fact that other people are as much individuals as you yourself are. They perversely insist on behaving like human beings. This means that they too have their strengths; they too have their ways of getting things done; they too have their values. To be effective, therefore, you have to know the strengths, the performance modes, and the values of your coworkers."

"The second part of relationship responsibility is taking responsibility for communication."

Wait! What? Is he saying that if I initiate a communication I am responsible for the success of that communication? Shouldn't it be the other way around? Surely, it's their problem to interpret what I say – and understand what I actually meant? Well, no. If you are part of a communication process it is your responsibility to communicate in as clear a manner as possible, to deliver the message in a way that the recipient can best hear it (i.e. in accordance with their profiles, not yours) and to check in on the correct and accurate transmission and interpretation of the communication.

Many managers and leaders become very surprised when we tell them their degree of responsibility; we often hear that their mental model is that it's up to their staff to adapt to their style. Wrong! We will cover this in a lot more detail in our next book, Your Brain With Another Person.

Bottom line summary

Drucker's comments are all pretty heady stuff – and this from one of the most well-known and respected leadership coaches. For example, lack of manners, intellectual arrogance and disabling ignorance – all as part of not being self-aware. It seems that it is a very important subject that we would all be wise to become better at.

Being self-aware seems to provide us with a wide array of advantages, both from a personal point of view and a leadership point of view. Becoming self-aware, however, requires a focus and a combination of self-reflection and seeking feedback from trusted others.

What's next?

What one or two things am I going to focus on in order to increase mt self-awareness?
What, specifically, am I going to do about it/them?
How will I measure whether I have been successful?

[5] Drucker, P. F. (1999). Managing Oneself. *Harvard Business Review*, 1–11.
[6] Eurich, T. (2017). Insight. Currency Books.
[7] Eurich, T. (2018). What Self-Awareness Really Is (and How to Cultivate It). *Harvard Business Review*, 1–8.
[8] Sedikides, C., Meek, R., Alicke, M. D., & Taylor, S. (2013). Behind bars but above the bar: Prisoners consider themselves more prosocial than non-prisoners. *British Journal of Social Psychology*, 53(2), 396–403. http://doi.org/10.1111/bjso.12060
[9] Utz, S. (2015). The function of self-disclosure on social network sites: Not only intimate, but also positive and entertaining self-disclosures increase the feeling of connection. *Computers in Human Behavior*, 45, 1–10.
[10] Eurich, T. (2017). Insight. Currency Books.
[11] Sassenrath, C., Hodges, S. D., & Pfattheicher, S. (2016). It's All About the Self. *Current Directions in Psychological Science*, 25(6), 405–410. http://doi.org/10.1177/0963721416659253
[12] Wilson, T. D. (2004). Strangers to Ourselves. Belknap Press.
[13] Burton, R. A. (2008). On Being Certain. St. Martin's Press.

[14] Created by Joseph Luft and Harrington Ingham in 1955
[15] Fields, E. C., & Kuperberg, G. R. (2015). Loving yourself more than your neighbor: ERPs reveal online effects of a self-positivity bias. *Social Cognitive and Affective Neuroscience*, 10(9), 1202–1209. http://doi.org/10.1093/scan/nsv004

Chapter 2:

Peeling Back the Layers
of
Your Personal Onion

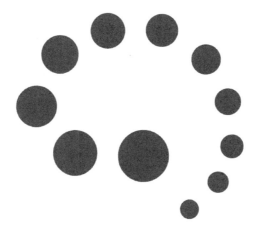

2. Peeling The Layers of Your Personal Onion

General comments

In *UYBFAC* we made reference to the process of looking at yourself being a little like taking the layers off an onion. This is what we suggest that you do as the beginning of understanding who you are, either as an individual or as a leader. Before you can start to look at what is going on in your brain, or indeed, in the brains of other people, you need to have done some internal reflection and measurement. It's a little like deciding to buy some new clothes. First you need to understand what size you are, whether you have plans to lose weight, what you want the clothes for and what is your overall fashion taste.

This section will mostly be a reminder or check list for your journey. I doubt whether any of us would choose to do all of the activities listed below, so select a sub-set. As you make your selection, think about why you are electing not to do the others. Is it because you don't have time, don't think that topic is important for you, or for some other reason? Maybe you might discover something that you would rather not? Just saying! ☺

Assuming that you decide to review your life and find out who you really are, there are a couple of words of caution. For many of us, as we start such a review, the voices in our head will start to judge or criticize. As we have mentioned, if we can sway these "inner critics" from *being judgmental* to *being inquisitive*, it opens the door to a more creative journey in effectively understanding your brain.

What works:

As a reminder, here's a list of the brain-oriented exercises that you could do to find out who you are:

➢ Take your Personal Threat Profile: Find out what threat/reward facets are important and unimportant to you and which of the 5 P's are your driving forces.
➢ Review your Personal Threat Context: Learn what overall stress factors you have going on
➢ Review how healthy you feel – physically, emotionally, and spiritually: What might get in the way of a growth journey to learn about yourself?
➢ Review the three different types of biases and identify the biases that you bring to the table. What could you do to limit any negative impact they may have in your future and that of others?
➢ Review the types of things that might cause you to behave 'irrationally': Identify where you might tend to make 'irrational' decisions and what impact that might have on you and others
➢ Review the stress curve: Identify where your natural 'set-point' on the stress curve is. What can you do to better manage your stress?

- Review how you tend to see and react to change – large and small: Understand the potential traps if you decide to make some changes
- Review your natural rhythms: Learn when you do your best work
- Review the section on the relationship between brain, heart and lungs: Remind yourself how to use simple deep breathing as a way to set yourself up to deal better with stress
- Review the amount of sleep you are getting: What actions might you take to get better sleep habits?
- Review the section on the Brain and Food: What you could you do to improve your diet?
- Review your exercise regime: What simple things could you do to improve it?
- Review your love and sex life: What changes could you or you and your partner engage in, if any?
- Review your spiritual life: What spiritual practices do you engage in on a regular basis? Do these practices work for you at this stage of your life?
- Review your overall attitude to life: What is your overall attitude? Where, for example, are you on the positivity-negativity spectrum?
- Review your family life: What is working in your family life? What are the pleasures? Where are the stresses?
- Review your mindfulness/meditation practices: What do you do in the way of mindfulness? What might be useful to add in?
- Review your habits with respect to music: Do you listen to music? Do you play an instrument? Do you congregate with others to sing? What additions would you like to make?
- Review your brain training regime: Do you have an explicit brain training regime? Do you use any of the more easily available games/exercises? Would an explicit regime be advisable?
- Review your use of technology: How much time do you spend staring at a screen? How much does your use of technology rule your life? How does your use of technology impact others?
- Think about which stage of life you are in – and the impact on the brain: Are there any practices or interventions that you could introduce that might increase your prospects on maintaining better brain health as you age?
- Review your ethical and moral practices: Are you satisfied with how you and the company that you work for approach ethics?

In addition, you might look at those things that are more self-oriented. Again, as a reminder, here are some of the things that you might look at:

- Take your brain profile. [16]
- Learn what brain exercises might give you better brain health.
- Review your chronotype [17] – see also your natural rhythms.
- Review what your tendencies are with respect to the eight focus areas in team conversations: Is that stance helpful for you at this stage in your career?

- ➢ Review where you spend your time with regard to advocacy or inquiry: Is that appropriate for you right now?
- ➢ Review your approach with regard to the TAPS model (Tell-Ask, Problem-Solution): Is that the best approach for you with what you will be facing in the future?
- ➢ Take a Five Factor Inventory test: What do you have to learn from these results?
- ➢ Take a Zimbardo Time Perspective Inventory: What are you learning from these results?
- ➢ Take a Social Style test: What are you learning from these results?
- ➢ Take a Belbin Team Inventory test: What are you learning from these results?
- ➢ Take a Leadership Work-Styles test: What are you learning from these results?
- ➢ Take the Extraordinary Leader test: What is there to learn from these results?
- ➢ Take the Leadership Circle test: What can you take away from these results?
- ➢ Assuming that you have reviewed your biases as described above, review the habit that you typically bring into your actions and reactions: Are they helpful for you and the people around you?
- ➢ Assuming that you have reviewed your biases as described above, review the habits that you typically bring into your actions and reactions. Are they helpful to you and the people around you?
- ➢ Review the patterns of behavior that you have had in your life up to this point: Do these patterns add value moving forward?
- ➢ Review what triggers you. What can you put in place to minimize the negative impact of these triggers?
- ➢ Review your worldview and personal paradigms: Do they still work for you with the stage of your life that you are in?
- ➢ Review the big six influencers (Reciprocity, Social Proof, Commitment and Consistency, Liking, Authority, Scarcity): How much do they (nonconsciously) influence you?
- ➢ Review the other things, or people, who influence you on a regular basis: What impact do these influences have on your actions, reactions or decisions
- ➢ Review what personal experiences might impact how you look at the world in general. Are you giving them the right amount of weight or attention when you are making choices?
- ➢ Review your purpose: Do you know what it is? Is it appropriate for you right now?
- ➢ Review your vision, passions, and dreams: Are they still true for you? Where are you in your journey towards them?
- ➢ Review the values that you hold: How well are you living up to them?
- ➢ Review the environment that you are in: What could be improved?
- ➢ Review your strengths and weaknesses: Do you ever overplay your strengths? What about those weaknesses? What could you do to minimize their negative impact?
- ➢ Review the players on your team: Identify the sub-personalities that are available to you. Are you using every one of them in an optimal fashion?

➤ Review your current outlook: What could you change to improve your success moving forward?

Brief examples or case studies

Let's now look at some examples of things that real people have discovered about themselves in doing this type of review.

Sitting in Rome, Italy a few years ago, Scott was with a business partner in an open-air café. It was summer, and the two had taken some time away from the busy schedule to enjoy a glass of wine and some wonderful Italian food. Leading up to this moment, Scott and Frank (not his real name) had been in several conversations about the intensity of Frank's work ethic. He was known for working to exhaustion daily, however, over the years he found it hard to enjoy any of his accomplishments fully. He had been working with Scott for a few weeks, and this subject seemed to keep coming up in their conversations. Finally, while sitting at this Italian café, Scott asked Frank to describe the three internal driving factors that motivated his work. Frank answered "First, I must make enough money to retire to Greece one day." Second, "I want to be revered by my fellow colleagues." And finally, "I never want to let my kids see me fail."

Scott made note of each driving force on three separate napkins and then placed them in front of him to see for himself. Scott then asked Frank how each factor was related to the others. As Frank thought about it, he looked at Scott and said, "Each one of these was something my father taught me." When Scott asked Frank if these driving factors were serving him, Frank thought a moment, and said sheepishly, "In some ways they are, but in other ways, I am not sure they really are". As the conversation progressed, Frank identified a mental model handed to him by his father that correlated his success as defined by where you lived, your status among your peers, and how failure should never be seen, much less talked about. In uncovering these underlying "rules," Frank found that there was a powerful mental model which was actively sabotaging his efforts. He looked over his glass of wine and said, "The lens that I have always experienced the world through is the lens of 'I am never going to be enough'."

After exploring how that model has actually served him in his career, and it has to some degree, Frank also lamented how that model has left a trail of broken relationships, debt, and a fair amount of self-loathing that has stolen his peace for years, and driven away people that mattered to him both personally and professionally.

After mentioning all this, Frank took some time with Scott to inventory the things in which he succeeded, and those things he had "failed" at throughout his life. Remarkably, through this process, Frank discovered that his successes, more often than not, were directly tied to his efforts to learn from his failures. At one point in the conversation he noted that every failure had been feedback which had ultimately led to one or more successes.

44

A few weeks later, Frank told Scott that he had elected to re-align his goals and his mental model in his mind, to make them more congruent with each other. When Scott asked what that was, Frank replied with, "for my kids to know themselves better through knowing me better." He then pulled out a paper from his pocket that read, "my failures don't tell me who I am, they tell me who I am not." Scott and Frank sat down and mapped out a plan centered on that new model.

Frank is now considered one of the most influential mentors in his field and sits on the board of directors for a nonprofit dedicated to the healing of broken families.

Some other examples stem from Phil's time at Apple, when they were running intensive Leadership Development programs. The first two were part of a group that was participating in a session with Tim Gallwey, and Phil was their coach. Tim used the metaphor of tennis as a way of learning – he had been a professional tennis coach, so that was a natural fit.

Tim had asked each member of the group that was working with him, what was their greatest weakness in their tennis game?

Let's take Margaret first. Margaret did not come across as the type of person who would be great on the tennis court. She was short, about five feet three inches and slightly overweight. But she was a natural for the game, was very aggressive in getting to the ball and returning it powerfully over the net. Everywhere that is, until she was actually playing at the net. There she changed character. She became timid and only made weak returns. That was what she wanted to work on.

Tim had her stand close to the net and, at least to start with, threw gentle balls at her. Her only job was to tell him exactly where on the racket the ball had hit – top, bottom, left, right or middle. If it hit the frame of the racket, that didn't matter, she just had to bring a level of awareness to the exact position that the ball had hit. This went on for several minutes, until he started to throw the balls harder and harder. She was perfectly describing where the ball had made contact with the racket, and every return was powerful and going back over the net, no matter where Tim threw the ball.

Then he picked up his racket and his shots were very powerful. She did perfectly at first, but then ducked as one of Tim's shots came straight at her face. Then, as she stood up, she burst into tears. She explained to Tim and Phil later, that she had had a sudden realization. When the ball came for her face, what she saw was her father's hand striking her when she was young and he was angry or drunk, not the tennis ball. That single realization enabled her to work on overcoming that mental hurdle.

Phil was happy to see that her learning proved positive in two ways. First, she became a much better player at the net, as reported by her tennis partner. The second was that she extrapolated that single piece of learning to other aspects of her relationship with her father, and how she responded to 'father' figures in the organization. It was a major breakthrough for her in learning to become a better leader.

The second example is Tony. Tony described that he had a weak backhand. He reported that he didn't know how to return an accurate, powerful, over-the-net backhand. Tim started to play a volley with him, asking him, en route, how he would do a powerful, over-the-net backhand if he did know how. And Tony showed him. Perfectly. Over and over again. Tony knew perfectly well how to do them but had convinced himself otherwise. Another case where there were two lessons, one in the game of tennis and one in the game of leadership. In fact, I should add a third lesson. One for the game of life.

The third person that Phil wants to report on is Michelle. She was part of a group exercise where the group had been given a hard task to do within a certain amount of time. In previous, private sessions, she had been given feedback that she was seen as a great leader – except that she always wanted to take control and didn't allow anyone else to step up and act as leader. She decided that the best way for her to experience a change of approach was to sit back and watch the group do the exercise – without her. She asked Phil, as her coach, whether that was acceptable. He replied that he thought it was perfectly acceptable if that's what she thought would be a good learning for her – but suggested that she tell the group why she was opting out. They were very supportive of her approach and assured her that they could manage without her.

It only took three minutes before she was anxious, pacing about and talking under her breath about what the group "should" be doing. Phil asked what was going on for her. Then she burst into tears. She related to him that her parents had always insisted that she be the one to lead by telling other people what to do. The act of not being there, not being seen as contributing, and not being seen as the achiever, brought a flood of issues back for her. It was, however, the first step in her transition into a more participative leader as she learned to step back and delegate.

As a final note, Phil describes a conversation with Tim regarding the game of tennis. Tim asked a group of people, why they played tennis. In addition, to the obvious things like exercise and the social aspects, several people said that it was about the need to win. And indeed, for some people that is an important facet. Then Tim suggested that if that were the case, why didn't they simply select opponents that were worse than they were. That gave rise to a discussion that it wasn't all about winning; for many people the challenge is just as important as the win. What about you? Which is more important? How relevant is that to the role you play in your organization?

The issue of finding out who you are is so important as the first step in addressing change, so let's look at a few more real-life examples.

Susan was an amazingly competent individual contributor; in all things, that is, except new things. Anything new threw her for a loop and took her almost into a state of paralysis. She was aware of it when she came for coaching but didn't know what to do about it. We discussed her worldview and mental models of "new things" – and identified that her parents had immigrated when she was fairly young, so everything was new to her. She withdrew for a while. Then when she did start to try new things her parents made fun of her when she didn't get them right first time.

She had grown up loving cars and all things mechanical. Phil happened to live on five acres and had a tractor. He asked whether she had ever driven a tractor before. No. Would she be willing to try? As part of the coaching process, she agreed to try to drive the tractor. Phil arranged for her to do a genuine piece of work around the property: moving the trunk of a tree that he had felled.

Within three minutes, she had successfully mastered all of the levers that she needed to accomplish the task, and within five minutes was competently driving the tractor. She translated this back into the work environment, by buying a model tractor, which she now keeps on her desk as a simple reminder that anything new is simply "a tractor that she hasn't driven before."

The next example includes a person whom we will call Bob. He was a mid-level manager in a growing organization and had been selected to be part of group that was to investigate and develop a five-year strategy for the company. Part of the initiative was to write a report and present a summary to the Board of Directors. When asked which part of the report he would be willing to present, he shied away, saying that he didn't think he was capable of presenting at that level. Needless to say, his self-confidence and self-esteem were pretty low.

Phil asked him one simple question. If he did a presentation, what would be the worst thing that could happen? He replied that he could completely mess it up, fumble over his words, get completely embarrassed and have to hand the presentation over to somebody else in the group. Phil then asked what Bob thought might happen then? Bob jumped to the worst-case scenario, in his mind, and replied that he could get fired as a result. Phil continued down the questioning pathway, and asked what he would do next? Bob replied that he would go out and look for another job. Phil asked how easy would that be, and Bob stated that it would probably be fairly easy considering all of the experience he had. Phil summarized the exchange by saying that it seemed that Bob was perfectly capable of being able to survive the worst-case scenario – in spite of what the internal voices in his brain were telling him. Bob finished by smiling and telling the group what part of the presentation he would take, and he did a great job.

It is probably not a coincidence that a little later, Bob met a new female friend, got a promotion, (several in fact), got married, and now has two wonderful children.

Lest you think that every intervention leads to great success, major change and a new life, let's take a look at T. In reviewing her life cycle T identified two major patterns. The first was that she had a habit of making decisions based solely upon emotion rather than a balance between emotion and rationale. Then she would spend time really regretting the decision and beating herself up over it. The second pattern that she saw was that she would run away from situations rather than face them. The need to change was clear. Unfortunately, when the next life choice point came up, T repeated her pattern. She was not yet ready to enter the change process.

Discussion

In the previous section we discussed several examples of change created through some simple and some complex scenarios. It must be noted here that change in and of itself does not happen easily and most especially if there is not a compelling outcome depending on it. Being able to put the outcome of change into a usable and sensory construct increases the likelihood that it can be accomplished. (We will come back to this in the chapter on Personal Change)

In the earlier section of "What works" we have given a large selection of tools that you can use to discover who you are. There are, of course, numerous other ways of discovering and reviewing that. We want to add two to our list; one is an assessment, and the other is a process.

An assessment and approach that has gained acceptance over the past several decades, both at the individual and the leadership level, is the concept of Emotional Intelligence (EI) [18] [19] or Emotional Quotient (EQ). In addition, to the concept itself, a plethora of assessments have been developed around it. A Google search will find many for you to choose from. The concept itself, the validity of the assessments and the possibility of 'faking' the answers to the assessments has caused some researchers [20] to cast doubt on the usefulness of the concept overall. In spite of these cautions, the use of EI and EQ has become widespread, and it has become a common tool for practitioners to use in this type of discovery and review. It's a good place to start from.

Another technique (process) is that of *identity constructs* i.e. how we, as individuals define ourselves. As you might imagine, in the field of psychology there has been much research on this subject, and here we are not about to embark on a review of all the approaches. If you are interested a simple Google Scholar review will give you plenty to get your teeth into!!! A few useful categories that we can use as a basis to start from are:

Personal identity	– I am a boy, black, tall, good-looking, old etc.
Relationship identity	– I am a father, girlfriend, wife, son etc.
Social identity	– I am a friend, a recluse, a butterfly etc.
Group identity	– I am a member of the rotary, a democrat etc.
Role identity	– I am a boss, a supervisor, an inspector etc.
Professional identity	– I am a doctor, an engineer, a cleaner etc.
Organizational identity	– I am a member of the IT department.
Workplace identity	– I am a creative member of a team.

The list does indeed go on, and we each have many identities, some of which are, at any place and time, in a constant state of flux. A change in our lives, even a small change, can often cause a change in our identity. Some of these have been marked by ritual and celebration in the past. Think about bachelorette parties, bar-mitzvahs, twenty-first birthday parties, weddings and so forth. Nothing inherently has changed, but we, and the rest of the world agree to change "our common narrative" about our identity.

In addition to the more definable identities that result from thinking about identity through some of the above lenses, there are other less tangible ways in which we develop identities, some real and others not so real. Many of us have a whole set of possible identities (or selves) that freely float in our imaginations. At the positive end of the scale, we might imagine ourselves as competing in an Ironman, or becoming the CEO of a major corporation or appearing as the lead violinist at the Royal Albert Hall. At the other end of the scale, in our less optimistic moments, we can sometimes see ourselves as destitute and drunk under a bridge!

The opposite of this, is when we have the concept of impossible selves. This is where we can never imagine those things. The background talk in our brains goes something like this like, "Oh, I could never imagine myself achieving partner status" or "I could never imagine myself getting a Master's degree" or "I could never imagine myself weighing only 80 kilos."

Another cut at this identity list, is the concept of multiple personalities that we introduced in *UYBFAC*. This is where we each have different aspects of our personality that can come out at different times. In *UYBFAC*, we gave an example of one of our clients, but think that the technique is valuable enough for us to repeat here.

It goes like this. Review the different characters that seem to exist as part of you. For example, a recent client identified the biggest character she sees in herself as that of "the eldest daughter." This character is very responsible, is adept at taking care of others, is a high-achiever, is a pleaser, a perfectionist and always executes a defined game-plan perfectly. She also saw another character – "The Hippy." This character is the diametric opposite of the eldest daughter. The Hippy is happy-go-lucky, irresponsible, devil-may-care and somewhat lazy. The two were in constant opposition in her life. She identified five more characters in the session. The following morning, she arrived back having identified an eighth character. The fighter.

Here are some more examples of other "characters" that we have seen in our work:

- A friendly parent
- A harsh parent
- A loving spouse/partner
- An indifferent or cold spouse/partner
- A happy child
- An unhappy child

- ➢ A playful child
- ➢ A sexual/sensual spouse/partner
- ➢ A sexually repressed spouse/partner
- ➢ A judge
- ➢ A perfectionist
- ➢ A flirt
- ➢ A lazy self

Once you have identified the major characters, then write down the following components for each of them

- ➢ Life purpose
- ➢ Motto(s):
- ➢ Core desire(s):
- ➢ Goal(s):
- ➢ Greatest fear(s):
- ➢ Strengths:
- ➢ Weaknesses:
- ➢ Strategy/Strategies:
- ➢ Talent(s):

Once you have identified them all, take a look at the following:

- ➢ Are there situations where two or more of the characters join together to make powerful allies?
- ➢ Are there examples where there is inner conflict between two or more of the characters?
- ➢ Which of the characters gets to make most of your decisions – and under what conditions?
- ➢ Which of the characters contributes most in your life?
- ➢ Which of the characters would you like to see more of as you move forward?
- ➢ Which of the characters would you like to see less of as you move forward?

Koerner [21] offers us an intriguing list of occasions where, when we engage in activities regarding our identities we might:

" … create, preserve, repair, revise, and strengthen our identities."

We have added to her list, but it includes:

- - transitions (promotions, mergers, new projects)
- - unexpected events
- - contradictions
- - tensions tend to elicit
- - emotional arousal
- - self-doubt
- - becoming open to new possibilities
- - creating a professional identity
- - experimenting with a new identity
- - transitioning to a new role
- - recovering from a workplace trauma, such as bullying, being fired or being demoted
- -

Bottom line summary

Make a choice. Do you want to find out more about who you are? If not, then go to the next topic. If you decide to find out more about yourself, review all the possible things that you might do, and select a handful. Or have someone else who knows you well, help you select a handful of options. Give yourself a date by which you will have completed the activities. Write down what you learn from each activity. Pick one thing that you will decide to address.

What's next?

What one or two mental models or identities do I want to examine and adjust?
How will I go about making these changes or adjustments?
How will I measure whether I have been successful?

[16] e.g. www.totalbrain.com

[17] At the time of going to press, the site for the Munich Chronotype online questionnaire was undergoing some change. An alternative is available at https://www.cet-surveys.com/index.php?sid=61524

[18] Goleman, D. (1995). Emotional Intelligence. Bantam Books.

[19] Goleman, D. (2006). Social Intelligence. Bantam Books.

[20] Grubb, W. L. I., & McDaniel, M. A. (2007). The Fakability of Bar-On's Emotional Quotient Inventory Short Form: Catch Me if You Can. *Human Performance, 20*(1), 43–59.

[21] Koerner, M. M. (2014). Courage as Identity Work: Accounts of Workplace Courage. *Academy of Management Journal, 57*(1), 63–93. http://doi.org/10.5465/amj.2010.0641

Chapter 3:

Mindfulness

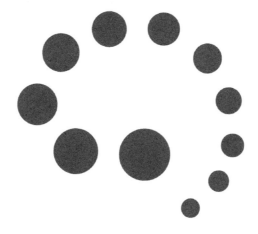

3. Mindfulness

General comments

Mindfulness has become one of the buzzwords in the Western corporate world over the past couple of decades. In many fields, mindfulness programs are being run to increase all sorts of things ranging from personal well-being to prosocial behavior. The good news is that, in general, these programs do seem to have a positive effect, even if we are not quite sure why or how much effect they have.

The data are impressive. Some research indicates:

> " ... over 13 percent of the working population has received some mindfulness training – and organizations from progressive Silicon Valley firms like Google to traditional corporate mainstays like General Mills train their employees by the thousands." [22]

And just in case you think that Mindfulness is a fuzzy or squishy word, there are at least six assessments out there for scientifically measuring mindfulness. [23]

For the analytical readers amongst you, take a look at this: one insurance company did a cost-benefit analysis of mindfulness programs. They determined that the productivity gains alone amounted to $3000 per employee, which was an 11-to-1 return on their investment, a significant ROI in anyone's eyes.

One word of caution. Many papers and books use "Meditation" and "Mindfulness" – synonymously. They are not synonymous. Mindfulness can simply be described as non-judgmental, present moment awareness. Meditation is one key approach to practicing mindfulness, but there are others.

What works

> ➤ Attend mindfulness workshops
> ➤ Develop a workshop for your organization
> ➤ Put what you learn into practice
> ➤ Find mobile app that works for you – some have been found to be useful for some people
> ➤ Remember to pay attention to what is occurring in one's immediate experience with care and discernment
> ➤ Allow other people to be who they are
> ➤ Practice being positive in life
> ➤ Recognize that there are many ways of getting things done – not just your way
> ➤ Focus on what is in-front of you ... not what might come along next week
> ➤ Take a non-judgmental approach to everything
> ➤ Allow time for yourself
> ➤ Give gifts not bribes

Here's a sample list of the topics that are addressed in one of the mindfulness assessments [24] (the short version) to show the type of things that work to enhance mindfulness:

1. I am open to the experience of the present moment.
2. I sense my body, whether eating, cooking, cleaning or talking.
3. When I notice an absence of mind, I gently return to the experience of the here and now.
4. I am able to appreciate myself.
5. I pay attention to what's behind my actions.
6. I see my mistakes and difficulties without judging them.
7. I feel connected to my experience in the here-and-now.
8. I accept unpleasant experiences.
9. I am kind to myself when things go wrong.
10. I watch my feelings without getting lost in them.
11. In difficult situations, I can pause without immediately reacting.
12. I experience moments of inner peace and ease, even when things get hectic and stressful.
13. I am impatient with myself and with others.
14. I am able to smile when I notice how I sometimes make life difficult.

Brief examples or case studies

Nina, a Chief Human Resource Office of a large and rapidly growing software company, was having a meeting with Peter, the Chief Technology Officer, a prince of a man. He was proposing to restructure his 300-person department and wanted to hear Nina's thoughts. He presented the outline of what he was trying to achieve by doing the restructuring, and then presented her with the new structure.

She listened and then responded that she thought that maybe there might be a different way of achieving his desired outcomes. She presented her ideas to him. He stopped and thought for a few moments. Then he replied: "I think your ideas are much better than mine. I will go with yours."

In talking with Peter afterwards, Nina learned a number of things. His response illustrated a number of things about what went on in his head: the ability to truly listen, the ability to understand the impact of what he was hearing, the ability to evaluate and compare Nina's new idea with his own, the ability to understand his own thoughts and feelings in connection with Nina's idea, the ability to let go of his own precept and adopt something new – and the mindfulness to do and be aware of all of this in real-time.

Andy is a COO for a rapidly growing defense contractor supplying mission critical parts for the United States Defense department. He has been in the role since 2008 and has seen several defense programs come and go during his very long career. For any of you that know about performance on government contracts, it is not for the faint of heart. In 2018 he suffered a mild heart attack and had to have a stent put into his heart to open one of his key arteries. When his doctor came in to talk about post heart attack recovery, he put heavy emphasis on stress management techniques that are not completely drug dependent. When Andy went through his post hospital therapy, one of the methods recommended for him to reduce his stress was to start with 5 min of mindfulness meditation per day and to work his way up to 20 min a day. Andy insisted that he had no patience for such things, but his wife agreed to join him in this rather esoteric approach. As he started making mindfulness part of his morning ritual, he noticed a change taking place at work. He was slower to get angry and frustrated, and he was less spent when he headed home at the end of the day. "It is like there is a traffic cop in my head and I am much more patient with others and myself. It's amazing what people will tell you if they trust you will not explode on them. I had no idea what was being held back from me due to my unpredictability with my team."

Even the US Military has explored the benefits of mindfulness training. In 2017 while working with a railroad company, Scott met Sam. Sam related a story that was surprising to many in the room. While working in Iraq in 2011-2013, as a military contractor and former special operator, Sam noted the enormous amount of time there was to sit and do "nothing" outside of training and remaining proficient. Unlike the movies, every day in Iraq was not full of shootouts and near misses, at least in his experience. Boredom and complacency are of particular concern for any military commander and not the least those in highly critical skilled roles such as the US Navy Seals or the US Army Delta Force. Sam noted that the special operations community had been on the front end of spending as much time training the brain as the body since its founding many years ago. Sam also noted that there is a tendency for soldiers of all types to get into mischief during the down time from combat while simply trying to occupy their time between highly stressful events. One of the tools that the military has introduced to these highly trained soldiers is mindfulness meditation. It is used today to enhance clarity and useful thinking in high stress scenarios where critical thinking is often suppressed, and reactionary thinking is predominant. Who knew that this often-dismissed practice has a place in today's military?

Discussion

The past two or three decades have produced a plethora of research papers on mindfulness; most address one of these questions:

- What is it?
- What impact does it have?
- How and why does it work?
- Why is it important for people and organizations?
- How do we train it?
- Are mobile apps an effective way of training?

Perhaps Jon Kabat-Zinn [25], a giant in the field of mindfulness, gives us the shortest and easiest definition:

" .... paying attention in a particular way: on purpose, in the present moment and nonjudgmentally."

On the other hand, David Black [26] gives us a definition of what it isn't:

"The term can be contrasted with experiences of mindlessness that occur when attention and awareness capacities are scattered due to preoccupation with past memories or future plans and worries; this, in turn, leading to a limited awareness and attention to experiences in the present moment."

So, does mindfulness work? Some researchers report that much of the research has:

" ... several key methodological shortcomings which preclude robust conclusions ..." and, even in 2019, *"while there has been considerable research into health outcomes, organizational mindfulness research is still developing a comprehensive case for the wide scale application of mindfulness."* [27]

In general, however, in spite of these reservations, much of the research supports that there are many positive benefits from mindfulness training both at the individual level and at the organizational level.

Let's take a look at some of the reported impacts:

"Methodologically rigorous randomized controlled trials have demonstrated that mindfulness interventions improve outcomes in multiple domains (e.g., chronic pain, depression relapse, addiction)." [28]

and

"Meta-analysis found eight brain regions consistently altered in meditators, including areas key to meta-awareness (frontopolar cortex/BA 10), exteroceptive and interoceptive body awareness (sensory cortices and insula), memory consolidation and reconsolidation (hippocampus), self and emotion regulation (anterior and mid cingulate; orbitofrontal cortex), and intra- and interhemispheric communication (superior longitudinal fasciculus; corpus callosum)" [29]

and

"Neuroscientists have also shown that practicing mindfulness affects brain areas related to perception, body awareness, pain tolerance, emotion regulation, introspection, complex thinking, and sense of self." [30]

The most complete report of the positive impacts of mindfulness that we can find was published by Cresswell [31] in 2017. Here's (a much-shortened version of) what he has to say with regard to physical health, mental health, cognitive and affective outcomes, and interpersonal outcomes:

"Physical health: Several large (studies) provide compelling evidence that mindfulness interventions improve chronic pain management" and *"There is also promising initial evidence that mindfulness interventions may reduce immune markers of proinflammation among stressed individuals."*

Mental health: Strong (study) evidence indicates that mindfulness interventions reduce depression relapse rates in at-risk individuals and improve the treatment of drug addiction and

There are also several well-controlled studies showing that mindfulness interventions can reduce anxiety, depression, and PTSD symptomatology.

Cognitive and affective outcomes: Among healthy young adult samples, mounting (study) evidence indicates that mindfulness interventions can improve attention-related outcomes (e.g., sustained attention, working memory) and affective outcomes (e.g., reducing rumination).

Interpersonal outcomes: There is currently little mindfulness intervention research on interpersonal outcomes, but initial studies suggest that mindfulness interventions may improve relational outcomes (e.g., relationship satisfaction and prosocial behaviors)."

That's all individually focused. How about the use of mindfulness training in organizations?

Sutcliffe et al. [32] provide us with a pretty good review of the state-of-the-art:

" ... research has found that, consistent with longstanding historical claims, mindfulness matters. Evidence shows that it is associated with some of the very outcomes - enhanced psychological and physical well-being - that people have long ascribed to it. Moreover, research indicates that mindfulness can prove beneficial in ways that even historical accounts of the phenomenon did not anticipate. To illustrate, researchers have demonstrated that mindfulness can slow aging, improve standardized test performance and produce measurable changes in the human brain. More germane to our review, organizational research indicates that individual mindfulness is positively related to employee outcomes such as work engagement and job performance suggesting that mindfulness contributes to an organization's bottom line."

"More recently, researchers have begun to investigate the employee and organizational consequences of collective mindfulness - defined as the collective capability to discern discriminatory detail about emerging issues and to act swiftly in response to these details - and, in doing so, have found an array of benefits. For employees, mindful organizing is associated with lower turnover rates and for organizations, collective mindfulness is positively related to salutary organizational outcomes including greater customer satisfaction, more effective resource allocation, greater innovation, and improved quality, safety, and reliability. Interestingly, these effects are most commonly observed in particularly trying contexts characterized by complexity, dynamism, and error intolerance."

How about leveraging technology as part of the mindfulness process? With regard to mobile apps, there is a lot of research going on. First, let's put the apps that are available in perspective; Mani et al. [33] published a report on the quality of mindfulness apps. They report that, although they found 560 apps on two app stores, by the time they focused on those that actually did mindfulness training and education, the number available dropped to 23. The rest addressed " ... *only reminders, timers or guided meditation tracks ...* " and hence were excluded. Of those 23 only four were deemed to be of high enough quality to be identified. Their names? Headspace, Smiling Mind, iMindfulness, and Mindfulness Daily.

"The intervention group reported significant improvement in well-being, distress, job strain, and perceptions of workplace social support compared to the control group. In addition, the intervention group had a marginally significant decrease in self-measured workday systolic blood pressure from pre to post intervention." [34]

In a very recent paper, Kudasia [35] took a slightly different approach. He describes mindfulness as a metacognitive process – i.e. a process whereby we think about our thinking. The abstract to his paper summarizes his approach:

"First, when seen as metacognitive practice, mindfulness is not a single mode of information processing to be applied in all situations. Instead, it is a metacognitive process by which people adjust their mode of information processing to their current situation.

Second, this metacognitive process is made possible by three specific beliefs that supersede lay beliefs about human information processing. A core function of mindfulness training, thus, is to provide a context that cultivates these beliefs.

Third, when these beliefs are put into practice, people gain greater agency in how they respond to situations. This matters for organizations, because as people interrelate their individual actions into a collective response, metacognitive practice can get embedded in amplifying processes that transform the organization—or in fragmentation processes that threaten it."

He expands the "three specific beliefs" as follows:

"First, when people monitor the state of their information processing relative to their current situation, they gain agency to adjust what information they process and how they process it.

Second, people's beliefs about information processing can enable or constrain their agency to make these adjustments.

Third, when people adjust their information processing, they respond to situations with more flexibility."

We should note that there are some indications that mindfulness and mindfulness training are probably not a one-size-fits-all panacea. A recent study [36] suggests that a general mindfulness meditation approach does not work, for example, with perfectionists. However, if a nonjudgmental element is added into the program, then the meditation approach did indeed prove effective.

Before moving to a summary, it might be worth taking a moment and look at downside risks. Not whether mindfulness and its training is, or is not useful, but whether there are any dangers that participants of such programs might face. Cresswell's 2017 paper [37] gives us a brief introduction to the downsides. He suggests that downsides might come in three forms, namely:

a) General adverse events such as such as agitation, anxiety, discomfort, or confusion
b) Specific significant adverse events
c) Negative cognitive impacts.

In a little more detail, with regard to general adverse events he suggests that:

"These negative reactions are viewed as an important feature of the psychotherapeutic change process in mindfulness interventions because sustained mindful attention to one's experience is thought to help participants explore and understand the full embodied experience of these reactions, to learn that the experience of these reactions is temporary, and to foster insight into how one reacts to these uncomfortable experiences."

In the case of more significant adverse reactions, he warns of some possibilities:

"For example, a participant who has a life history of trauma might experience the resurfacing of these trauma memories during mindfulness training exercises, potentially triggering a major

depressive episode. Researchers have also voiced the concern that individuals who are at risk for psychosis (e.g., schizophrenia) or seizures (e.g., epilepsy) might put themselves at elevated risk for exacerbation of these symptoms if they participate in formal mindfulness exercises."

and adds

"Some observational research suggests that these severe adverse events can occur (albeit infrequently) among individuals going through more intensive residential mindfulness meditation retreats lasting from 2 weeks to 3 months."

He finishes this part of the analysis by offering some positive thoughts:

"The current evidence-based mindfulness interventions which are offered in smaller-spaced doses by trained instructors, carry minimal risks for significant adverse events."

Finally, with regard to negative cognitive impacts:

" … the possibility that the conscious effort at maintaining awareness on present moment experience might have cognitive costs among individuals who are new to mindfulness interventions. Some studies suggest that training in mindfulness can be initially cognitively depleting."

and

" … it is also possible that the cognitive demands of adopting this more reflective awareness of one's present moment experience might disrupt, slow, or bias one's responses on cognitive tasks."

So, all in all, there is a risk factor to be taken into account, but a minimal one.

Bottom line summary

Mindfulness really is a case of "What's not to like?" It seems that mindfulness training has a wide array of positive impacts ranging from physical health to better organizational results. Maybe it is best summarized by the last chapter of the Congleton et al. HBR article: [38]

"Mindfulness should no longer be considered a "nice-to-have" for executives. It's a "must-have": a way to keep our brains healthy, to support self-regulation and effective decision-making capabilities, and to protect ourselves from toxic stress. It can be integrated into one's religious or spiritual life or practiced as a form of secular mental training. When we take a seat, take a breath, and commit to being mindful, particularly when we gather with others who are doing the same, we have the potential to be changed."

What's next?

What one or two things am I going to focus on in order to increase my mindfulness?
What I am going to do about it/them?
How will I measure whether I have been successful?

[22] Kudesia, R. S. (2019). MindfulnessAs Metacognitive Practice. *Academy of Management Review, 44*(2), 405–423. http://doi.org/10.5465/amr.2015.0333

[23] Kentucky Inventory of Mindfulness Skills (KIMS), Toronto Mindfulness Scale (TMS), Cognitive and Affective Mindfulness Scale (CAMS), Five Facet Mindfulness Questionnaire (FFMQ), Freiburg Mindfulness Inventory (FMI), and the Philadelphia Mindfulness Scale (PHLMS).

[24] Freiburg Mindfulness Inventory

[25] Kabat-Zinn, J. (1994). Wherever you go, there you are: Mindfulness meditationin everyday life. Hyperion Books.

[26] Black, D. S. (n.d.). A Brief Definition of Mindfulness. Retrieved October 13, 2019, from www.mindfulexperience.org

[27] Passmore, J. (2019). Mindfulness in organizations (part 1): a critical literature review. *Industrial and Commercial Training, 51*(2), 104–113. http://doi.org/10.1108/ICT-07-2018-0063

[28] Creswell, J. D. (2017). Mindfulness Interventions. *Annual Review of Psychology, 68*(1), 491–516. http://doi.org/10.1146/annurev-psych-042716-051139

[29] Fox, K. C., Nijeboer, S., Dixon, M. L., Floman, J. L., Ellamil, M., Rumak, S. P., et al. (2104). Is meditation associated with altered brain structure? A systematic review and meta-analysis of morphometric neuroimaging in meditation practitioners. *Neuroscience Biobehavioral Review., 43*, 48–73.

[30] Gongleton, C., Hölzel, B. K., & Lazar, S. W. (2015). Mindfulness Can Literally Change Your Brain. *Harvard Business Review*, 1–5.

[31] Creswell, J. D. (2017). Mindfulness Interventions. *Annual Review of Psychology, 68*(1), 491–516. http://doi.org/10.1146/annurev-psych-042716-051139

[32] Sutcliffe, K. M., Vogus, T. J., & Dane, E. (2016). Mindfulness in Organizations: A Cross-Level Review. *Annual Review of Organizational Psychology and Organizational Behavior, 3*(1), 55–81. http://doi.org/10.1146/annurev-orgpsych-041015-062531

[33] Mani, M., Kavanagh, D. J., Hides, L., & Stoyanov, S. R. (2015). Review and Evaluation of Mindfulness-Based iPhone Apps. *JMIR mHealth and uHealth, 3*(3), e82–11. http://doi.org/10.2196/mhealth.4328

[34] Bostok, S., Crosswell, A. D., & Prather, A. A. (2018). Mindfulness on-the-go: Effects of a mindfulness meditation app on work stress and well-being. *Journal of occupational health psychology.*

[35] Kudesia, R. S. op cit

[36] Cardiovascular effects of brief mindfulness meditation among perfectionists experiencing failure".Hannah R. Koerten, Tanya S. Watford, Eric F. Dubow, William H. O'Brien. *Psychophysiology* doi:10.1111/psyp.13517.

[37] Creswell, J. D.op cit

[38] Congleton, C. op cit

Chapter 4:

Purpose

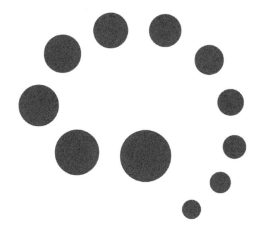

4. Purpose

General comments

Take a moment and think back to the last time you took a vacation. Think about that vacation and what it meant to you. Now think about how much time you spent planning it. Some of you will simply say, "Oh I woke up one morning and took off – there was no planning needed." Let us assure you that you are in the minority! Most people spend a large amount of time in the planning and preparation of a two-week vacation, especially here in the United States. Typically, people spend anywhere between 12 hours and 10 days to do that planning

We contend that if you are going to spend that amount of time to plan a two-week vacation, surely it must be worth taking at least that amount of time in planning your life and its purpose?

Phil describes an occasion when he came across a quotation from a kitchen and bath magazine, (Yes, we know, an unlikely place to look for articles on personal development) but we think it gives a succinct description of why we should plan our future:

> *"In 1974, I started a unique, life-long and life-changing investigation of motivational psychology, which is the study of what makes people do what they do.*
>
> *"The one thing that stands out for me from all of those years of research, writing, presenting and applying success principles is that you must have a plan and a personal creed to live by in order to succeed. If it's not in writing, it's only a dream. Things in writing must be consciously dealt with. Dreams vanish into the air."*(39)

This chapter is about consciously planning your life and its purpose and recording it. The bottom line though is this: Finding our purpose is not a mandate, but an extremely important navigational tool when trying to put the events of our lives into a context which we can understand and apply. Purpose is extremely brain-friendly. Without purpose, the brain can spend a lot of time simply searching for threats and defending against them, rather than progressing to a higher and more meaningful existence. Keep in mind that purpose also puts our threat profile into a useful context rather than a solely hedonistic defense posture.

The intent of this chapter, therefore, is to provide you with an approach to thinking about the future that you wish to create. In addition, we will attempt to stimulate and challenge you. Maybe the chapter will bring out what has been in your head or your heart for some time. Maybe, it will take you places in your thoughts that you haven't been before.

For some people, their purpose on the planet became very clear to them early on in life, and hence, they were, and are, able to very easily line up their studies, pursuits, work and energies behind that purpose, and can pursue that purpose in everything they do. Their life's work is clear to them.

But we don't all have that level of clarity – in fact, our suspicion is that there are many more of us who are not clear on our purpose, than there are those who are clear. Most self-help books don't help either – they suggest that you find it – but don't offer a great deal of help in doing so. What if you can't identify or describe your purpose – or at least can't yet?

For example, Phil describes that, many years ago, when he started down the road of self-discovery, he realized that not only was his life's purpose not clear, but he had no idea of how to go about getting clarity. He had identified some goals early on in life and had achieved most of them – but they certainly weren't in support of some greater life-long purpose. He describes that he was, and to some extent still is, envious of those people who have theirs identified – or somehow could step back and pull one out of their heads and hearts when required or asked.

Sometimes our purpose, or some might define it as "calling," comes gradually; we recently read an article in Vanity Fair magazine that talked about the work that Bono and Sir Bob Geldorf had done some time ago in pulling together a commitment from the G8 group to give $25 billion to Africa to overcome poverty. We sincerely doubt whether, when these two gentlemen were 21 years old, that the concept of raising billions of dollars in this manner was in their sights. Maybe it was. For many of us, however, these things come to us gradually.

If you have your life's purpose identified, then great. Write it large and often. If you don't have one, then don't worry. It will become apparent at some stage in the future (maybe while you read this book and plan your journey, but maybe not.)

As an initial exercise, write a succinct answer to the following:

My life's purpose is:

_____

If you can complete that exercise to your own satisfaction, then it is probably time to jump to Chapter 5. If not, then keep reading. ☺

In *UYBFAC*, we identified "Purpose" as one of the five drivers of the brain. We broke this domain down into the following set of statements:

1. We want to achieve mastery in our fields and have an opportunity to practice it on a regular basis
2. We want to develop ourselves and self-actualize
3. We want to have a Mission/Purpose/Meaning
4. We want to live in accordance with our core values and work with people/organizations that align with those values
5. We want to be able to express ourselves artistically
6. We want to explore and live our spirituality
7. We want to feel passionate about something
8. We want to have a challenge
9. We want to seek the truth

In an ideal world, our overall Life's Purpose would probably include all nine of these aspects. In reality, however, for many of us they are separate activities.

What works

- Identify what values are most important to you.
- Identify what you want people to say about you in the future.
- Make a list of behaviors that you value in a mentor and write it down.
- Describe a unique gift that you have which is valuable to yourself and others.
- Describe one or two aspects of your life that you want more of in the future.
- Describe one or two things that you would add to your current life.
- How will those one or two things serve you?
- Describe one or two things that you would like to remove from your current life.
- How are those one or two things not serving you?
- Identify who you are passionate about helping.
- When you think in private, what one or two things would you change about yourself?
- Do you live your life in accordance with your credo or value set? If not, what would have to change?
- Think of someone you admire. What one or two things about them would you want to add into your life?
- Just write thoughts down about your purpose without filtering them
- Write a letter to yourself from the future
- If you don't know your life's purpose, do you have any clues or inklings about what it might be? If so, write them down.
- If you don't know your life's purpose, do you know any of the attributes that it might consist of? If so, write them down.
- Ensure that any life purpose that you land on is aligned with your strengths and values for you as well as something that has a personal element … and not something that you are doing to satisfy someone else's demands on you.
- Take a look at the Purpose statements below – and write down those that are already part of your ideal world and then add those that resonate with you.
- Create a compelling future for yourself

Brief examples or case studies

Examples of purpose statements

- *To inspire creative change through teaching children around the world.*
- *To bring personal value and psychological safety to every employee I encounter.*
- *To encourage, engage, and equip others to pursue their dreams.*
- *To educate the uneducated of the harmful effects of drugs on the brain of an unborn child.*
- *To heal the hurting by using my education through medicine and empathy.*

> ➢ *To help others discover their best and elevate to their full potential.*
> ➢ *To bring smart technology into every home on the planet.*
> ➢ *To inspire hope and healing to every person that I encounter.*
> ➢ *To mend broken relationships for myself and others.*
> ➢ *To open the eyes of a child to see their potential in a positive and healthy light*
> ➢ *To demonstrate forgiveness to others, starting with myself.*

These are just a few examples of Purpose statements. Please note, however, that they all have two attributes: 1) All of them are easy to remember and 2) they are all are written in a way that will act as a litmus test to determine if how you are spending time serves this statement. Having a purpose does not require that everything you do serves that purpose, but you may find that it will save you from spending a lot of time on those things that do not serve your purpose. You may also find that things that you do that do not serve your purpose fail to create a reward for the brain. Remember what you learned in *UYBFAC*. Our brains are driven by chemical rewards.

On a personal note, Scott spent the better part of 2007 doing some serious self-reflection and found that ultimately his purpose was to "To Teach and Inspire Executive Leaders To Lead From Their Heart As Well As Their Head". This came as a result of over 20 years in leadership on the battlefield and in Corporate America. After his stroke in 2003, he knew that there was something special about the brain as he went through his recovery. Finally, in 2007, he acted on developing his purpose. After some help from several friends and some honest conversations with trusted colleagues he took the risk of putting his Purpose statement on paper. Now the game was on. He was gainfully employed but knew that he was growing restless and needed to do something that brought him greater satisfaction. His wife, Stephanie suggested that he consider doing something directly related to his Purpose. Well, the rest is history and he has not looked back. This is not a suggestion that you should quit your day job to go chase a purpose, but it may help to know that when living with purpose, change may or may not be required. That is up to you.

Discussion

In order to find purpose in our lives we must first address some fundamentals that, when adopted, will start to clear the path to a meaningful outcome when it comes to Purpose.

We are not our mistakes or successes

We must first understand that our trials, tribulations, failures, success and accolades are not necessarily a reflection of who we are, but more, a way that we have catalogued the events and experiences and our subsequent responses to them. None of us are born "Failures" or "Winners". We are constantly exposed to circumstances by which we are making rapid and often nonconscious decisions that lead to outcomes. Some of us come from very stable and healthy upbringings while other of us come from less than healthy and stable upbringings - both of which serve as a basis for the filter by which we experience the world. Both scenarios provide an opportunity to create value in those events which can lead to a meaningful purpose. When things go wrong or right in our lives, there is a natural tendency to associate our personal value to the outcome. It is very important to find the separation of the event and the identity we find in that event so that we can process the lesson for future application and purpose.

<u>Every experience has value - how we label it matters</u>

From the time we are born we are exposed to circumstances that shape the way we experience the world around us. Psychologists have spent years trying to help us make sense of the world and many of them have done great work in creating models that allow us to put our experiences into a useful context vs. simply taking them on as our identity. With that said, one of the largest barriers to defining Purpose in anything is our inability to separate our label of the event or circumstance from our label of who we claim to be in the context of that event. Scott had a stroke in 2003 and he attributed his success in recovery to the fact that he never allowed himself to claim he was a stroke victim, but that he had "experienced a stroke". Doctors credited much of his rapid recovery to the way he labeled his role in the event and his subsequent actions that lead to healing.

Scott met a young man in December of 2019 who described himself as a champion. When Scott asked about the details of the claim, he said that he had won his high school MVP award for the swim team that year. Scott delighted in his success and asked what he learned from the experience. His answer, "I am better than any of my high school teammates". Clearly, he had taken on the title of champion and it reflected in his mirror of himself. (Now, before anyone gets the wrong idea, we all are excited for our seventeen-year-old champion.) What our young man had not realized at this point in his journey, is that this label could possibly become a limitation for him unless he transcends how he can apply it to a larger more dynamic objective that compels action. The label of champion is based on a historical event, whereas, left where it is, it may serve as a false predictor of future events.

One must examine the event from a perspective of how the brain creates value of success and failure as to its application when discovering purpose. Remember, the brain is constantly learning to apply survival skills in the myriad of threats (Protection, Participation and Prediction. Without purpose, the brain spends a great deal of time passively defending against threats to basic survival. With the development of purpose, the brain will quickly find lessons learned from pain and pleasure and apply them for progress.

Since we were just talking about swimming, Michael Phelps once said " *I want to test my maximum and see how much I can do. And I want to change the world of swimming.*" Mr. Phelps found purpose in his many successes or perhaps more aptly, his purpose drove his continued success.

Finding meaning in our experiences - for future use

Now, before you say to yourself, "I have a lot of experience failing, so how is that going to help me find my Purpose?" Keep in mind that failure is nothing more than feedback to the brain, just as success is nothing more than feedback to the brain. Identifying what you love or dislike, are passionate about or uninterested in, along with knowing where you naturally sparkle, and you naturally retreat, is a very important step towards finding purpose.

There often is an assumption that our purpose is fixed from an early age. This could not be further from the truth. Mother Theresa was born in 1910 in obscurity and was 36 years old before she found her true purpose. Still, it took her several more years before she become well known for her charity work. In fact, her fame on the international stage started small and not until the 1980s (70 years into her life) was she such a force that influential leaders and politicians would stand in line for just a moment of her time. What truly makes her story remarkable is that she suffered greatly as a child and her purpose came from her suffering. While not all of us will have lives as well-known as Mother Theresa, we can learn a great deal about how getting to purpose may involve a series of steps that include intermediate purposes for where we are at that time in our journey through life.

We would be remiss if we did not address the differences between goals and purpose. Goals themselves are measured milestones along the journey which are congruent with the ongoing purpose. For instance, the energy drink company "Red Bull" is a sponsor of two Formula 1 racing teams. Their goal is to see their cars win the championship, while their purpose is to bring more awareness and sales to Red Bull, the drink.

Purpose evolves from our ability to inventory the lessons and learnings from both success and failures and applying those lessons in a way that provides motivation to pursue something inside or outside of ourselves. Our brains are built to sort for useful information once we tell it what is important. By creating a well-defined purpose, that is easy to remember, and in a context that makes sense, we will find our brains sorting for roads that lead to the fulfillment of that purpose. We are handsomely equipped with a mechanism in our brain called the Reticular Activating System (RAS) and it naturally will sort for things that serve what we identify as important to us. Therefore, when Scott's wife told him about a new car she wanted and showed him a picture of it, he started seeing that model of car everywhere he went. He later joked that his wife has influence because she arranged for that car to be everywhere he went. Scott's RAS was working overtime making sure he fulfilled a purpose to keep his wife happy. (Now <u>that</u> is purpose ☺)

Your purpose at work

Much has been made over the years about finding "purposeful work". Buried in that phrase is an assumption that the work itself is the purpose, whereas we argue that work is a way by which our purpose can be fulfilled.

Scott met a firefighter a few years ago that, when he was defining his purpose, he said it was "To bring restoration to the wounded". He could have easily said, "My purpose is to put out fires" but he admitted that he felt being a firefighter was just a mechanism for his true purpose. When he was not at work, he spent time working at a charity where single parents came to find safety and a chance to get back on their feet. Both roles allowed him to enjoy a purposeful life, however, it expanded beyond a job title.

Oprah Winfrey has publicly stated that her purpose is "To be a teacher and to be known for inspiring my students to be more than they thought they could be." In an interview with "O" magazine she reflected that she had no idea that it would be on TV. The brain does not care if it is on TV or in a living room by itself; having a well-defined purpose creates value to our tribe and the brain likes the prospect of being valuable to self and to others.

In Austin, Texas, Scott and his wife have facilitated a 501c3 program called "Discovery Programs" (www.discoveryprograms.org) in which an individual spends three weekends spread over about 90 days, to explore their past, present and future through a series of games in order to identify a purpose that is congruent with their skills, experience and passion going forward. This is just one example of such a program – programs like this are a good resource for people who might need a formal structure to come up with a meaningful purpose.

Before moving on to the rest of the chapter, as you think about your Life's Purpose, we wanted to draw your attention to the Japanese concept of Ikigai – or finding Purpose in Life; it is represented by the following diagram:

IKIGAI
Your "reason for being"

Delight and fullness, but no wealth

Excitement and complacency, but sense of uncertainty

what you LOVE

PASSION   MISSION

what you are GOOD AT   IKIGAI   what the world NEEDS

PROFESSION   VOCATION

Satisfaction, but feeling of uselessness

what you can be PAID FOR

Comfortable, but feeling of emptiness

Defining purpose can often feel like trying to define distance when it comes to the universe. This is further complicated by the standard that we often put on ourselves that our *Purpose* must rival some significant historic event or have a headline on Google news for it to have any meaning or any significance. (This is the availability bias at work). During the 2020 Covid-19 pandemic there was a lot of talk and news coverage about the significance and purpose that the medical community found in their quest to heal and comfort those that were facing a cruel and deadly virus. What was equally interesting was the number of people finding purpose in their own small communities not necessarily related to the sick but to those that were trying to remain healthy and connected to others from a distance.

We would like to dispel the notion that the brain needs to have a headline worthy *Purpose* for it to find significance and value. Keep in mind that the brain is focused on survival first, so any purpose that creates a sense of progress and enhances wellbeing, serves the brain nicely while yielding short term and long-term benefits.

Purpose itself does not always come from victories or sunny days. Victor Frankl, psychologist and author of the well-known book *"Man's Search for Meaning"*, wrote about man finding purpose in the direst of circumstances.

As a prisoner of the Nazi Death Camps in Auschwitz spanning over several months from 1944 to 1945, he observed himself and his fellow man stripped of all that they held dear including their families and their possessions, leaving only "naked" existence. His observations are too long to list here but It boils down to this: Finding the meaning (Purpose) in suffering gives one the choice to *respond* to their circumstances. His premise is clear - even in suffering we can find purpose which then gives meaning to the suffering itself. He offers us suggestions that there are three parts to it, through work, through love and through courage in adverse times. We strongly recommend reading Frankl's work in your search for Purpose.

Over the past several decades there have been numerous studies published about the positive contribution that having a worth-while purpose or meaning in life has on our brains. Having a worthwhile Purpose brings a host of benefits. Maybe these results are best summarized by a recent (2019) study of over 7300 men and women [40] that reports:

> *"We show that independently of age, sex, educational attainment, and socioeconomic status, higher worthwhile ratings are associated with:*
>
> - *stronger personal relationships (marriage/partnership, contact with friends)*
> - *broader social engagement (involvement in civic society, cultural activity, volunteering)*
> - *less loneliness*
> - *greater prosperity (wealth, income)*
> - *better mental and physical health (self-rated health, depressive symptoms, chronic disease)*
> - *less chronic pain*
> - *less disability*
> - *greater upper body strength*
> - *faster walking*
> - *less obesity and central adiposity*

- more favorable biomarker profiles (C-reactive protein, plasma fibrinogen, white blood cell count, vitamin D, high-density lipoprotein cholesterol)
- healthier lifestyles (physical activity, fruit and vegetable consumption, sleep quality, not smoking)
- more time spent in social activities and exercising
- less time spent alone or watching television."

In a slightly older article Ashton Applewhite [41] summarizes a number of studies in a compelling manner:

"When scientists at Chicago's Rush University Medical Center in Chicago dug deeper, they uncovered another, overarching factor. They examined the brain tissues of 246 people who died during a long-term study of more than 1,400 older men and women. The autopsy results, reported in Archives of General Psychiatry, were striking. People who exhibited very different levels of cognitive decline often showed similar levels of damage from Alzheimer's. The brains that functioned better, it turned out, belonged to people who had indicated more purpose in life over the course of the study."

"In other words, having a goal in life actually affects cellular activity in the brain. Plaques and tangles still form, but having a goal seems to increase the brain's protective reserve. Not only that, the stronger the purpose, the more it adds to the reserve. The results held up even after the researchers controlled for differences in exercise levels, education, and other factors. Other studies link a sense of purpose not only to slower rates of cognitive decline but to lower rates of disability and death."

She adds that the study defined purpose in life as

" ... the tendency to derive meaning from life's experiences and possess a sense of intentionality and goal directedness that guides behavior."

Schaeffer et al. [42] suggest that having a purpose may

" ... afford protection from negative events and confer resilience through enhanced automatic emotion regulation after negative emotional provocation."

If you are still not convinced take a look at a 2008 paper by Koizumi et al. [43] where they report that a strong sense of purpose resulted in a 72 percent lower risk of a stroke and a 44 percent lower rate of cardiovascular disease.

Before we end this chapter, we also want to address the concepts of "vision" and "mission," or the combination which we call a "compelling future." The brain gets some reward from looking at positive futures, so the creation of a personal, compelling future, is a brain-friendly act. Once a compelling future has been identified, and committed to, the brain aligns behind it to make it happen. The brain loves consistency.

You can have a purpose without a vision. And the other way around – a vision without a purpose. However, we think that it goes without saying that it is ideal that you have both, and that your vision aligns with your purpose.

Each one of us has a different "definition" of what a personal vision is. It doesn't matter whether or not your definition fits any given standard. It just needs to provide you with a guiding and exciting direction. It can be as long or as short as you want it to be. Here are a couple to illustrate. At the "short" end of the spectrum, the vision of a non-profit that Phil is on:

"To develop and support a vibrant and creative arts community for the people of our two counties and for our visitors."

At the other end of the length spectrum:

"Develop commission from $200 million in revenue
Some athletic activity every day
Significantly improved diet and complexion
Soulmate to share life with
Optimally functioning brain
Quality time and trips with family
Write a best-selling book
Create a financial legacy for my family
Build a world-class team
Develop a coaching program to assist other senior females to become better leaders
Develop greater personal confidence, greater reliance on my intuition and trust in myself
Develop a powerful personal voice
Become debt-free and create a secure financial future for my family
Develop personal discipline to accomplish my vision and goals
Develop peace within
Maintain a healthy relationship with friends"

Bottom line summary

Having a purpose in life and a vision gives us some major advantages, not least of which are slower rates of cognitive decline and lower rates of disability and death. Seems like a worthwhile endeavor to us.

What's next?

What one or two things am I going to do to better define my purpose?
What I am going to do about it/them
How will I measure whether I have been successful?

[39] Oxley, R. (1997, January). The Designer's Creed for Success. *Kitchen Bath Design News*.

[40] Steptoe, A., & Fancourt, D. (2019). Leading a meaningful life at older ages and its relationship with social engagement, prosperity, health, biology, and time use. *Pnas, 116*(4), 1207–1212. http://doi.org/10.1073/pnas.1814723116

[41] Applewhite, A. (2016, November 23). How Having A Purpose In Life Impacts Your Brain — In A Big Way. Retrieved March 23, 2020, from wwwhuffpost.com

[42] Schaefer, S. M., Morozink Boylan, J., van Reekum, C. M., Lapate, R. C., Norris, C. J., Ryff, C. D., & Davidson, R. J. (2013). Purpose in Life Predicts Better Emotional Recovery from Negative Stimuli. *Plos One, 8*(11), e80329–9. http://doi.org/10.1371/journal.pone.0080329

[43] Koizumi, M., Ito, H., Kaneko, Y., & Motohashi, Y. (2008). Effect of Having a Sense of Purpose in Life on the Risk of Death from Cardiovascular Diseases. *Journal of Epidemiology, 18*(5), 191–196. http://doi.org/10.2188/jea.JE2007388

Chapter 5:

Personal Change

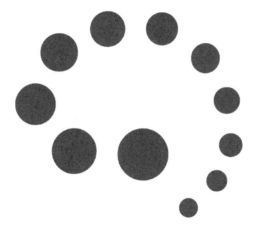

5. Personal Change: Adoption of new ideas and approaches

"When we are no longer able to change a situation, we are challenged to change ourselves."
Viktor Frankl

General comments

As we were finishing the process of writing this book, the world was faced with a challenge, the like of which we hadn't seen: Covid-19. This forced every country and every person in each country, to face some things which caused us all, to have to change. Some of the things which we were required to do were new to us - self-isolation, social distancing and not shaking hands, were new concepts. Some, like coughing into your sleeve or washing your hands more frequently, were not. For many people the changes, while not particularly welcome, were easy to adopt. Other people had significant trouble with the new requirements. So, what was going on? In this chapter, we are going to explore what happens when people decide to change.

For those of you that have not read *UYBFAC*, let's do a quick recap of a central and important matter. Your brain generally dislikes change. Change disrupts established patterns of thinking which are quick and efficient for the purposes of survival. Now, to be clear, your brain can handle small change much easier and will resist less, however, change for change sake is generally much more difficult to accomplish. Change for well-defined benefits that are locked into the future-state expectation stand the greatest chance of taking hold.

Before embarking on or incorporating something new, it is easier to understand yourself and to ensure that you are aware of how you are feeling. If you haven't taken the time to understand yourself, we strongly recommend either reading and acting upon the previous three chapters or, if you haven't already done so, read *UYBFAC*.

What works

Here's how to incorporate something new:

➢ Use the transition map, p 84, as the basis for adopting something new
➢ Be very clear about what it is you want to implement.
➢ Write it down – in as much detail as possible
➢ Create well-formed outcomes using kinesthetic, visual and auditory anchors
➢ Tell your close friends – if they are part of your future
➢ Get some support
➢ Review your progress
➢ Plan for some celebrations
➢ Carefully plan to avoid the traps outlined in the dynamics behind adopting something new
➢ Review your Personal Threat Profile to see where you will resist new things

- Be well aware of your current Personal Threat Context
- Use your strengths
- Be clear about your personal vision of the future
- Be clear about what you are dissatisfied with in your current environment
- Identify a few small first steps
- Identify what you will have to give up or lose in order to move to the new you – and ensure that the cost associated with those losses is not too great.

Brief examples

During the process of writing this book, Scott experienced a series of changes in his life which included becoming a Grandfather, moving to a new location and changing several critical routines all in a two-week period. With this many changes happening at once it is understandable that his threat level was a bit higher than normal (to put it mildly). He noted a lower sense of patience with those around him as well as with himself. He was having a hard time concentrating on his work and was overreacting to less than perfect outcomes when it came to his new role as a Grandfather. All of this was at its peak when he received a phone call telling him that an important piece of business he was working on, had just fallen though. Months of planning down the drain. He felt more out of control than ever before and it was driven by the sequence of changes which made his life almost unrecognizable (at least in that moment). He was having a hard time embracing the changes as positive.

One morning his wife said to him, as she prepared breakfast for them both, "I think I would like to try something new for breakfast". Scott responded, without much thought, that he did not want another change and that he would prefer to take breakfast just as he had done every day for the last two years. His wife smiled and said, "What else around you has remained the same?" It was a light bulb moment for him. He began to take inventory of those things that had not changed and identified those over which he had total influence. As the list grew, his anxiety shallowed, and he started listing out the benefits for the recent changes. "I was reminded that every one of the changes had long term value, but I had not allowed for the transition for that value to emerge fully from behind the curtain of loss." The frustration subsided by identifying what had remained the same, that which he had chosen to change and the subsequent need for the transition period in order to embrace fully the benefits of the changes. By identifying what had not changed first, he set the stage for the real value of change to become obvious. "I felt I had choice in the matter once I could anchor into my patterns and habits first, then I could examine the benefits of change in the context of that steady framework."

Discussion

For many of us, the thought of change brings out some of our very base characteristics, most of them driven by the fear of change. Remember:

- We are driven by bias, habits, patterns etc.

- ➢ We act irrationally
- ➢ Many of us are experiencing major stress
- ➢ The brain doesn't like change
- ➢ There are many aspects of our Personal Threat Profile model which will cause us to get triggered when we attempt to go through change

OK. So, you have decided to do something different. As we mentioned in *UYBFAC*, a colleague of Phil's once said, "The difference between an expert and a novice is a model." [44] Here we are going to help you become experts by giving you several models to help deal with various aspects of doing something different i.e. changing. They are adapted from a variety of sources including Dan Millman, [45] Bill Bridges [46] and Friedman and Gyr [47]

The first distinction that we are going to introduce you to is with regard to some common words. Let's start with the word "Change" Changes are normally instantaneous. You get a new boss. You hand in your notice. You make a decision to lose weight. You decide to live a healthier lifestyle. We often call these "Change triggers." The change, however, doesn't mean that you are now different and have moved into a future state. What has happened is that you have taken the first step of a Transition.

The change itself triggers off some Endings. You know that there is another life out there, sometime in the future, but you are not there yet. You may have left some things behind, but you need to go through a Transition before you reach the new Beginnings, or the Future.

If we look at a simple model of the process it looks like this:

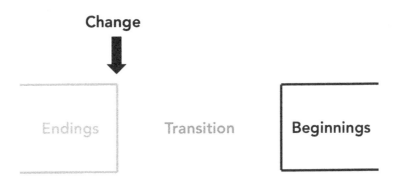

For most of us, the Transition process involves some losses, some ambiguity, some internal reflection, a period of uncertainty etc. before we embark on the new chapter in our lives. And, as you now know, most peoples' brains really dislike being in that state. It feels uncomfortable, scary, and fraught with potential danger, although when asked to describe the danger we're often at a loss for words. When we examine "What's the worst that can happen" it's very often not that bad. It certainly isn't as bad as our brain tries to tell us. This Transition time is sometimes referred to as the Neutral Zone, the Wilderness, or the Tar-Pit. In contrast to those descriptors, however, many people also report that it was a very inventive, creative time in their lives where they gave themselves permission that they never had given themselves before.

We're now going to look at the various parts of this fundamental diagram and start to understand what goes on in each. We're going to look at an expanded model, superimposed on the basic transition model shown above.

As you will see, we have added in, or expanded the model into seven parts, namely

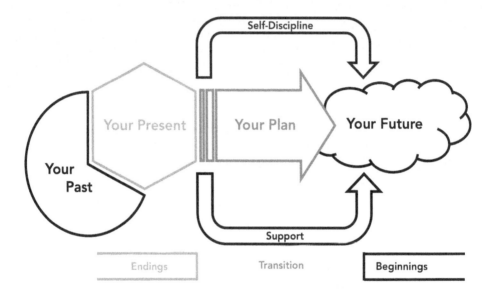

> ➤ Your future
> ➤ Your present
> ➤ The pathway that you will select to get to the future i.e. Your plan
> ➤ Your past
> ➤ The self-discipline you will need
> ➤ The support you will need.
> ➤ Your first step (s)

It is tempting to think of this as a linear model. However, as you think about your future, your brain is just as likely to think about the different parts at random. As you think about the future, part of your brain will be distracted to think about something that is going on for you in the present moment. And then that will trigger off a thought about the past. And so, it goes on.

The good news is that if you have read our first book, *UYBFAC*, you will have already started thinking about all of the components of the change model. There are some parts that are especially useful - the section on the Self, for example and the 5 P's. If you haven't read these …. a small hint. It will be easier to go back and read them. ☺ Understanding yourself i.e. gaining self-awareness, is a crucial first step in creating a personal platform for change.

We just have to add one more statement in here. This is just one model of change; if this one doesn't resonate with you, there are plenty more to find on the Internet. But having a model to base your transition upon, is very helpful.

The Dynamics of adopting something new

Before we start, however, we want to give you a heads up that there are a couple of dynamics that tend to occur when people are thinking about change. The first and biggest of these is your very own Background Talk.

Background Talk. Most of us have several 'voices' in our heads, which give us 'advice.' When we hear someone say something, these voices, or background talk, are making judgments - constantly. These voices do the same with our own activities, statements, thoughts, ideas or plans.

The messages that arise from this background talk otherwise known as "belief systems" are often grounded in deep lessons from our past – or statements that we have heard in the past, that might have been true then, but are not necessarily true now. Early in our life we are taught, either intentionally or unintentionally, that certain things are true, and we accept them without any evidence for or against their validity. These are often hidden influences, much like software, running in the background of our daily experiences.

Sometimes these voices are useful and helpful to us – they provide good cautious wisdom and can nudge us in the right direction. They are often the voices that make us do the right thing, even when no-one is watching! These are the voices of our empowering beliefs.

Sometimes, however, these background voices get in our way. They get in the way of doing something that we could do, might do, or need to do. Sometimes these voices get in the way of taking that step which would move us forward in our lives. Sometimes they get in the way of taking the risk that we've never taken. Sometimes they get in the way of changing a habit that has been there for a while and needs to be changed. These are the voices of our limiting beliefs.

Here is an example of how one of these cautionary voices works in practice, concerning the issue of how we make the future happen. Many people will shy away from saying or writing something about their future because they can't immediately see how to make it happen. When new thoughts or ideas come into our head, or we hear them from other people, we tend to judge them quickly – and harshly. We follow up with thoughts or statements like, "Well, that'll never happen" or "I tried that before and look at where it got me." We're sure you can come up with many, many more of your own.

We tend to view these thoughts in three ways - immediately and, mostly, nonconsciously!

> 1. We evaluate the thought or idea's <u>feasibility</u>, or whether we can see how to get it done

> 2. We evaluate the <u>appeal</u> of the thought or idea i.e. do we like it?

> 3. We evaluate the degree that we will have to <u>change</u> what we are currently doing in our lives.

Then we make a decision – again, mostly nonconsciously, and often focused only on the thought or idea's feasibility, no matter how appealing it is to us. And this goes on rapidly in our brains – often before the thought or idea is fully formed or evaluated. And certainly, before it ever comes out of our mouths, or takes residence in our head.

Let's draw this out in diagrammatic form, using a scale of 0 to 10 where 0 means "None" and 10 means "High," using the following diagram as a basis:

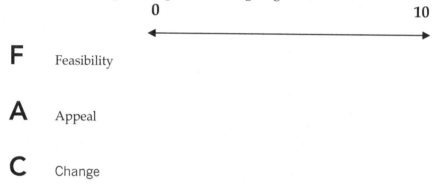

Let's look at what happens when we come up with about a new thought or idea. Typically, although it might be very appealing to us, it is likely to involve a lot of change, and, in the first instance, on most occasions, we probably have no idea how to go about doing it. In this instance, the FAC diagram looks like this:

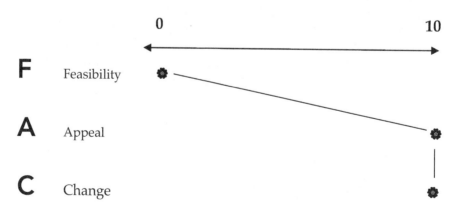

The sad thing is that we tend to make our decision based on the fact that we haven't got a clue how to go about it, and/or it will involve a lot of change. We often go through this process before the idea has even come out of our mouth. Unfortunately, many new ideas never get past the 'feasibility' or 'change' evaluation stage - regardless of how appealing the idea might be – and hence do not get acted upon. Your specific background talk (Your Limiting or Empowering Beliefs) will depend upon all sorts of factors - many of them based upon your worldview, your Personal Threat Profile and your current Personal Threat Context.

On the other hand, ideas that are easy to do, i.e. high in feasibility, are frequently low in appeal because we've heard about them before or they are not breakthrough ideas. The upside is that they often don't involve much change. These are the ideas that tend to get acted upon. They offer the path of least resistance. They tend to look like this:

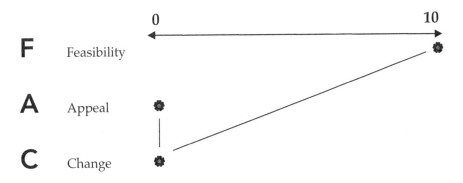

For the time being, as you start thinking about change, give yourself permission simply to think about and evaluate any of your thoughts or ideas <u>solely</u> based upon their appeal and, again for the time being, forget about their feasibility or the change aspects involved. We'll figure out how to make them work later.

As you think about and plan out a change, be aware of the influence of all this background talk – catch yourself when listening to this background voice - and bring it out to the open. Ask yourself, "Is this a limiting or empowering belief that is talking to me?"

Each of us has different background conversations – the one described above is just a typical one. Take a moment to think about your own background conversations.

The next thing that tends to happen is that we rapidly have our own personal failure talk.

<u>Failure talk.</u> Nowadays, we have a high expectation that everything happens immediately. It surrounds us. We call it "the immediacy of time." We can get (most) things delivered within 24 hours. We expect responses from our e-mails, voicemails, texts, Instagram messages etc. within minutes, and often get frustrated when the recipient takes longer to respond. Some of us start to feel guilty if we haven't responded to a text within a couple of minutes. We expect soundbites that are not too long, yet long-enough to capture our attention. Unfortunately, when it comes to changing something material and worthwhile in our lives, it takes longer than the

currency that we currently measure our time in. Much longer. Especially if you are changing an old habit and replacing it with a new one.

Over the past three decades, we have both watched many people start off on a change initiative, only to get frustrated with themselves in a very short time. They haven't been able to fully master the new way of doing things within the first week. Or they keep making mistakes. Or they keep reverting back to old behavior. You name it. The exact failure talk depends on the individual, their specific Personal Threat Profile and the change that they are trying to enact. We set up expectations for ourselves that are almost impossible to meet. And we give up, driven by failure talk. It's our brains again. They want to be able to predict what's happening. Or be in control. Or be right. So, when you catch your brain acting up and attempting to move you away from the change that you are embarking on, congratulate yourself. If you worked on the section on subpersonalities in *UYBFAC*, you can use one of those subpersonalities to set you back on track. ☺

Another dynamic that tends to happen as we enter into this change path, is that we discover that not all is wonder and light. There are a few things that we are going to have to give up or lose as a result of the change

Grieve the losses. One thing that is common in our dissection of change is that there are always losses associated with change. *"This sense of loss is present even when the change is obviously for the better"* writes Bridges [48] a master of studying change and transition. For example, promotions, although ostensibly positive, will often mean having a different relationship with, or even losing a relationship with, past co-workers. They can often mean going from a role in which you felt competent, to one in which you feel incompetent. Even the upgrade of a piece of software can make people feel very uncomfortable [49].

Bridges identifies six categories of loss:

> ➢ Loss of Attachments/Relationships
> ➢ Loss of Turf/Territory
> ➢ Loss of Structure
> ➢ Loss of a Future or a Dream
> ➢ Loss of Meaning/Purpose
> ➢ Loss of Control

Several senior practitioners that Phil was in conversation with recently have used this list as a starting point but have added to it when working with their clients. They have added the following:

> ➢ Loss of a feeling of Competence or Mastery
> ➢ Loss of a sense of Security
> ➢ Loss of a sense of Direction.

One can easily see that all of these losses relate back to the 5 P's we described in *UYBFAC*. It is also easy to imagine that the threat to any of the many facets of the 5

P's could easily lead to a loss. The degree to which that loss affects any one of us will depend on the weight that the individual ascribes to that facet. If, for example, being in an in-group is important for you, then loss of those attachments/relationships will be hard.

Many years ago, Phil heard a phrase that has stuck with him. He cannot remember who said it, so if you know, then please let us know. It is probably a well-known idiom in the psychotherapy field. It goes like this: "All change is loss, and all loss must be grieved."

There are many models of grief or mourning, all described in terms of stages. The common ones are:

D.A.B.D.A	S.A.R.A.H.
Denial	Shock
Anger	Anger
Bargaining/Betrayal	Rejection
Depression	Acceptance
Acceptance	Help

It seems that D.A.B.D.A is more common in the US and S.A.R.A.H. is better known in the UK, but we have no scientific data on that. The "no scientific data" is also true for the debate that ensues around the 'stage' model of grief. There are wide ranging discussions about its validity and usefulness ranging from one supportive piece of research that aligned the model with the user reaction when the iPhone 5 was released [50] through to a plea that *"stage theory should be discarded by all concerned (including bereaved persons themselves); at best, it should be relegated to the realms of history."* [51] Whether it is a valid and complete model, or whether indeed it is a dangerous model – we will let you make up your own mind.

These tips for how to use the model might be useful, however: [52]

1. These stages are not meant to be complete; i.e. there may be other dynamics that occur. Bridges suggests numbness, yearning and searching, disorganization and despair, and a degree of reorganization. The addition of shock, rejection and a request for help in the SARAH model seems to be useful.

2. These stages are not meant to be chronological: i.e. this is not a defined sequence. Many people will find that, if they can identify the stages, which some people cannot, then they experience them cyclically or at random.

3. Not everyone who experiences grief will feel all five stages nor will everyone who does go through that experience do so in any particular order.

4. Elizabeth Kubler-Ross " *... originally applied these stages to people suffering from terminal illness, ... she did not discard the possibility of applying this theoretical model to any form of catastrophic personal loss*" i.e. it was never intended to be an all-encompassing theory.

5. The theory was oriented towards a negative change/loss that has been imposed on a person, rather than one which he/she elected.

That all being said, we have found that using these models as a basis for understanding your own process of change (or indeed, when working with others) does help. To know that the anger you are feeling is not unique to you, or that the sense of "why me" is "normal" and helps us through those uncertain times.

The next dynamic is something we call the need to "learn how to change" as this ability does not necessarily come naturally to us:

Learning to change. We are going to adapt and leverage a model offered by Dan Millman. [53] At one time, he was an Olympian gymnast and an instructor for trampoline. He noticed a learning process that his students typically went through. His name for it was the Ladder of Learning. It consisted of eight steps, as follows:

1. The bottom of the ladder is where the student is unable to recognize the new behavior in a professional even when it is deliberately illustrated.

2. The first step is to be able to recognize it in a professional when it is being deliberately illustrated.

3. The next step is to be able to recognize it in a fellow student.

4. Then the student is able to recognize it in himself – but after the event e.g. watching a replay.

5. Then the student is able to recognize it in himself – but immediately after the event.

6. The next step is for the student to able to recognize it in himself as it is happening – and, maybe, correct it.

7. Then the student is able to prevent it from happening, but with conscious effort.

8. The final step is for the behavior to become nonconscious.

We include a picture of a ladder on the next page for those of you that are more visual and hate lists!

In our experience of assisting and supporting people going through change, this process is what happens most of the time, when people are successful in their change initiative. It has proven a useful tool to be able to identify which step in the ladder they are on. In some ways, however, the picture of a ladder, with equal steps is misleading. It is a relatively quick and easy step to go from the bottom of the ladder on to the first step. And the step to the third and fourth rung is fairly easy too. Then the going gets a little tougher. The step to the fifth rung happens fairly soon. But many people find the jump to the sixth rung more difficult. Seven gets more difficult and taking it to a nonconscious habit can take much longer.

So, how long does it take to make a change? There are many schools of thought about that number. Some people believe that once you have done something three times,

8. It has become nonconscious behavior

7. Able to consciously prevent it from happening

6. Able to recognize in self – as it was happening and correct it consciously

5. Able to recognize in self – immediately after the event

4. Able to recognize in self – long after the event

3. Able to recognize in other students

2. Able to recognize in a professional

1. Unable to recognize in a professional

then you have started to change. Gordon [54] suggests what he calls the 1000x rule. You have to do something a thousand times before it becomes ingrained.

That's the bad news. But, there's good news. Imagining doing it is almost as good as actually doing it.

The next dynamic comes down to your own style. One of the factors in the Neo-FFI is Agreeableness and it seems that it might have an impact on people's ability to change.

Agreeableness. Phil's thesis for his Master's degree was focused on what made people adopt a change when they had been given feedback. It turns out that, for many people, they reject the process of being given feedback – and react in the opposite way. Phil states that he learned many things in the process of researching his thesis but was unable to come up with a set of factors that he could correlate with people's success in changing. One thing he did find out, though, was the exact opposite. He discovered a trait that seemed to be associated with people not changing. For the cohort (a fancy word for a specific group of people) that he was studying, all the people who did not change, all had a high score in Agreeableness. (Reminder: Agreeableness is one of the Neo-FFI factors that you read about in the Self section of *UYBFAC*)

Scientific proof? Far from it. First, it was a very small cohort. It was twenty people in total. To have any validity, it would have had to have covered a much larger cohort. Second, 10 changed and 10 didn't. The 10 that didn't, all scored high in Agreeableness. That doesn't prove that it caused them not to change. Again, it would require a lot more research to make those types of conclusions. It's just interesting that there was a 100% match. Also, it doesn't prove that if someone is more on the Disagreeable end of the Agreeableness spectrum that they are more likely to change.

But it might be an indication that people who are high in the Agreeableness score might have a tougher time changing. It also suggests that if you are a person with a high Agreeableness score, or if you are coaching or assisting someone like that, you might want to ensure you take that into account.

That's a conclusion about one specific measure of behavior. The more general conclusion is that, from a brain and behavioral perspective, not all of us will approach change in the same way.

Until this point, we have referred to change as a single generic process. And from an overall perspective, it is. The models for all changes are similar. But there are different types of changes.

Type of change. The major differences in type of change, lie in the timeframe of the change and the scale of the change. Clearly, largescale changes over longer periods of time, tend to be more difficult than smaller more immediate changes. But, having spent thirty years helping people go through change, small changes are where the action is. Most, if not all, large scale changes are made up of a series or cascade of small changes. Having a compelling vision of the future is essential. Gleicher's formula, which we will address below, indicates that change is difficult without such a vision. Having a set of clearly identified first steps, is where the small change process kicks in.

Scott was working with a senior leader, we will call David, at a well-known bank. David struggled to understand why one of his direct managers, Bob, was not willing to change his focus from providing private mortgages, which he had done for 20 years, to offering services beyond mortgages which included small business loans, treasury management as well as fraud protection, mitigation and prevention. Six months earlier the bank had been acquired by a competitor and this model fit the acquiring bank's operations. As they worked through the resistance David realized that Bob's threat was tied to his insecurity in promoting products that he knew very little about. He was also looking at a new bonus structure based on this change and Bob knew he would not be able to maximize his earnings while taking on the new product line. David finally came to understand that Bob needed to see a vision where he was part of the future, whereas Bob was convinced that this new role was intended to remove him and have him retire earlier than planned. There was also another factor. Bob had watched several of his friends from Wells Fargo go through a scandal from 2011 through 2015 which involved fraudulent cross selling. It was a mental barrier. It is no wonder that Bob was faltering.

David came to the conclusion in order to get the best out of Bob he needed to feed the changes in small doses which allowed time for competence and success to take hold thereby quieting the voice inside that told Bob this was a set up. Two years later, Bob was making more money than ever before and was a very active member of the change committee which he set up as a support system for the growth strategy.

One of the things that we know about the brain is that it seeks, and is influenced by, consistency. If we can adopt a small change, which is in the right general direction, then the brain wants to be consistent and is more likely to adopt the next change, and one following that … until the vision is fulfilled.

Whenever we listen to people talk about change, the conversation invariably turns to everyone's resistance to change. We know that the brains of many people do resist change. And we know why.

Resistance to change. There are many, many books devoted to why people resist change. A review of these books would take between two decades and forever, so we are not going to attempt it. ☺ These books do, however have useful models for people going through change. A Google or Amazon search will give you plenty to choose from. We have found one, in particular, that provides a useful basis for discussion. Gleicher's Formula. [55]

The latest version of this formula identifies four factors that must be present for change to actually occur. These are:

Dissatisfaction with the Status Quo (D) multiplied by

A Compelling **Vision** (V) multiplied by

Clearly defined **First Steps** (F) multiplied by

Believability (B)

must be significantly greater than

Personal Cost to Change (PC)

The formula is represented by the following equation:

$$D \times V \times F \times B \gg PC$$

Personal Cost of change may have many attributes including time, money, psychological, emotional, losses and social attributes.

Sorry to bring this up now, but we are going to tread into the field of algebra, which we suspect is not, to say the least, everyone's favorite topic. The fact that the above change formula is expressed as an algebraic equation, implies that, under the laws of algebra, if one or more of the factors on the left-hand side of the equation is less than "1" then the resultant product will become very small and is unlikely, therefore, to overcome resistance to the change or personal cost. Clearly, according to this formula, if any of the factors is zero, or non-existent, then no change is likely to occur.

So, what does this mean for personal change? It means that if you are about to embark on a change you need to be able to say a wholehearted "yes" to each of the four items identified above. Yes, I am dissatisfied with what is going on today. Yes, I have a clear picture of what I want in the future. Yes, I know what I am going to do first, and yes, I believe all of the above, at both a conscious and nonconscious level.

The language we use (and the attitude we hold)

Phil holds two sayings or mantras dearly.

The first will be well known to many of our readers. "Do. Or do not. There is no try." Yoda! (The Empire Strikes Back) It seems to make a subtle but important difference in our ability to act. It seems that, if we use the word "try," then the nonconscious part of our brain gives us an "out" if we fail in what we were going after. Our background conversation goes something like this: "I just said that I was going to try. I am OK if I didn't manage to succeed." In our work with helping people through change, this has been one of the more useful tools when helping people identify exactly what they are going to do. The use of the word try can be insidious. It just creeps in there. It helps if you have someone else to help keep watch for you.

Other words that seem to have a similar impact are "Can't" and "Never." Be really careful with their use.

The second of Phil's mantras goes back a little further. In general, it is attributed to Johann Wolfgang van Goethe. [3] It is a mixture of dream and commitment.

> "Until one is committed, there is hesitancy, the chance to draw back, always ineffectiveness. Concerning all acts of initiative and creation, there is one elementary truth the ignorance of which kills countless ideas and splendid plans: that the moment one definitely commits oneself, then providence moves too."

> "All sorts of things occur to help one that would never otherwise have occurred. A whole stream of events issues from the decision, raising in one's favor all manner of unforeseen incidents, meetings and material assistance which no man could have dreamed would have come his way."

> "Whatever you can do or dream you can, begin it. Boldness has genius, power and magic in it. Begin it now."

Amazingly, this was written in the 18th century. We have used this on countless occasions, to help people become clear on what it is they are planning, and then deciding to commit to that plan, no matter how small the change or goal.

Our last comment on the words that we use, is subtle and somewhat more difficult to identify, but equally powerful. Once you understand it, you will never go back. It rests on the difference between the use of the word "I" and the use of the word "You."

Before we explain further, we are NOT talking about the explicit difference between "I" and "You" which has become the focus on many training sessions over the past decade. The theme in these sessions is that "You" statements can make people feel accused, inferior, guilty etc., for example, "When you are late with the project, we all suffer." The suggestion, supported by research, is that these type of statements make people defensive – and feel threatened, and as we now know, that is not a good brain state to put people in. Better to take ownership yourself and use "I" statements. "I start to get worried when I don't have the report. How can I help?"

---

[3] There is some debate as to whether he actually was the originator or not – but the power of the statement still remains, regardless of the origin.

These are all good techniques and need to be incorporated by all of us.

But we want to dig deeper.

Eavesdrop on a cocktail party conversation. Or simply keep quiet next time when you are in a conversation which involves several people. And listen closely to what they are saying and the pronouns that they use. Or, more specifically, when they change back and forth between the two pronouns "I" and "You." Let's look at an imaginary conversation, and, as they say in modern parlance, unpack it.

"I really had a great time at the cinema the other day, except at the very end. I was standing up to leave, when I went to turn and knocked over the box of popcorn of the guy next to me. You know the sort of thing. When you're not paying attention to where you are going. You know those occasions when you should apologize, but don't because of the look on someone's face."

Let's pull this apart. All the while our narrator is having a good time, he/she uses the pronoun "I" – "I really had a good time …" or "I was standing up to leave" etc. Then when something goes wrong, he/she changes the use to that of "you." "You know the sort of thing." Or "When you're not quite looking where you are going."

At some nonconscious level, this person knows that they were at fault. They even know why. They weren't paying attention to where they were going. They even knew that they should apologize. Our language, however, changes to something else. We alleviate our guilt or sense of accountability by passing that feeling on to "You."

That was a fictitious example. Here's a recent, real-life example. [56] This concerns the feelings of Christopher Steele, "the former M.I.6 spy turned private investigator" who wrote a dossier on Donald Trump, only to learn that U.S. politicians were accusing him of being a criminal. In describing his feelings to his co-founder, Christopher Burrows, this is what Burrows recalled:

"You have this thudding headache – you can't think straight, you have no appetite, you feel ill."

Now, we don't know whether the "You" pronoun was used by Steele, or was introduced in the recall by Burrows, but it is a stark demonstration of distancing oneself from the real, unpleasant feelings which were swirling for him at the time.

We have found that when we are helping people to change, challenging people in conversation over their use of "I" vs "You" can have a very powerful impact on their ability to get their arms around what they need to address.

OK. Let's move on to the next dynamic we see. Are you ready?

Readiness for change. There is an old adage "Ready, willing and able." These three factors are important in the world of change. If you are not ready for a change, don't attempt to do so, regardless of what your friends and significant others say, or your horoscope says, or what you think you should do just because it's New Year's Day and you need to make a resolution.

James Prochaska [57] has spent a good deal of his career in studying change. While the focus of his studies has generally been about things like smoking cessation, his theories have been applied to many change processes, so we think his models are worth reviewing. He identified five stages for change as follows:

1. *Pre-contemplation:* this is the stage in which there is no intention to change behavior in the foreseeable future.

2. *Contemplation:* is the stage in which people are aware that they need action, and/or are seriously thinking about doing something about it but have not yet made a commitment to take action. People at this stage struggle between their positive evaluations of changing their behavior versus the amount of effort, energy, and loss it will cost to overcome and solidify the change.

3. *Preparation:* this is the stage in which individuals are intending to take action in the next month and are reporting some small behavioral changes ("baby steps").

4. *Action:* is the stage in which individuals modify their behavior, experiences, and/or environment to address the change that they are wishing to make. Action involves the most overt behavioral changes and requires considerable commitment of both time and energy. Individuals are classified in the action stage if they have successfully altered their behavior for a period from 1 day to 6 months.

5. *Maintenance:* is the stage in which people work to prevent relapse and consolidate the gains attained during action. This stage extends from 6 months to an indeterminate period past the initial action.

If you are in the first of these stages, you should definitely not embark on a change. If you are in the second, then consider very carefully whether this is the right time to invest that amount of effort and energy, and whether you are willing to incur the losses involved. If you are in stages three or four, then you are on your way to change.

Other researchers have expanded Prochaska's work. In the preparation phase and in the action phase, we often see an "Experimentation" component, that is trying out different ways of attempting the change. Seeing what works best.

In addition, some researchers add on a "Relapse" phase. In the smoking, or addiction field, this has different consequences and meanings than it does in the arena that we are focusing on, but it is valuable to talk about the fact that ... well it doesn't always go well. You are not going to get it right the first time. And you aren't always going to maintain positive forward momentum. When we are attempting to change long-standing habits and replace them with new ones, it takes a while.

Another important dynamic that we need to address is, of course, the impacts of the nonconscious brain.

Conscious and nonconscious modes. In *UYBFAC* we introduced the suggestion that, if you are to approach a change then you need to take both the conscious and the nonconscious modes of the brain into account. We also said that we would come back and address it in more detail. Now is the time.

The problem, as with all things brain related, is that it is not as simple as addressing just one Brain Principle; there are, however, a number of the brain principles and brain dynamics that we now need to address in order to assist ourselves in effecting change. Let's look at them all:

> We are primarily driven by the nonconscious mode of our brain
> There is an on-going struggle between the PFC and the Limbic system
> We are driven mostly by our biases and our habits
> We are irrational
> We are less effective when under stress
> Change is an anathema to the well-constructed, and in some cases, life-long schemas that are a fundamental part of how our brains process information.
> Brain Rhythms – we less likely to have full control of our PFC at the 'wrong time' of the day
> We all are driven by our own Personal Threat Profile
> We are all driven by all of the aspects of the Self

In fact, there is an argument to be made, that in looking at change we need to bring together all of these aspects. But, at a minimum, we need to address the conscious and the nonconscious modes.

The lack of this two-part approach is one of the biggest failings of most approaches to change. We believe this to be true at every level whether it is at the individual level or at the organizational level, and everywhere in between.

Let's take a look at what this means in practice.

If you make a statement, say for example, a New Year's Resolution, that you intend to make a change, the likelihood of that change occurring is increased if you write it down. So far, so good.

There is also some evidence that suggests if you make the resolution public you also increase the chances of success in making the change. Now we are starting to work on the nonconscious aspects. Your public commitment seems to introduce into the brain the Consistency dialog. An internal 'narrative' arises that says, "I need to have my external and internal commitments aligned."

In addition, it is clear that the more specific you can make your "goal intentions" the greater the chances of actually introducing the change that you wish to bring about. The old "S.M.A.R.T." goals approach is a good starting point. The use of "Goal Intentions" has been widely studied in the research literature. [58] Research has shown that the addition of "Implementation Intentions" significantly increases the chances of achieving the goal (or desired change.) It seems to work as follows:

The problem:

The PFC, the center of our Executive Function, is fully able to grasp the need to achieve a goal or make a change. Indeed, it is gung-ho to do so. For a very brief period of time! Then it gets distracted and moves on to something else. Then the over-riding change or goal, gets lost in the myriad of other items that it chases. Until something reminds the PFC that it should be paying attention, and so the loop starts all over again. The ability of the PFC to self-regulate our actions is, at best, tenuous.

That is when we are in top form. In practice, however, our susceptibility to stress and energy cycles means that, as the day goes on, we are less and less able to self-regulate. As that happens, we are more and more inclined to react out of habit. Which is what gets most individual change programs in trouble. (And probably many organizational ones, too). We simply revert back to our old patterns and often justify what we are doing. "Well I have been so good on my diet all day, that it is OK if I have a bowl-full of ice-cream now."

The solution:

Create an "instant habit" which runs in parallel to those already in place. The overall construct is to create an "Implementation Intention" in the form of an "If-Then" statement. It's a sort of preview of what can go wrong, a preventative contingency plan and a reminder of the overall goal, all in one. It looks like this:

"If I am in (*circumstance a*) then I will do (*b*) in order to achieve (*c*)"

"If I find myself at the freezer, picking up the carton of ice-cream, then I will replace it on the same shelf, and, instead, pour myself a glass of orange juice, in order to develop a healthier life-style."

By forming this detailed mental image, then the specified situation or cue becomes more accessible and increases the chance of making the appropriate change stick. It turns out that this self-regulatory act has an impact, even if the individual doesn't remember that they have put the instant habit in place. Saying the sentence three times, seems to also have a major impact on the instant habit's efficacy.

> *"The act of making the statement seems to help the brain automatically trigger the top-down control when it needs to trigger it and removes or lessens the burden for the person (i.e. the PFC) to be continuously monitoring their behavior."*

There has been a large amount of research into how to make these implementation intentions more effective. We will add two items in here:

1. If the statement is around "inner states" then the intention has a greater chance of being useful in a variety of circumstances. So, the statement above could be changed to:

> *"If I find myself tempted to fall off the wagon of my diet, then I will replace the temptation with something healthier instead, in order to continue a healthier life-style."*

2. If the "then" part of the statement is action-oriented rather than simply internally reflective.

The more specific you are in the identification of the temptation, and the more specific you are with your prescribed response, the greater the chance that you can create a predictive outcome which serves your needs. It removes the ambiguity and allows the top down approach to be more efficient.

So far so good. But can you do it on your own?

<u>You need a friend – but the right type of friend</u>

There is much research that shows that who you hang out with impacts many aspects of your life. Part of the Participation domain is that we want to be with people that we like and that are like us. In an obvious way, if you want to make a change, for example, to quit smoking, then it's best not to hang around with smokers. If you want to make a change to a healthier lifestyle, hang out with people who are living a healthy lifestyle.

The downside of this is that it can mean increasing the 'losses' associated with the change, for example, losing some of the 'past' friends that you associate with the 'old' habits.

<u>Resistance from others</u>

In some ways, this is an extension of the previous dynamic. Surround yourself with supporters, at least in the short term. The story goes something like this. One of the problems with personal change is that, very often, even when we have figured out how to work on ourselves, we get resistance from the 'system' around us. Other people are used to us being the way we are – and when we change, especially if we don't let them know we are attempting a change or going through a change, they will push back on us when they see us doing things differently or behaving differently. These pushbacks can be subtle or direct.

The subtle ones are often the curious or disbelieving look. Nothing is said but you know that they have noticed a change in you, and are reacting to it, but not saying anything. The more direct ones are comments, often supposedly as a joke, but delivered with a sarcastic tone or a barb. "Hey, what side of the bed did you get out of this morning?" As a reminder, we have discussed the impact of being rejected, albeit subtle and how that can impact our primary threats thus impacting our ability to maintain change. Remember the "Agreeableness" discussion earlier? If you or someone you know has a high level of agreeableness you may find this resistance working against you or them and it increases the likelihood of a failure to maintain change. The system surrounding you or them must be modified to make sure that change can take root.

Let's look at a diagram of what it feels like to go start the journey of a change. Let's say we have decided that we need to be a more assertive and less passive in our behavior. And we have worked with a coach, made a few plans and defined some first steps. And we have executed our first new behavior. The outside world sees a small change in us. This can be shown in the following diagram. Our starting point is shown as "A" in the diagram, and the results of our new behavior are shown as "B."

That is what the rest of world sees. But, internally to us, where we have been used to behaving in a more passive manner, it feels like we have taken an incredible jump – and we are acting in a crazy, uncontrolled and dominant fashion! It feels more like position "C" below.

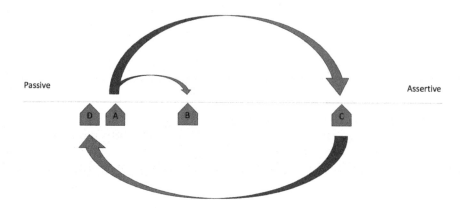

This is one of the danger points. If, at this fragile moment, we get ridicule, opposition or negative pushback, we can often 'cave in' under the pressure. We don't typically have the resilience to 'protect' our new position. In many cases, we revert slightly further back, feeling that nothing we do will ever be good enough, as shown in "D."

Surrounding yourself with people that know you are going through change, whom you have asked for help, and are mostly supportive can mitigate against this.

As you find yourself gradually going down the change journey, it is important to recognize progress.

<u>Use your strengths</u>

As you review your Personal Threat Profile, some of your scores will show up as being of assistance in helping you do something different; others will hinder you. You may have taken other assessments which outline your attributes, both positive and negative. Pull together all of your positive attributes and strengths; most people who adopt a change, tend to use and leverage their strengths.

<u>Celebrate successes</u>. All of them. No matter how small. Give yourself a reward for achieving a goal. Provided that reward is in line with your overall vision. Celebrate that success with someone else, who knows of your change and is in support of it. Research shows that a positive reward for success is a much more effective means for changing behavior, than punishing yourself for failure. One word of caution. Be sure that celebration is congruent with the change you seek. If you are learning to stand your ground in executive meetings and you celebrate by going to the pub and bragging about it to your colleagues that also work for that boss, it may not serve you in the long run. Find a reward that does not set you back on your change but enhances your motivation to continue the change.

Bottom line summary

There is much to think about with regard to adopting something new. Not just what it is that you want to adopt, but how you can increase the chance of being successful. We strongly recommend completing your own version of the transition map we outlined above. In as much detail as you can.

What's next?

What one or two things am I going to focus on in order to be more flexible in change?
What I am going to do about it/them?
How will I measure whether I have been successful?

---

[44] Thank you, Dr. Evian Gordon.

[45] Millman, D. (1991). The Warrior Athlete. Stillpoint Publishing.

[46] William Bridges, (1988) Surviving Corporate Transitions, William Bridges & Associates

[47] Friedman, L., & Gyr, H. (1997). The Dynamic Enterprise. Wiley, John & Sons, Inc.

[48] William Bridges, (1988) Op cit

[49] Bryson, P. (1999). The Nudist on the Late Shift and Other True Tales of Silicon Valley. Random House.

[50] Lim, W. M. (2013). Revisiting Kubler-Ross's five stages of grief: some comments on the iphone 5. Journal of Social Sciences, 9(1), 11–13. http://doi.org/10.3844/jsssp.2013.11.13

[51] Cautioning Health-Care Professionals: Bereaved Persons Are Misguided Through the Stages of Grief, Margaret Stroebe, Henk Schut, and Kathrin Boerner

[52] These notes are extracted from Lim's paper aligning the DABDA model with user complaints with the iPhone 5 release.

[53] There is an almost parallel but less detailed change model in common use that is referred to as the Competence-Incompetence/Conscious-Unconscious model. We have abandoned that. Being referred to as Unconsciously Incompetent is about as unfriendly to the brain as you can get.

[54] Gordon, Evian, (2012) Brain Revolution, Brain Revolution Publications

[55] A number of people have been credited with this formula, but all of the versions appear to be derivatives of the work done by David Gleicher of Arthur D Little, in the 60's

[56] The Man Behind the Dossier. Jane Meyer. The New Yorker, March 12 2018.

[57] Prochaska has published many papers on Change – a Google scholar search will be very rewarding

[58] Gollwitzer has published many papers on Goal Intentions - a Google scholar search will be very rewarding

Chapter 6:

Stress Mastery

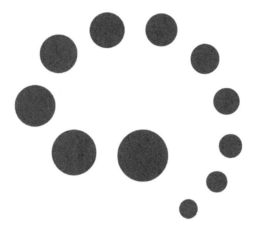

6. Stress Mastery

General comments

So, why all the fuss about stress? We thought it useful to put the impact of stress in perspective – and hence explain why it is important to understand and 'master' it. A recent paper from Harvard and Stanford Business schools [59] assessed the impact of work-place stress on mortality in America. The ten stressors that they studied were:

> *"Unemployment, lack of health insurance, exposure to shift work, long working hours, job insecurity, work-family conflict, low job control, high job demands, low social support at work, and low organizational justice."*

And the results? Pretty staggering:

> *"We find that more than 120,000 deaths per year and approximately 5-8% of annual healthcare costs are associated with and may be attributable to how U.S. companies manage their work force."*

Please note that they don't explicitly include "my boss" as part of the analysis; one's boss has been shown by Hogan etc. [60] as one of the biggest stressors for most people who work in corporate America. The actual impact of stress might be greater if you consider the overall impact on employee morale, employee turnover, workplace hostility etc. And, by the way, if your mind doesn't immediately calculate what 5-8% of annual health care costs, another paper estimated it at $180 billion.

In another even more recent article, Tomiyama [61] summarizes for us some of the impacts of chronic stress:

> ➢ *First, stress interferes with cognitive processes such as executive function and self-regulation.*
> ➢ *Second, stress can affect behavior by inducing overeating and consumption of foods that are high in calories, fat, or sugar; by decreasing physical activity; and by shortening sleep.*
> ➢ *Third, stress triggers physiological changes in the hypothalamic-pituitary-adrenal axis, reward processing in the brain, and possibly the gut microbiome.*
> ➢ *Finally, stress can stimulate production of biochemical hormones and peptides such as leptin, ghrelin, and neuropeptide Y.*

So, it seems that if we can have some impact on reducing the impact of stress, it is a worthy cause. The importance of this as an issue, is one of the reasons why this is one of the longest chapters in the book.

The term "stress" has become widely bandied about over the past couple of decades; in some sense it has become overused and hence needs a little more clarification before it can become a useful term again. So, once again, we will look to providing a definition.

First of all, there are different types of stress McEwen [62] provides us with a useful classification and explanation, as follows:

"Good stress: the experience of rising to a challenge, taking a risk, and feeling rewarded by an, often positive outcome. Healthy self-esteem and good impulse control and decision-making capability, all functions of a healthy brain architecture, are important in this scenario. Even adverse outcomes can function as growth experiences for individuals with such positive, adaptive characteristics."

So, not all stress is bad.

"Tolerable stress: situations where negative events occur, but the individual with healthy brain architecture is able to cope, often with the aid of family, friends, and other individuals who provide support. Here "distress" refers to the uncomfortable feeling related to the nature of the stressor and the degree to which the individual feels a lack of ability to influence or control the stressor."

Once again, this stress is not too bad - if you have a healthy brain.

Toxic stress: situations in which negative events are experienced by an individual who has limited support and may also have brain architecture that reflects the effects of adverse early life events that have impaired the development of good impulse control and judgment and adequate self-esteem. Here, the degree and/or duration of distress may be greater. With toxic stress, the inability to cope is likely to have adverse effects on behavior and physiology.

This one is the killer. Whether something is perceived as good, tolerable or toxic will depend on many, many factors, including your Personal Threat Profile and Personal Threat Context; indeed, one of the phrases used by McEwen in describing tolerable stress, *"the ability to influence or control the stressor"* directly calls into account Predictability. So, whether you see something as tolerable or toxic will also depend on your sense of whether you feel the need and ability to influence or control. If this facet of Predictability is not important to you, then a particular stressor may not impact you much. If, on the other hand, your need for influence and control is high, then you may experience a high degree of toxic stress.

We can now look at what can be done about them. While those three distinctions are helpful, however, before we move ahead, a cautionary word of warning from the abstract from McEwen's article: *" ... there are no magic bullets"*

Brief examples

Phil and Scott have a colleague that they have both known for some time. She recently took a job at a widely known company. It was a perfect job for her. She knew the brand, she knew the people and is one of the leading experts in the topic that she had been recruited for. The role is a senior role, reporting to the COO, who also knows her well. A couple of months later, in a telephone conversation, it became very clear that, even though she teaches managers on how to manage stress, she was clearly very stressed by her new role. Phil noticed a couple of items that seemed to be in conflict. On the one hand she was excited about contributing to the overall direction and strategy of the company and aligning her department behind that strategy. On the other hand, one of her passions and strengths is delivering in front of a room. She reported that she had just completed another certification, was excited about that new knowledge and looked forward to doing some more in-the-front-of-the-room delivery.

Phil asked her how she was doing with the balancing act of "working on the business" versus "working in the business," a simple question which stopped her in her tracks. She was trying to do both roles at the same time – and becoming highly stressed in doing so.

Many of us fall into that trap. We call it "walking into the future backwards;" in a new role, which is inevitably going to bring with it a whole new set of stressors, we tend look back at what made us successful and continue to do our past work, rather than turn around and face our new challenges.

Another colleague developed a very simple thinking structure to help her master some of her stress. Once she recognized her stressor, she would ask herself a couple of questions so that she can allocate any given issue to one of four buckets:

Is this primarily an internal issue of my own or is it primarily due to my external environment?
If it was an internal issue, then she would develop an appropriate strategy based on her PTP.
If it was an external issue, then she would ask the next three questions:
      Is this something that I have control over?
      Is this something that I can influence?
      Or is it simply something that is subject to the laws of physics, and I have no control or influence whatsoever?

With the issue assigned to one of those buckets, she could take appropriate action – and not stress about things that she has no control or influence over.

The last bullet point of the "What Works" section states: "Tweak the Dragon's nose." You may have wondered what the heck we were talking about. Here's the explanation! In many situations, we worry about what might happen. Our brains, sometimes consciously, and sometimes nonconsciously, develop all sorts of scenarios. By the very nature of the brain being survival oriented our brains will wander unchecked into a wide-ranging set of worst-case scenarios, without thinking deeply about their reality and likelihood.

Our recommended approach is to, deliberately and explicitly, explore the things that could really go wrong. And take a look at what you could do to prevent them from happening, what you would do if you experienced one of more of them actually happening, and if they did happen, what you would do to recover. If you cover all of these bases, and you can live with everything that you discover, then it tends to settle the brain down. This is what we mean by Tweak the Dragon's nose – explore the worst case that can happen in some detail. Most of the time, you will find the dragon is nowhere near as ferocious as it first seemed.

The final example that we want to give you, is based upon that approach, and concerns a female executive who was stressing over getting married. Not just the details of the wedding itself, but whether she should even be getting married. Her boyfriend had proposed, and she had accepted, but later was getting worried about whether she had done the right thing. She used the exercise described above to look at what she was about to do. Based upon that exercise she realized that "when she tweaked the dragon's nose" her fears were unfounded, and she went ahead. This occurred at least twenty years ago, and to our best knowledge the two are still happily married.

Discussion

We need to remind you of the impact of chronic stress on the brain. The Hippocampus (associated with learning and memory) and the Pre-Frontal Cortex (Executive Functions) both experience deterioration as a result of chronic stress. This can be seen in a number of ways, most obviously a reduction in the length of the neurons and the number of branches of the neurons in both of these areas. The amygdala on the other hand, experiences a corresponding increase in both the length of the neurons and the number of branches.

Amy Arnsten [63] summarizes the impact on the PFC and the amygdala for us:

> "Studies of the molecular pathways activated by stress exposure have begun to explain why PFC circuits deteriorate in so many cognitive disorders. The presence of intrinsic mechanisms to actively weaken connections during stress exposure in these newly evolved circuits renders them particularly vulnerable when they are dysregulated owing to genetic or environmental insults. This contrasts with the stress effects on subcortical regions such as the amygdala that are strengthened by stress exposure, thus switching the brain into a more primitive, reflexive state."

and this paper [64] summarizes the impact on the hippocampus and amygdala:

> "These results point to a role for BDNF in stress-induced structural plasticity across both the hippocampus and the amygdala, two brain areas that have also been implicated in the cognitive and affective symptoms of stress-related psychiatric disorders."

In other words: Chronic stress diminishes our executive functions, learning and memory, but enhances the amygdala, which sets off a vicious cycle of making the brain more aware of stress, and hence better able at detecting stress and that's where the cycle starts again. You get the picture?

As if this isn't bad enough. Take a look at this study. Dias Ferreira et al. [65] indicate that:

> " ... chronic stress leads to a bias in behavioral strategies toward habit."

So, in addition to impacting executive functions, learning and memory, chronic stress tends to make us revert to old habits. Hmmm. Not good.

It is worth taking a moment and understanding the fundamental message from Robert Sapolsky's book, Why Zebras Don't Get Ulcers. [66] Sapolsky has spent much of his life studying animals, both human and non-human. He makes it very clear that we are (seemingly) the only species that plans the future, regrets (or not) the past and ruminates over both. Much of our stress comes from "anticipatory" stress i.e. worrying over what could happen.

When looking at the things that stress us, it is also important to look at where the sensitivity to those stressors came from. In some instances, we can assist this process by examining early child-hood experiences. There is growing evidence, as illustrated in the following two references, that early child-hood experiences have significant impact in adulthood. We'll look at two references, one in some detail.

In the first case, Shonkoff et al., [67] draw the conclusion for us:

> *"A scientific consensus is emerging that the origins of adult disease are often found among developmental and biological disruptions occurring during the early years of life. These early experiences can affect adult health in 2 ways - either by cumulative damage over time or by the biological embedding of adversities during sensitive developmental periods. In both cases there can be a lag of many years, even decades, before early adverse experiences are expressed in the form of disease."*

In the second case, Felitti et al. [68] give some explicit details of the impacts of early child-hood experiences, which are of such severity we cite their study and methods, their conclusions together with the complete results of the study. (For the sake of clarity, we have changed some of the sentence structure, but the wording and content is intact)

> ***Methods****. A questionnaire about adverse childhood experiences was mailed to 13,494 adults who had completed a standardized medical evaluation at a large HMO; 9,508 (70.5%) responded. Seven categories of adverse childhood experiences were studied:*
>
> - *psychological, physical, or sexual abuse;*
> - *violence against mother;*
> - *living with household members who were substance abusers, mentally ill or suicidal, or ever imprisoned.*
>
> ***Conclusions****: We found a strong graded relationship between the breadth of exposure to abuse or household dysfunction during childhood and multiple risk factors for several of the leading causes of death in adults.*
>
> ***Results****: More than half of respondents reported at least one, and one-fourth reported 2 or more, categories of childhood exposures. We found a graded relationship between the number of categories of childhood exposure and each of the adult health risk behaviors and diseases that were studied.*
>
> *Persons who had experienced four or more categories of childhood exposure, compared to those who had experienced none, had:*

- *4 to 12-fold increased health risks for alcoholism, drug abuse, depression, and suicide attempt*
- *2 to 4-fold increase in smoking, poor self-rated health, > 50 sexual intercourse partners, and sexually transmitted disease*
- *1.4 to 1.6-fold increase in physical inactivity and severe obesity.*

The number of categories of adverse childhood exposures showed a graded relationship to the presence of adult diseases including ischemic heart disease, cancer, chronic lung disease, skeletal fractures, and liver disease. The seven categories of adverse childhood experiences were strongly interrelated and persons with multiple categories of childhood exposure were likely to have multiple health risk factors later in life."

And please note that this list of adverse early child-hood experiences, does not include the impact of negative socioeconomic status, or adoption, both of which are known to have significant impacts later in life.

Gender and stress: We want to start this portion of the discussion with some disclaimers. We researched this area with some trepidation. Part of that reluctance was due to the sheer volume of research in this domain. Huge numbers of papers. The other part of our reluctance was based upon the fact that we don't want to negatively contribute to the myth that we refer to on page 19 i.e. that men's brains and women's brains are different. Having said that, it does appear that women and men react differently to stress; this difference manifests itself, not only in differences of behavior, but also in differences of areas of brain activity. However, and this is very important; many of the research papers say that it seems as though there's a difference, but further exploration is necessary before we can reach any firm conclusions. Let's explore.

As regards the behavioral aspects, one place to start is with the following question(s): when and why does the difference in stress response start? Jose and Brown [69] give us an initial clue:

"The onset of the gender differences in stress and depression occurred at age 13 years, and for rumination one year earlier at 12 years. Significantly, also from 13 years, rumination explained the gender difference in depression by showing that it significantly mediated the effect of gender on depression. Gender moderated the rumination to depression relationship; specifically, the association was stronger for females than males."

And what is the impact? How do men and women behave differently under stress? Here's one difference. Tomova et al. [70] indicate that under acute stress, women tend to have a heightened awareness of needing to be careful in social interactions and men have a decreased awareness.

Taking another tack, Kivlighan et al. [71] examined the endocrine responses to stress in a competition ... and found that there were differences, but that the specific differences depended on a large number of variables:

"Men's and women's endocrine responses to this competitive setting were more different than alike and varied by level of competitive experience, the specific phase of the competitive event, and the particular hormone measured. Inter-individual differences in testosterone and cortisol were differentially associated with social affiliation with teammates."

Olff [72] reviewed the differences in terms of PTSD and reported the following:

"In the acute phase, women generally score higher than men on acute subjective responses, e.g. threat perception … Women handle stressful situations differently and have evolved differentially to support these different behaviours. For instance, women in stressful situations may use a tend-and-befriend response rather than the fight-or-flight response that is often assumed. Emotion-focused, defensive and palliative coping are more prevalent in women, while problem-focused coping is higher in men. Women seek more social support, the lack of it being the most consistent predictor of negative outcome of trauma."

In an earlier paper, Matud [73] described the differences as follows:

"Although there was no difference in the number of life events experienced in the previous two years, the women rated their life events as more negative and less controllable than the men. Furthermore, we found gender differences in 14 of the 31 items listed, with the women listing family and health-related events more frequently than the men, whereas the men listed relationship, finance and work-related events. The women scored significantly higher than the men on the emotional and avoidance coping styles and lower on rational and detachment coping. The men were found to have more emotional inhibition than the women. And the women scored significantly higher than the men on somatic symptoms and psychological distress. Although the effect sizes are low, the results of this study suggest that women suffer more stress than men and their coping style is more emotion-focused than that of men."

With regard to the difference in brain activity, here's a summary of what Lee et al. [74] have to say:

"Activation of areas involved in inhibitory control and sensory awareness might contribute to the significantly lower stress ratings in males."

We could go on, but for a change we won't. ☺ There are many more research papers identifying that there are differences in male and female behavioral responses to stress. While we have learned that we have to be careful about jumping to conclusions, it does seem reasonable to assume that there are significant differences between the way that men and women respond to stress. When planning your personal stress management strategies, it would, therefore, seem reasonable to take these differences into account.

Age and stress. As we age, do we get more tolerant of stress or less tolerant? Once again, we can look at from the same two aspects: behaviorally and neurologically.

One recent study [75] summarizes the situation as follows: from our 20's to our mid-50's we see ourselves as having a relatively constant amount of stress. Then our perceived stress levels rapidly decline through to our mid 80's. That's good to know, but do we know why? Well, probably not:

" ... none of the variables tested provided a compelling explanation for the pattern of decline ... Remarkably, factors such as employment, social support, marital status, health conditions, health insurance, and church attendance, which conceptually appeared to be logical candidates given their association with age and stress, did not appreciably flatten the slope of stress over age. This regardless on one's social and health situation stress is reported much less frequently from middle age onward."

Note what they don't say! They don't say that we have less stressful events – just that we don't report them as stressful, which presumably means that we have a natural way of dealing with them as we age.

Provable reasons for this apparent acceptance of stressful events has eluded many researchers who are still looking for that magic bullet combination of factors. In his recent book, Levitin [76] describes:

" ... that social support is a strong predictor of allostatic load (total accumulated stress), with those having less social support showing the highest load. This is another case of not knowing the direction of the causality - does having few or no friends increase stress? Probably. Does being stressed to begin with drive friends away? Probably. Does not having friends to comfort you cause that stress to linger instead of dissipating? Again, probably."

From a neurological perspective Bloss et al. [77] launch in with a relatively major blow, admittedly with research on rats:

"It is known that in young animals, stress causes morphological remodeling of prefrontal pyramidal neurons that is reversible. ... in contrast, middle-aged and aged rats failed to show reversible morphological remodeling when subjected to the same stress and recovery paradigm. The data presented here provide evidence that aging is accompanied by selective impairments in long-term neocortical morphological plasticity."

What does that mean? When we are young our brains bounce back from stress, but that capability goes away when we are older.

Now let's look at some activities to increase your stress mastery. There are numerous sites on the Internet that will give you (mostly good) advice on how to help you; here we've just picked a few strategies here that will head you in the right direction.

Developing awareness and understanding. This is the first step, as you have heard us say before. Understanding your own make-up, behaviors and the types of stressors that impact you. We covered that process in the section on Peeling Back the Layers of Your Onion, page 49. Fully understanding your triggers, and what your habits and patterns are, is a good first-step in managing your stress.

Avoidance. We know that this approach might be so obvious and simplistic to address that it is not worth saying, but once you know something stresses you then: avoid it! If being with people of a certain behavioral type stresses you, then avoid being with that type of person. If tight deadlines cause you stress, then take a job which has more flexible deadlines. If working on your own stresses you out, then ensure that you are always part of a team. We understand that avoidance is not always possible, but be aware that it is, in some instances, a legitimate strategy for stress management.

Personal self-regulation

Over the past four decades or so, there has been a lot of research into the impacts of self-regulation. Two of the giants in this field are Walter Mischel, who pushed forward the field of delayed gratification in kids [§] and Roy Baumeister, who developed much of the theory about the depletion of our ability to self-regulate. Much of the subsequent research has been based upon their bodies of work.

The abstract of one of Mischel's papers [78] eloquently describes the self-regulatory process as follows:

"A 2-System framework is proposed for understanding the processes that enable – and undermine – self-control and willpower as exemplified in the delay of gratification paradigm. A cool, cognitive "know" system and a hot emotional "go" system are postulated. The cool system is cognitive, emotionally neutral, contemplative, flexible, integrated, coherent, spatiotemporal, slow, episodic, and strategic. It is the seat of self-regulation and self-control. The hot system is the basis of emotionality, fears as well as passions – impulsive and reflexive – initially controlled by innate releasing stimuli (and, this literally under stimulus control); it is fundamental for emotional (classic) conditioning and undermines efforts at self-control. The balance between the hot and the cool systems is determined by stress, developmental level and the individual's self-regulatory dynamics."

Although they (Metcalfe and Mischel) refer to the two systems as "cool" and "hot" it is one of the best descriptions of the struggle between the PFC and the limbic system that we have seen.

Baumeister and Vohs, [79] on the other hand, explain the individual's self-regulatory dynamics with the strength model of self-regulation which holds that:

" … self-regulation operates by consuming a limited energy resource, thereby producing a state called ego depletion in which volition is curtailed because of low energy."

In other words, our ability to self-regulate is reduced when we are tired, stressed or have made lots of self-regulated decisions already. The resource that the brain needs to self-regulate has been depleted. While there have been many challenges to this theory over the past couple of decades, Baumeister and Vohs claim that *"the strength model is much better able than the rival accounts to explain all the available evidence."*

Lest we think that there is only one approach to self-regulation, it must be said that there are a number of mechanisms for coping with stress, some of them positive and some of them not so. Mezuk et al. [80] give us eight self-regulating activities that people frequently use for dealing with stress, namely, on the negative side, smoking, alcohol,

---

§ If you have not yet seen some of his work, then look him up on YouTube … his videos showing delayed gratification in kids are hilarious

drug use, and overeating, and on the positive side prayer, exercise, social support, and talking with a counselor.

Let's be clear about our approach. When we talk about self-regulation, we are referring to that mental function of controlling yourself through your own volition by actively using the PFC. ☺

Shields et al. [81] have introduced "inflammation" as another lens through which to look at self-regulation. They first emphasize the importance of self-regulation:

> "*Whereas superior self-regulation predicts better academic achievement, relationship quality, financial and career success, and lifespan health, poor self-regulation increases a person's risk for negative outcomes in each of these domains and can ultimately presage early mortality.*"

They then go on to say:

> " *... that components of the immune system involved in inflammation can alter neural, cognitive, and motivational processes that lead to impaired self-regulation and poor health. Based on these findings, we propose an integrated, multi-level model that describes how inflammation may cause widespread biobehavioral alterations that promote self-regulatory failure. This immunologic model of self-regulatory failure has implications for understanding how biological and behavioral factors interact to influence self-regulation. The model also suggests new ways of reducing disease risk and enhancing human potential by targeting inflammatory processes that affect self-regulation.*"

In other words, there may be other biological issues at play that affect our ability to self-regulate. Watch this space.

In chapter 3, we addressed the benefits of a mindful approach to life; it turns out that it a mindful approach supports self-regulation, and that self-regulation is more effective than imposing restraints.

Understand your brain. If you can understand the fact that you are (or really, your brain is) reacting exactly the way you were/it was designed to. The problem is that the design was laid down many millennia ago – and may not be the best design for what you are facing right now! Until we get Brain 2.0, however, we need to work with what we have. For example, the internal message some of us get from our brain if we miss a deadline is that "we are all going to die!" You're not.

Understand your stressors. We cannot emphasize this enough. Get to know what causes your stress. Your own Personal Threat Profile and your own Personal Threat Context. If there's anything in your context that you can change to reduce the stress, then do so.

Putting things in perspective. We have a colleague who, when something drastic goes wrong, will ask the question "Will this mean some unfortunate person somewhere in the world is going to die?" or some such equivalent. Most of the time, this enables her and us to reframe what is going on.

<u>Ask yourself, what's the worst that can happen?</u> Most of the time, our brains project doom and gloom into the future, far worse that what is likely to happen. Some of us play mental what if games. Over and over again. We referred to it earlier as the 'rehearsal' mode.

<u>An attitude of gratitude.</u> Appreciating what you have and what's positive, tends to increase your mood, your energy, your physical well-being, your subjective well-being and a whole host of other things. Or at least mostly. It's complicated. Most of the research suggests that this is the case, but there is some research out there that says that it depends on numerous other factors as well. But, just as important, none of the researchers suggests that practicing gratitude has any harmful effects.

There's plenty of research, but let's look at just three pieces of research. In a recent article, Valikhani et al. [82] summarize their abstract thus:

"It can be concluded that gratitude not only has direct effects on quality of life, but also has indirect effects through perceived stress and mental health."

Disabato et al. [83] add:

"Our findings suggest the potential for gratitude and meaning in life interventions to facilitate depression remission."

And this from Leary and Dockray [84] :

" … a growing body of gratitude research has found robust and consistent associations with well-being. It is associated with reduced anxiety; stress and depression; and increased life satisfaction, positive affect, and health behaviors."

So, what do we mean by an attitude of gratitude? Leary and Dockray give us a nice approach:

"Gratitude interventions tend to involve thinking or writing about things one feels grateful for over a period of time. Such single-component gratitude interventions are usually quick to complete, easy to use, and cost-effective."

There you have it. Keep a gratitude journal.

<u>Reframing</u>

There are many names for this approach, for example looking at things through another lens, taking another point of view or simply exploring the positive possibilities rather than focusing on the negative. Reviewing what could happen, might happen, is happening, or just happened, in a different way. You can look at something that didn't work as a failure or that you have learned another approach that you won't have to repeat.

A couple of years ago Scott was working with a client on his mental models of the world and one of them had to do with him being convinced that he was "Not Smart Enough". This unfortunate model becomes a filter and every experience is impacted

115

by it. One day, during their coaching session, Scott asked him what evidence he had that he was not smart enough and his client said, "I am learning every day". It took exactly 13 minutes for this executive to discover the reframe of "I am not good enough" to "I am learning every day" and write it down, put it on his computer screen and put it at the end of his signature block on his email. Soon his executive team adopted it as part of their rally cry when solving a problem. A reframe does not solve the problem itself, however, it does offer a different light that can inspire positive results.

Phil recalls an ancient story about a farmer and his son. We suspect it is a fable, but like many of its kind, it is nicely illustrative. The farmer and his son and their trusty old steed, were ploughing the "back forty." They stopped for lunch and while they were eating lunch, their horse ran away. The son had not secured the horse well enough to the tree and it had gotten loose. The son was chagrined, apologized to his father and said what a terrible thing it was to have happened.

The farmer's reply was that maybe it was and maybe it wasn't.

A week or so later, the horse came back, and it is followed by four mares. The farmer and son are both delighted, of course, and the son explains what a wonderful thing it was.

The farmer's reply was that maybe it was and maybe it wasn't.

Over the next several weeks the son starts to break-in the mares, one by one. When he starts work on the last mare, she is particularly resistant, and throws him off, breaking his leg. The son is not only in pain but realizes what a terrible blow this will be to his ability to work. Once again he states what a terrible thing it was to have happened.

You've guessed it. The farmer's reply was that maybe it was and maybe it wasn't.

The next week, the recruiting team for the army comes around looking to press-gang young males into joining … and, of course, they don't take the son because he has a broken leg.

At any given point in time, there are always many ways to look at the same situation.

Positivity. When you are in a relaxed mood, think of a picture or image that conjures up warm, positive feelings. Practice bringing that picture or image to mind. Do this again and again, so it comes into your mind very easily. If you can, get an actual example or artifact of your image. Put it somewhere where you see it frequently. We are flooding and priming your brain with that image. When you find yourself getting stressed, either before an event, during an event or after an event, bring this image to mind.

In addition, there are several apps that you can use that prime your brain with positive words. It turns out that simply focusing on positive words reduces the stress experienced by the brain.

Labeling. Labeling (or affect labeling as it is known in the literature) is very simple. It is the act of putting emotions into words. The overall approach is that if you are experiencing an emotion, describe it in words. What you did made me angry. Made me sad. Whatever. Then move on. Don't dwell on it. Research has shown that this approach has a similar result to stress management as other emotion regulation approaches. The biggest downside, it seems, is that even though in the laboratory and under fMRI scans, it can be shown that the approach reduces arousal in key areas of the brain like the amygdala, for some people it doesn't feel effective as a tool. Try it for yourself.

Give up hope for a better yesterday. Once the moment, hour, day, week has gone there is no reliving it. And no changing it. All you can do is make a determination about what you are going to do moving forward. Dwelling on the "woulda, coulda, shoulda" won't change the facts. Looking back and ruminating is only useful if you can do so with a learning mindset. This process of looking back and wishing that you had done something different is often associated with negative self-talk. Give up the hope that yesterday might change.

Unwind. This approach is simple. Deliberately take time for yourself. Even if it's a small break, get up and walk around. Go outside. Do something different, especially if it can be the opposite of what was stressful. If it can also take you away from your digital interactions, so much the better.

Identify the Protocols. Every business, group, or family has a series of protocols and paradigms that they operate under. Rieger [85] calls them rules and breaks them into four types:

➢ Gospels – rules that must be followed, with no exception
➢ Guidelines – rules that apply only under certain conditions
➢ Ground rules – rules that don't dictate specific behaviors
➢ Ghosts – rules that are not really rules, but apply anyway – or are no longer relevant

In any group, knowing what the rules are is important to understanding what is expected of you and what you may or may not do. In the cultural sense, it manifests itself in "that's the way you get things done around here."

Rules come up in all sorts of unexpected ways. Scott describes a recent house move. Their dog had a tough time with the move and was obviously stressed by all the changes. They decided that, although he normally sleeps in his kennel, he should be allowed to sleep in the bed until he was in a better shape. Scott describes how the ghost rule from his father echoed around his head "Dog's shouldn't be allowed to sleep on the bed."

As Rieger states "auditing every rule and policy in an organization, is impossible." In fact, had we tried to audit Scott's rules, we probably wouldn't have predicted one about "dogs in bed." But noticing what seems to be causing stress and/or is getting in the way can be a starting point to identifying rules. Then you can make a judgment as to whether the rule is still useful.

We recently met a new mother who was struggling as to when to return to work after having her first child. She struggled with two opposing ghost rules. The first was that no one can take care of a three-month old properly except the Mom and the second was that a Mom staying home with their newborn child means that she will be left behind regarding her career. As you might imagine, these two opposing rules created plenty of conflict for her when making a decision to return or not to the workplace.

Drink carefully. This is probably another one of those that is simplistic and may not be worth addressing, but just in case – be careful about drinking coffee and alcohol. For different reasons, they may not be a good way of combating stress.

Language. The language we use, especially when we are "talking to ourselves" is extremely important. It can impact our nonconscious brain in unpredictable and unexpected ways. In particular, be sensitive to the following two pitfalls:

> Use realistic rather than extreme statements. It is way better to remind yourself occasionally "that you may have to focus on clarity" rather than saying, "I never seem to be able to make myself clear." "Never", "always" and "should" set up some pretty unreasonable expectations in our brain.

> Use positive words rather than negative words. Better to say, "I will remain calm" rather than "I won't get upset." Giving the brain the choice to do something proactive is always a much better strategy than telling the brain what not to do, especially if the brain is responding to a perceived threat. The rational action of "remaining calm" is a planned response to an anticipated trigger and it calms the brains need for prediction. Phrases like "I won't get upset" optimistically relies on "Willpower" to avoid a response that is tied to the most primal of responses to a perceived threat. Telling the brain not to do something it is naturally designed to do, can be stressful...and that defeats the point.

Sense of humor. Did you hear the one about three guys that ...? We won't complete the story, leaving it to the imagination of the reader. But starting off that way, belies the question. Does humor help relieve stress? Like many other things with regard to people and the brain, it depends. In general, the answer is yes, as illustrated by Newman & Stone [86]:

"These results suggest that humor production may be an effective coping strategy, even for individuals who do not typically use humor to cope with stress."

And take a look at the following generally positive results associated with positive psychology interventions (PPIs) focus on humor [87]:

"Previous research provides support for the notion that they can enhance well-being in the general population and also in clinical samples. There are group-administered training programs for humor that were found to be effective for enhancing emotional well-being, life satisfaction, psychological well-being, subjective health, positive mood, optimism, and lowering depression, feelings of stress or suicidal tendencies. Thus, humor-based PPIs are expected to be well-received by the participants and enable a higher commitment to continue practicing and incorporating the activities into daily life. It has been shown that humor induces amusement, an important facet of positive emotions (the one that most frequently goes along with laughter) Given that the elicitation of positive emotions is one of the proposed working mechanisms of PPIs humor seems to be particularly well-suited for incorporation in PPIs."

Immediately, however, we have to start making some qualifications as we take into account the following type of results [88] that indicate that (a) humor did help Australian employees deal with stress over time, but not Chinese employees , and (b) that it helped Australian employees less if they had a greater sense of humor that those who had a weaker sense of humor.

And now we have to start to qualify the type of humor that is used. Let's look at two models for differentiating between types of humor.

Ruch & Heintz [89]	
Benevolent humor	*" ... a humorous outlook on life that entails the realistic observations and understanding of human weaknesses (and the imperfections of the world) but also their benevolent humorous treatment."* *" ... positive correlations with most of the 24 character strengths and uniquely related to the strengths of several virtues (justice, temperance, and transcendence)"*
Corrective humor	*" ... akin to satire, uses wit to ridicule vices, follies, abuses, and shortcomings with the intent of shaming individuals and groups into improvement."* *" ... related most strongly to the strengths of wisdom, courage, and justice"*
Oktug [90]	
Self-enhancing humor	*"As the level of self-enhancing humor increases, the effect of job stress on emotional exhaustion is attenuated"*
Self-defeating humor	*"As the level of self-defeating humor increases, the effect of job stress on emotional exhaustion is intensified."*

So. Humor? Good or bad. As we said above, it is probably mostly good, but be careful what type of humor and with whom.

<u>Get good at what you are going to have to do.</u> The stress curve diagram that we identified in *UYBFAC* as Brain Dynamic # 4, indicates that when you are faced with a new or unusual task, the curve moves to the left. i.e. when facing a new task, you become more stressed, more easily. The more you practice, the better you become and the less stressful the task appears to be. Have you noticed that when you drive in a new town, the first couple of times, you are on full alert, turn the radio down or off and focus on what you are doing? By the time you have traveled the route three times, your brain is back to its normal functioning … i.e. most of the process being handled by the nonconscious – and you travel the route with the radio turned up.

So, when you are faced with something new, if it something that you are going to have to do again and again, then, and we know this seems obvious to say, the quicker you learn it, the less stressed you will be.

<u>Engaging in regular physical activity.</u> Pretty much all of the research data shows us that physical activity and exercise increases our ability to deal with stress and reduces the impact of it. Let's turn to McEwen again:

> *"Regular physical activity has effects not only on cardiovascular and metabolic systems but also on the brain, with improvements seen in the blood flow of prefrontal and parietal cortices and enhancement in executive function. Moreover, regular physical activity, consisting of walking (1 h/day, 5 out of 7 days/week) increases hippocampal volume in previously sedentary elderly adults. … regular physical activity is an effective antidepressant and protects against cardiovascular disease, diabetes, and dementia. Moreover, intensive learning has also been shown to increase the volume of the human hippocampus."*

If you find yourself under stress, incorporate exercise into your daily regime.

<u>Reframing early child-hood experiences.</u> Levitin [91] provides us with a great summary of the impact of early child-hood experiences, and puts them into context from the brain's perspective:

> *"Part of effective regulation is the reduction of uncertainty. Our brains try to anticipate the outcome of future events, to anticipate our needs and plan how to satisfy those needs in advance. Doing this is metabolically expensive if your life is marked by great uncertainty, and the brain can easily use up its resources, resulting in a harmful increase in allostatic load* [**]

> *Because allostatis is a predictive system, it can be influenced or mis-calibrated by early life stressors or extreme traumas. A stable fetal and early childhood environment can lead to a well-functioning allostatic system. But adverse childhood experiences can result in a system that either overreacts or just shuts down in response to what might otherwise be considered normal daily ups and downs, creating hypervigilance, reduced resilience, and sometimes wild mood swings – a lifetime in which normal allostatic regulation is never reached. Someone how has grown up in adverse conditions will have long-term memories that contain threatening and stressful information; their default prediction for even neutral events is that something bad could*

[**] The total load of all stress

happen, and this kicks in their stress response, releasing cortisol and adrenaline in advance of a great many situations that are benign."

Digging a little deeper, what do we mean when we refer to these early-childhood experiences? Again, Levitin comes to our rescue – and we show some of his list:

" … it's not just the obvious things like a mother who took drugs during pregnancy, or an early toddlerhood surrounded by domestic violence, but include:

➢ *demographics such as age, sex, socioeconomics, education;*
➢ *developmental conditions, such as poor parental attachment, chronic illness, being bullied;*
➢ *genetics;*
➢ *environment, such as culture. Extreme climates, smoking behaviors, famine;*
➢ *psychological factors, such as locus of control, and the tools we bring to emotional regulation."*

Why do these factors affect some people much more than others? We don't know.

"The prized combination that allows some people to live more positive lives, to turn lemons into lemonade, is still unknown and an active topic of research."

Clearly, compensating for these experiences is not easy. The first part is to acknowledge those experiences and recognize that they might be having a number of impacts on you, including your ability to manage your stress. Some people are reasonably good at doing this on their own, or with the help of a trusted friend. On the other hand, others need help. There are a number of therapeutic models being developed e.g. Cognitive Behavioral Therapy, which might bring some advancement – but most of these approaches take effort and the willingness to step into, sometimes, unknown waters.

Mindfulness-based stress reduction. We examined the positive impact, in general, of mindfulness and mindfulness-based stress reduction programs in Chapter 3. In addition to that information, one study [92] ties the impact of such a program directly with a positive impact on the amygdala:

"Following the intervention, participants reported significantly reduced perceived stress. Reductions in perceived stress correlated positively with decreases in right basolateral amygdala gray matter density."

A review of the literature shows that in the early 2000's, scientists were reluctant to endorse the effectiveness of mindfulness-based stress reduction (MBSR) programs; times have changed but not much! Science moves slowly. There is a lot of anecdotal evidence that suggests that MBSR programs have a positive effect in reducing stress. Scientific "proof" is less easy to come by, with many articles suggesting support for the approach but only lukewarm endorsement. The summary of a 2018 review [93] of 23 studies is a typical example:

"Based on our analysis, the strongest outcomes were reduced levels of emotional exhaustion (a dimension of burnout), stress, psychological distress, depression, anxiety, and occupational stress. Improvements were found in terms of mindfulness, personal accomplishment (a dimension of burnout), (occupational) self-compassion, quality of sleep, and relaxation.

Conclusion: The results of this systematic review suggest that MBSR may help to improve psychological functioning in employees."

So, what can we definitively say about MBSR programs and stress management? Not much, other than they probably work, we cannot prove it yet, but well-designed and managed programs probably can't hurt.

Deep breathing. Let's start with a summary of one article on deep breathing as an approach to stress reduction:

"... a portable intervention which is an innovative, safe, inexpensive and friendly technique."

From the research literature we could add descriptors such as easy to learn, easy to use, highly effective and probably the highest ROI based on the time involved in learning and using the technique.

Let's go back to basics. What do we mean by deep breathing? Taking deep breaths, far into the belly, five or six times a minute for a number of minutes. There is a body of research, for example, [94] [95] [96] that supports the use of deep breathing as an effective technique for stress management. What this research has done is validated what has been known by many practitioners for hundreds, if not thousands of years!!! The research has explained what those practitioners intuitively knew i.e. that there was a linkage between the lungs, the heart and the brain. Deep breathing causes the brain to feel less stressed, and heart rate variability to increase (a measure of calmness).

Some studies have shown that even a minimal amount of deep breathing e.g. two minutes, can have a profound effect on one's ability to deal with stress for the next two hours. There is some evidence that ten minutes of deep breathing sets you up to deal better with stress for twenty-four hours and repeating this three-times a week for six weeks increases your threshold of dealing with stress. [97]

How to use this nugget of information? If you know you are going to have stressful day, take out ten minutes in the morning and breathe deeply. If you are about to go into a stressful meeting, breathe deeply for a couple of minutes.

Stress-reduction apps

There is an ever-growing number of apps, videos and websites that are specifically focused on deep breathing and other stress reducing activities. Like anything these days, a couple of minutes on Google will show you more than you can imagine, so we are not going to review them here. We will simply cite one piece of research. Dillon et al. [98] found that:

" ... smartphone applications combined with a skin conductance biofeedback device significantly reduced stress."

Sleep. In UYBFAC we went to some length to illustrate the dangers of too little sleep. In the context of this chapter, the lack of sleep negatively impacts our ability to deal with stress. In turn, increased stress negatively impacts our ability to get a good night's sleep. The combination of these tends to take us into a vicious downward spiral. We need to find a way to break the cycle. Sleep therapies, and stress management therapies are, of course, useful approaches.

There is, however, another way. Positivity and . It seems that becoming more positive and demonstrating gratitude has an impact on both stress and sleep … and it's a cheap, non-invasive and easy way to tackle the issue.

Pay attention. Notice what you notice. Write down, of journal, the things that you notice. Make a stress journal – and see what patterns you have noted down. What are you noticing again and again? What's the impact of those things on your stress levels.?

As we reviewed this list, we decided that there were many more that we could introduce but decided that enough is enough. If you want to explore the whole topic of stress and stress management in a greater level of detail, there is a vast amount of information on the Internet. Be careful though, as not all sources are of equal validity. There are a number of peer-reviewed journals available e.g. The International Journal on the Biology of Stress, so they would be a good place to start.

Bottom Line Summary

Make a choice. Do you want to reduce your stress? If not, as we have said before, then go to the next topic. If you decide to do so, review all of the possible things that we have listed under "what works" and select a handful. Try them out and see how you do. Not all of them work for everybody. Try a few. If they work for you, integrate them into your life. If not, try some different ones.

What's next?

What one or two things am I going to focus on in order to better manage my stress?
What I am going to do about it/them?
How will I measure whether I have been successful?

[59] Goh, J., Pfeffer, J., & Zenios, S. A. (2015). The Relationship Between Workplace Stressors and Mortality and Health Costs in the United States. *Management Science*, 608–628.

[60] Hogan, Robert & Hogan, Joyce. (2003). Assessing Leadership: A View from the Dark Side. International Journal of Selection and Assessment. 9. 40-51. 10.1111/1468-2389.00162.

[61] Tomiyama, A. J. (2019). Stress and Obesity. *Annual Review of Psychology*, 70(1), 703–718. http://doi.org/10.1146/annurev-psych-010418-102936

[62] McEwen, B. S. (2016). In pursuit of resilience: stress, epigenetics, and brain plasticity. *Annals of the New York Academy of Sciences*, 1373(1), 56–64. http://doi.org/10.1111/nyas.13020

[63] Arnsten, A. F. T. (2015). Stress weakens prefrontal networks: molecular insults to higher cognition. *Nature Neuroscience*, 18(10), 1376–1385. http://doi.org/10.1038/nn.4087

[64] Lakshminarasimhan, H., & Chattarji, S. (2012). Stress Leads to Contrasting Effects on the Levels of Brain Derived Neurotrophic Factor in the Hippocampus and Amygdala. *Plos One*, 7(1), e30481–6. http://doi.org/10.1371/journal.pone.0030481

[65] Dias-Ferreira, E., Sousa, J. C., Melo, I., Morgado, P., Mesquita, A. R., Cerqueira, J. J., et al. (2009). Chronic Stress Causes Frontostriatal Reorganization and Affects Decision-Making. *Science*, 325(5940), 621–625. http://doi.org/10.1126/science.1171203

[66] Sapolsky, R. M. (2004). Why Zebras Don't Get Ulcers (Third). Holt Paperbacks.

[67] Shonkoff, J. P., Boyce, W. T., & McEwen, B. S. (2009). Neuroscience, Molecular Biology, and the Childhood Roots of Health Disparities: Building a New Framework for Health Promotion and Disease Prevention. *Jama*, 301(21), 2252–2259. http://doi.org/10.1001/jama.2009.754)

[68] Felitti, V. J., Anda, R. F., Nordenberg, D., Williamson, D. F., Spitz, A. M., Edwards, V., et al. (1998). Relationship of Childhood Abuse and Household Dysfunction to Many of the Leading Causes of Death in Adults. *American Journal of Preventive Medicine*, 14(4), 245–258.

[69] Jose, P. E., & Brown, I. (2007). When does the Gender Difference in Rumination Begin? Gender and Age Differences in the Use of Rumination by Adolescents. *Journal of Youth and Adolescence*, 37(2), 180–192. http://doi.org/10.1007/s10964-006-9166-y

[70] Tomova, L., von Dawans, B., Heinrichs, M., Silani, G., Lamm, C. (2014). Is stress affecting our ability to tune into others? Evidence for gender differences in the effects of stress on self-other distinction http://dx.doi.org/10.1016/j.psyneuen.2014.02.006

[71] Kivlighan, K. T., Granger, D. A., & Booth, A. (2005). Gender differences in testosterone and cortisol response to competition. *Psychoneuroendocrinology*, 30(1), 58–71. http://doi.org/10.1016/j.psyneuen.2004.05.009

[72] Olff, M. (2017). Sex and gender differences in post-traumatic stress disorder: an update. *European Journal of Psychotraumatology*, 8(sup4), 1351204–3. http://doi.org/10.1080/20008198.2017.1351204

[73] Matud, M. P. (2004). Gender differences in stress and coping styles. *Personality and Individual Differences*, 37(7), 1401–1415. http://doi.org/10.1016/j.paid.2004.01.010

[74] Lee, M. R., Cacic, K., Demers, C. H., Haroon, M., Heishman, S., Hommer, D. W., et al. (2014). Gender differences in neural–behavioral response to self-observation during a novel fMRI social stress task. *Neuropsychologia*, 53, 257–263. http://doi.org/10.1016/j.neuropsychologia.2013.11.022

[75] Stone, A. A., Schneider, S., & Broderick, J. E. (2017). Psychological stress declines rapidly from age 50 in the United States: Yet another well-being paradox. *Journal of Psychosomatic Research*, 103, 22–28. http://doi.org/10.1016/j.jpsychores.2017.09.016

[76] Levitin, D. J. (2020). Successful Aging. Dutton.

[77] Bloss, E. B., Janssen, W. G., McEwen, B. S., & Morrison, J. H. (2010). Interactive Effects of Stress and Aging on Structural Plasticity in the Prefrontal Cortex. *Journal of Neuroscience*, 30(19), 6726–6731. http://doi.org/10.1523/JNEUROSCI.0759-10.2010

[78] Metcalfe, J., & Mischel, W. (1999). A Hot/Cool System Analysis of Delay of Gratification: Dynamics of Willpower. *Psychological Review*, 106(1), 3–19.

[79] Baumeister, R. F., & Vohs, K. D. (2016). Strength Model of Self-Regulation as Limited Resource (Vol. 54, pp. 67–127). Elsevier. http://doi.org/10.1016/bs.aesp.2016.04.001

[80] Mezuk, B., Ratliff, S., Concha, J. B., Abdou, C. M., Rafferty, J., Lee, H., & Jackson, J. S. (2017). Stress, self-regulation, and context_ Evidence from the health and retirement survey. *SSM - Population Health*, 3, 455–463. http://doi.org/10.1016/j.ssmph.2017.05.004

[81] Shields, G. S., Moons, W. G., & Slavich, G. M. (2017). Inflammation, Self-Regulation, and Health: An Immunologic Model of Self-Regulatory Failure. *Perspectives on Psychological Science*, 12(4), 588–612. http://doi.org/10.1177/1745691616689091

[82] Valikhani, A., Ahmadnia, F., Karimi, A., & Mills, P. J. (2018). The relationship between dispositional gratitude and quality of life_ The mediating role of perceived stress and mental health. *Personality and Individual Differences*, 141, 40–46. http://doi.org/10.1016/j.paid.2018.12.014

[83] Disabato, D. J., Kashdan, T. B., Short, J. L., & Jarden, A. (2016). What Predicts Positive Life Events that Influence the Course of Depression? A Longitudinal Examination of Gratitude and Meaning in Life. *Cognitive Therapy and Research*, 41(3), 444–458. http://doi.org/10.1007/s10608-016-9785-x

[84] O' Leary, K., & Dockray, S. (2015). The Effects of Two Novel Gratitude and Mindfulness Interventions on Well-Being. *The Journal of Alternative and Complementary Medicine*, 21(4), 243–245. http://doi.org/10.1089/acm.2014.0119

[85] Rieger, T. (2011). Breaking the Fear Barrier. Gallup Press.

[86] Newman, M. G., & Stone, A. A. (1996). Does humor moderate the effects of experimentally-induced stress? *Annals of Behavioral Medicine*, 18(2), 101–109.

[87] Wellenzohn, S., Proyer, R. T., & Ruch, W. (2018). Who Benefits From Humor-Based Positive Psychology Interventions? The Moderating Effects of Personality Traits and Sense of Humor. *Frontiers in Psychology*, 9, 1–24. http://doi.org/10.3389/fpsyg.2018.00821

[88] Wang, R., Chan, D. K. S., Goh, Y. W., Penfold, M., Harper, T., & Weltewitz, T. (2017). Humor and workplace stress: a longitudinal comparison between Australian and Chinese employees. *Asia Pacific Journal of Human Resources*, 56(2), 175–195. http://doi.org/10.1111/1744-7941.12157

[89] Ruch, W., & Heintz, S. (2016). The virtue gap in humor. Exploring benevolent and corrective humor. *Translational Issues in Psychological Science*, 2(1), 35–45. http://doi.org/10.1037/tps0000063

[90] Oktug, Z. (2017). The Moderating Role of Employees' Humor Styles on the Relationship between Job Stress and Emotional Exhaustion. *International Business Research*, 10(4), 131–8. http://doi.org/10.5539/ibr.v10n4p131

[91] Levitin, op cit

[92] Hölzel, B. K., Carmody, J., Evans, K. C., Hoge, E. A., Dusek, J. A., Morgan, L., et al. (2009). Stress reduction correlates with structural changes in the amygdala. *Social Cognitive and Affective Neuroscience*, 5(1), 11–17. http://doi.org/10.1093/scan/nsp034

[93] Janssen, M., Heerkens, Y., Kuijer, W., van der Heijden, B., & Engels, J. (2018). Effects of Mindfulness Based Stress Reduction on employees' mental health: A systematic review. *PLoS ONE*, 13(1), Article e0191332.

[94] Perciavalle, V., Blandini, M., Fecarotta, P., Buscemi, A., Di Corrado, D., Bertolo, L., et al. (2016). The role of deep breathing on stress. *Neurological Sciences*, 38(3), 451–458. http://doi.org/10.1007/s10072-016-2790-8

[95] Varvogli, L., & Darviri, C. (2011). Stress Management Techniques: evidence-based procedures that reduce stress and promote health. *Health Science Journal, 5*(2), 74–89.

[96] Naik, G. S., Gaur, G. S., & Pal, G. K. (2018). Effect of Modified Slow Breathing Exercise on Perceived Stress and Basal Cardiovascular Parameters. *International Journal of Yoga, 11*(1), 53–58. http://doi.org/10.4103/ijoy.IJOY_41_16

[97] Private conversations with Dr Evian Gordon

[98] Dillon, A., Kelly, M., Robertson, I. H., & Robertson, D. A. (2016). Smartphone Applications Utilizing Biofeedback Can Aid Stress Reduction. *Frontiers in Psychology, 7*, 94–7. http://doi.org/10.3389/fpsyg.2016.00832

Chapter 7:

Time and Energy Management

7. Time and Energy Management

General comments

As a somewhat amusing anecdote to start off this section, Phil was once asked to deliver a brain-science based, day long workshop on Time & Energy Management to about thirty people, mostly engineers and scientists, in a federal agency. It was well-received, and all the individual end-of-session reports were 4 or more out of 5. As required in the contract, we did a post-mortem with the client and the purchasing officer a week or so later. The client was the boss of all the people who had attended, but he, himself, had not attended the workshop. He gave us low marks, saying that as far as he could see, we had just made them more effective and more efficient but hadn't taught them Time Management!

So, in a way, that is the crux of the problem. The Time Management or Energy Management aspects are simply a means to an end. In the sales construct of "Features, Advantages and Benefits" they are simply Features. The Advantage is that you become "more effective and more efficient." The Benefit? When we're in control of our time, we often feel less stressed, get more done, get to look at a greater number of long-term, important issues, feel happier, more engaged and, maybe, get to take a little more time-off for ourselves. ☺

As an example, this was reported by Macan et al. [99]:

> *"Students who perceived control of their time reported significantly greater evaluations of their performance, greater work and life satisfaction, less role ambiguity, less role overload, and fewer job-induced and somatic tensions."*

Managing our time, however, is something where even the best of us frequently fall short; and, once again, there are no magic bullets. What we offer here are simply some ideas that may resonate with you. We have said before; everyone's brains are so different, not only from one to another, but across months, weeks, days and hours. We may all need different things at different times.

What works – external factors

- ➢ Be aware of what and who wastes your time – and take action to avoid those activities or people
- ➢ Only attend well organized meetings – beware of FMS/FOMO [f]
- ➢ Learn techniques for managing virtual meetings
- ➢ Learn to say no – use the request/counter-offer methodology
- ➢ Avoid taking on too much – beware unnecessary monkeys
- ➢ Learn to delegate effectively

---

[f] Fear of Missing Something/Fear of Missing Out

What works – internal factors

- Focus – switch off electronic interferences – emails, texts, IM's, DM's etc.
- Break up your time – learn the optimal time span that works for you. It's probably less than you think.
- Then do something which involves a change, movement, and, if possible, going outside.
- Find a "system" that works for you for daily lists, prioritizing, important vs urgent review, etc.
- Learn to be self-aware. Ask the question – is what I am doing right now the optimum use of my time?
- Communicate well – avoids the need to do it again
- Determine the level of perfection that is required for any given task – good enough is sometimes just that and sometimes it needs to be better than that!!!
- Eat and drink (water) at appropriate times – getting too hungry is very inefficient
- Put everything on your calendar – everything!!! Free up the PFC for remembering more important things.
- Carry a small notebook with you for random thoughts, ideas and commitments
- Reward yourself
- Consider the two-minute rule – if you can do something in two minutes or less, then do it rather than writing it down on a to-do list.
- Develop your own set of tools – practice them
- Avoid the temptation to 'multitask' – the brain is really bad at it
- Book times on your calendar for your own work – treat yourself as important as everyone and everything else
- Be aware of when you are at your best – and use that time for your most difficult, creative or energy absorbing work.
- Be aware of your own mental time default.

Brief Examples

A client, who we will call Wolfgang, was recently working with Phil. Wolfgang had decided to become aggressive in terms of his sales revenue. He wanted to increase it by a factor of 10. As he investigated what barriers there would be in achieving that goal, he started to think about where and how he spent his time. He realized two major aspects to this analysis. The first was that he had a large number of clients that were not adding much to his portfolio, and they took up a lot of his time. The second was that he was on a large number of boards and committees which also took up a large amount of time – not just the meetings but the activities that went on behind the scenes, such as fund-raising. Once again, they did not seem to add to his portfolio.

When he dug in further, he realized that the reason he was in the situation he was in, was because of a reluctance to say no. He worked on ways that he could be comfortable saying no and found a technique that would work for him. When asked whether he would do something, rather than simply say no, he would structure one of two replies:

"… I am sorry, but I cannot do that at the moment as my life has become incredibly busy. Ask me again in 6 months when I anticipate life will be a little easier."

"… I am sorry, but I cannot do that at the moment – but here's what I can do: … "

… and makes an offer of what he is able to be accountable for.

During the 2020 pandemic Scott held a virtual session with a group of 60 account executives from Mexico, El Salvador and the United States. The subject was on working from home vs in the office and the challenges of remaining focused, along with time management. One account manager called him after the session and said, "I struggle with my work-day at home because there are so many interruptions". As they discussed the situation, Scott discovered that she lived alone, did not have pets, and was not having contact with anyone outside of the virtual world of zoom. This was a head scratcher….at least for a moment. When Scott asked her to describe what was happening in her day that created disruption she said, "My phone keeps alerting me to an email, Facebook post, LinkedIn post, Instagram post, and WhatsApp post. And this is all before I get out of bed at 9 AM." You can imagine how much fun Scott had with that conversation. We are easily distracted and led off course on our time management when we are allowing things to dictate where our attention goes vs setting up protections that create boundaries around our schedules.

Discussion

If you do a Google search on Time Management, you will find plenty of tools, tips and techniques. If you are investigating this topic from scratch, you will find plenty of offerings this way, and it's a good way to begin. We will mainly restrict our offerings to those aspects of time management that have something to do with our brain and our behavior. We will divide the topic into three areas:

- ➢ External aspects that impact your time and energy – and what you might be able to do about them
- ➢ Internal aspects that impact your time and energy – and what you might be able to do about them
- ➢ Time Management Systems

There is some really good news, however. Many of the things that help with Time and Energy Management, are the same things that help with Focus and Attention, and with Stress Management. So, some of the things that we will be covering in this section, will give you several bangs for the buck! If you haven't already read those two sections, we would strongly recommend doing so, as the topics covered there bleed over into the topic of Time and Energy Management.

External factors

A quick definition here. External aspects are those that are either a) out of your control and you have no influence over them or are b) out of your control but might be able to have some influence.

Let's take a moment and look at an example of influence and no influence. If you are a first responder, you probably have little or no control over when you will be called upon to do your primary job. On the other hand, you do have some influence over who gets to interrupt you when you are sitting in your office, at your desk or in your cubicle.

So, strictly speaking, this part of the discussion should be in the book about "Your Brain with Another Person," the next book in the series, but for the sake of continuity, we will deal with it here.

Interruptions - regardless of their source, whether by other people dropping by, telephone calls, by e-mails pinging on your computer or mobile phone, the need to drop what you are doing in order to attend a meeting, or indeed anything else that stops one train of thought and requires you to attend to something different – is one of the single biggest drains on our time and effectiveness. Someone dropping by and spending just two minutes, doesn't occupy just two minutes. It takes your mind away from the collection of thoughts and data that were present in your brain at the time of the interruption. Getting all of those back, takes time to "reboot." There are many estimates with regard to how long the recovery process takes – some people say as low as five minutes; others say as much as twenty-five [100]. One person that we were talking to recently described that when he is doing really difficult work, it can take him an hour to get back on track. And this doesn't take into account the possible psychological cost of what happened during the interruption! What occurred during the interaction might still linger in your brain, causing you to continue to be distracted.

The research shows that these impacts are very bad. Here's one simple statement showing the level of impact that an e-mail interruption has on our efficiency: [101]

   "A typical task takes one third longer than undertaking a task with no e-mail interruptions."

All of the research suggests that we all suffer from these interruptions; in some cases, we are actually addicted to the interruptions: [102]

   "The questionnaire data show clinical characteristics classify 12 per cent of e-mail addicts, and behavioral characteristics classify 15 per cent of e-mail addicts in the workplace."

And take a look at these findings:

   ➤ Interruptions consume 28% of a knowledge workers' day. [103]
   ➤ Interruptions caused (just) by email arrival alerts can take an additional 5%. [104]

132

> - Interruptions not only require extra time to get back on track, but impact the quality of the work as well [105]
> - Frequent interruptions increase exhaustion, annoyance and anxiety [106]

Please note that this last finding was reported in the International Journal of Stress Management, so we could have included it in that chapter as well. ☺

The aspects which we identify above are only those that are known as active interruptions; there's also a class of interruptions which are more passive – for example background noise, passing sirens, or someone else's phone, together with distractions like our own internal worrying.

Whichever way you look at it, managing interruptions is a high leverage point to managing our time and our energy.

Let's start with the people side of the equation. Let's call them the usual suspects. You know who they are. Those people that interrupt you for the slightest reason, often manufactured, and once they have your attention, it is impossible to get away. At least that's what it feels like at the time. The answer? The first thing is to differentiate between interruptions from those people that have a legitimate reason to do so – and those people who just 'waste' your time. These latter people are those with whom you have a polite but definitive conversation. If that seems like a difficult thing to do, take a look at your Personal Threat Profile – and see whether you are being triggered in some way. An investment of time in preventing these people interruptions, or at least controlling them in a better way, will show huge returns.

Now for meetings; there are many suggestions with regard to meetings, most of them suggesting not to go to them unless you absolutely have to. ☺ Many of us have found that we have attended a meeting only to realize that we didn't need to be there … or it didn't need to be a meeting in the first place. [g] And if that happens to you a lot, then take a look at why you say yes to meetings. If you review your Personal Threat Profile, there may be some clues. Maybe you don't say no, when it would be beneficial for you to do so, because you are afraid of disappointing someone that is important to you. Or maybe you have a high need to know what is going on. Attending every meeting known to mankind is one way of finding out. Or maybe you like being with your "in-group" and attending meetings is one way of feeling rewarded in that context.

As regards "effective" meetings, there is a huge amount of research and training about how to hold effective meetings – so if you find that you are being requested to go to those that are ineffective, then stop going to them. Or push for some changes in the way that the meetings are handled. There are numerous checklists available on the Internet. Even minor changes in meetings and meeting processes can have huge positive impacts on their effectiveness.

---

[g] Phil has a mug with the following inscription: "I survived another meeting that should have been an email."

Virtual meetings are a different animal; they require a new set of skills for most people, both technologically and culturally. Technologically, life is getting easier. The use of real-time videoconferencing has become common place over the last decade or so. That has meant that is easier to set up multiple real-time attendees with relative ease, and we no longer have to get over the one or two second delays which tended to mess with our brains. But, in some cases, that delay still occurs … so just recognize that it is not the fault of the person on the other side – they are just as smart as can be! The fault is with the technology, not with them.

The more important issue is the cultural side of the equation. Do you understand the subtleties of the culture of the people that are on the other side of the video – and possibly the other side of the world? This starts with a very simple, but very important, question. What time is it? For them and for you. So often, people set up multi-national calls for the convenience of the initiator - rather than taking into consideration that the timing might mean the person at the other end has to get up at 4.00 a.m. or stay up until midnight in order to participate.

Now compound this with all types of different cultural approaches to problem solving, debating and contributing. This is not the book to delve into those things in detail … a Google search will point you in the right direction. Our job here is to flag the issue.

We mentioned above the, apparently simple, concept of saying no. Some people do it well. Others are almost petrified to say no. Clearly, we are all at a different place on this spectrum, and, as we suggested earlier, understanding your Personal Threat Profile might offer some help. In addition, however, there are some techniques that can be used that prove effective for many people. One such technique is what we refer to as the request/counteroffer methodology.

This methodology suggests that we reframe the interruptions, demands, suggestions, shoulds etc. that are presented to us, simply as requests. Like any request, we can accept it or refuse to accept it. If we accept it, then life goes on – and you have the accountability for whatever you accepted. If you deny the request, then it means saying no, which is difficult for many of us. However, we can add to the "no" response with a counteroffer. In its simplest form, your response of "No" becomes "No I cannot do that, but here's what I can do." If someone interrupts your concentration, rather than say yes to the interruption and get taken completely off track or say no and risk your own discomfort and maybe their displeasure, you offer a third alternative. It goes something like this: "Sorry, Fred. I am really slammed right now, but I will be free early this afternoon. I can get back to you at two." Request and counteroffer.

Most of us these days have too much to do. The changes in our work and social lives over the past couple of decades has meant that it is almost impossible to get everything done on a daily basis. Understanding what is expected of you from all of your stakeholders, how your activities or results will be measured, and what degrees of freedom you have within your role, is one of the critical components of time and energy management. Getting very clear on the goals or objectives of any given project or task will help avoid wasted effort and missed opportunities at a later stage. For some people, these aspects are so important, that their brains constantly feel in a threat state if they are not defined. This in turn leads to stress, which leads to yet a further decreased ability to manage time. So, it becomes a vicious cycle.

Let's stop a moment and examine one of the statements in that previous paragraph "… from all of your stakeholders." Your job overall has many stakeholders, some of the more obvious ones being you, your boss, your direct reports, your internal and external clients, your vendors and your family. And within that, there might be additional stakeholders for specific projects. Understanding who they are is the first step in understanding what is expected of you. Understanding who they are also helps to put a ring-fence around who you can say "no" to, how you can say no, and to whom you cannot. Spending time, up front, figuring out what is expected of you can help make your job and your tasks more manageable.

With regard to the tasks that are legitimate for you to do, Oncken and Wass wrote a classic article in 1974 [107] the lessons from which are just as applicable today as they were then. The title of the article is Management Time: Who's Got the Monkey? but the approach became known as Monkey Management. The basic metaphor is that every task that you have responsibility for, or that the people that work for you have responsibility for, or your colleagues have responsibility for, is a monkey. And monkeys have a habit of leaping from the back of the person that has responsibility for them onto someone else's back. Maybe yours. And this can happen quite by accident! Or at least, it can happen to the unwary.

The leap from one back to another occurs something like this: You bump into one of the people that work for you and he/she asks a follow up question to a discussion that you had prior. "Did you make a decision on which approach we should use for Customer X?" Now, you have been thinking about it but haven't yet reached a conclusion. So, you reply to that effect. Then you add. "I'll think about it this weekend." So, the underlying question is "Whose Monkey is it?" Should it be you making the decision or the person who works for you? The monkey is now clearly on your back.

The metaphor continues by saying that there are only three humane things to do with a monkey – feed it, give it to someone who will feed it, or shoot it. Don't let it starve. By being careful of what additional tasks you inadvertently commit to is a key technique in time and energy management.

This technique naturally leads to the issue of delegation. We will go into more detail about techniques for delegating in our next book. For the time being, lets restrict our discussion to what goes on in our brains when we consider that act of delegation.

So, what is delegation? Delegation means giving someone the responsibility and authority to perform a task or make a decision on your behalf, while you remain ultimately accountable for the final result. Wow! That means, if I delegate then I lose control.

Finally, a comment on personal technology. At one level it is easy. Turn your technology off for critical periods. Turn off the phone, your email, your text messaging systems. Relax. It is easy to turn them back on and you will give your brain the luxury of some complete thoughts.

If necessary, recognize and manage your technology addiction. We know. Easier said than done. But, once again, the rewards in terms of time management and energy management are huge.

The first item in the "What works" section above, states "Be aware of when you are at your best." In *UYBFAC*, we suggest that one of the aspects that you might learn about yourself is your chronotype – that's a fancy way of saying that you have a pattern of when your energy is up and when it is not. This pattern tends to be impacted by three main rhythms, all of which interact:

➢ Whether you are an owl, a lark or neither
➢ The up and down cycle of the day
➢ 90-minute cycles during the night and day

Some people have a marked tendency to do better work in the early morning – they are larks. Most larks know that and will get up much earlier than the rest of us. Female larks tend to have their peak of energy half an hour before male larks. On the other hand, owls tend to do their best work late in the evening. Some people seem not to have a preference. Identifying your own preference – and ensuring that you use the optimum part of your day for the most difficult or challenging tasks is one way of managing your energy – and, as a result, better managing your time.

Like all living creatures, we are subject to a twenty-four-hour rhythm, called the Circadian Rhythm. This rhythm dictates many, many aspects of our body, including our energy levels. It looks like the diagram on the following page. What this shows is that, at the beginning of the day, we have a relatively low energy level that rises gradually during the day, peaking at around twelve, noon. Then our energy levels gradually lessen during the first part of the afternoon, with some of us getting a 'second-wind' later in the afternoon. Then they further reduce until it is time to go to sleep and the cycle begins all over again.

In practice, what this means is that there are better and worse times to do things during the day. If you have tough, logical challenges, then devoting time to them when you are your best, i.e. in the morning, seems to make sense. Tasks that require less attention or logic would be better left to when you are in the valleys, for example early to mid-afternoon.

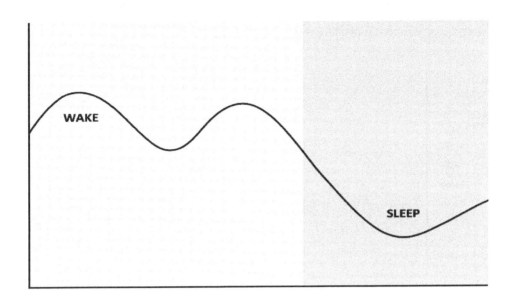

The third of the three cycles, the 90-minute cycles that run through the night and the day, are called Ultradian Rhythms. By themselves they look like the diagram on the next page.

The impact of these ultradian rhythms is that you can feel engaged and energetic at a given point in time, and yet forty-five minutes later it feels like you are running out of steam.

The shorter length, ultradian rhythms are superimposed on the longer cycle, circadian rhythms, resulting in an integrated energy diagram that looks like this:

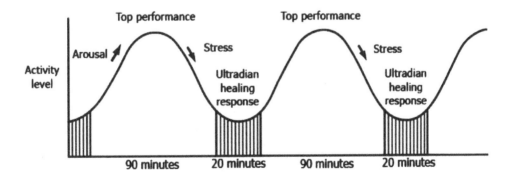

The ultradian rhythms are superimposed on the circadian rhythms, resulting in an energy diagram that looks like this:

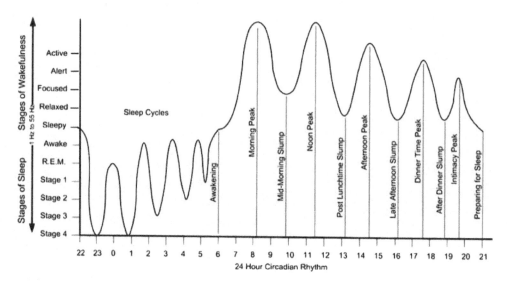

Once you learn how the combination of these rhythms impacts you, you can adjust what you do throughout the day

In addition to these three rhythms, there is a strong indication that the PFC (Pre-Frontal Cortex) gets depleted during the day. [108] It seems to act like a muscle in that it gets tired. It gets depleted by a number of things – including having to make lots of decisions, being stressed, or exercising a lot of self-control. The impact of this, is that it is easier to exercise self-control earlier in the day than later.

When we focus on people who get a lot done, it seems that they are always very clear on their goals. They have identified their immediate, short-term, medium-term and long-term goals, and often have them displayed where they can see them on a frequent and easy basis. At any point in time, with reference to these goals, they are very clear about the next step they have to take in order to move toward the goal. As their day progresses one of the questions that is dominant for them is:

"Is what I am doing right now leading to the accomplishment of one of those goals?"

In addition, when they are faced with a task, they clearly identify it with regard to the following two questions:

"On a scale of 1 to 10, how important is this task?"
"On a scale of 1 to 10, how urgent is this task?"

If you want to be geek and nerdy like Phil, you could develop a two by two matrix for this ☺

People who get a lot done also realize that they need to give themselves a break. Literally! Our brains need a change of pace every so often. We all differ slightly, but many people find that doing something different after 45 minutes or so, can help keep the brain from becoming over tired. Use the break time to give yourself a reward – either for having achieved something or having tackled it in the first place.

What about daily to-do lists? Are they a good thing or a bad thing? It depends. It depends on your traits and your state. In terms of traits, some people live their lives through to-do lists and couldn't function during the day without one. Other people hate the very thought of them. Yet others use them from time to time, but not consistently. Remember – it's all about you and your preferences, not about the latest fad or app.

From a brain perspective, there are some good arguments for the good old to-do list – whether it's written out on a piece of paper or spoken into an iPhone. Here's a couple of them:

- As you know if you have read *UYBFAC,* our dear old friend, the PFC, gets easily distracted. The act of writing something down, (or recording it) means that you can free up the PFC from attempting to remember what needs to get done.
- The simple of act of writing it down assigns some level of import to the task – and this registers in our brain
- The act of crossing something off from that list is rewarding for some people

Some additional tips:

- If you use a to-do list, record results rather than activities. "Produce the next chapter of the book" is better than "write some of the book."
- If you can only describe the task in terms of an activity, find a way of putting some other boundary condition; for example, "write three pages of the book" or "spend one hour researching the brain and art."
- If the task appears to be able to be done in two minutes or less, then consider doing it rather than writing it on the list
- Put some simple success criteria around the task; this will be based upon a number of considerations but typically they might be comments around quality, quantity, effort, cost, time or the approach you want to take.
- Remember that not all tasks have to be done to perfection; good enough is sometimes good enough.
- Consider the need for the brain to be rewarded. Take time to inventory things that you have done that were not on your list and write them down. Allow your brain to enjoy the reward of an easy win.

What about those days when your to-do lists finish up longer at the end of the day than at the beginning? Not many people these days actually get through their to-do list. For some people this drives them crazy. For others, it's easy just to reassure yourself that you got done what you could, and the rest will be there tomorrow. Taking a leaf from Drucker's journaling approach, you might start to monitor how many items you start with, how many you do and how many are left at the end of the day. Review once you have sufficient data and see whether you can detect any patterns. Maybe you are simply taking on too much and the issue is the need to learn to say no, rather than the need to become more efficient. Or maybe you are taking on too much because you haven't trained the people that work for you or that you haven't learned to delegate effectively.

Taking on something new can be exciting and yet can be very frustrating. As we described in the chapter on personal change, some of us have an expectation that when we start, we will have success immediately. But that is rarely the case. We need to practice. If we can use golf as a metaphor, if a golfer identifies the need for an improvement in some aspect of her/his game, she/he will go to the range and practice. If a carpenter wants to try a new technique or tool, they will practice on a waste piece of wood. Not on the next commissioned piece of furniture!!!

Time Management Systems

Our experience is that, with a few exceptions, typical time management systems don't work over a long period. We all start off with good intentions, but, very soon their usage falls by the wayside, like most New Year's Resolutions.

Let's take a look at some possible reasons why. First, maybe each one of us actually needs different systems at different times, depending on the state of our brain and the context we are operating in.

Consider the following. You wake up in the morning and are full of the joys of spring. You are alert and ready to tackle the world full on. This most definitely happens for the larks amongst us. Maybe less so for the owls.

Your PFC is in full control. You make your to-do list, or ABC list, or COZI list, or Franklin-Covey entries, or whatever, and you are off and running. The first three or four get knocked off in rapid succession. You feel good. Then comes the first unplanned interruption. Or a tough decision that you have to make. Or the first put down or criticism of the day. The story goes on.

Within a few short hours, the ability of your PFC to self-regulate, focus your attention on those things that you deemed important, and maintain concentration, goes to hell-in-a-handbasket. We become driven by interrupts and our limbic system rather than by our priorities or plans. It would probably be difficult for any single system to cater for all these dynamics.

The second reason might be that there is no one-size-fits-all system that works for everyone. Phil reports that he worked with a colleague that drove his life with a blank-sheet sketch book, filled with Mind-Maps. And got on just fine. On the other end of the scale, Phil had a realtor once, who had been using her Franklin-Covey equivalent for over ten years and wouldn't go anywhere without it. And she got on just fine. In many cases, these systems appear to have been designed and developed with one brain profile, or behavioral profile in mind.

If you find one that works for you, then use it. Some of us have a hard time with anything that doesn't fit our personal brain profile.

Bottom Line Summary

There are a number of tools and techniques that are useful to help in time and energy management. Pick some that interest you and try them out. Keep using them if they are useful for you, but don't be afraid to throw them away if they don't end up working for you.

What's next?

What one or two things am I going to focus on to better manage my time and energy?
What I am going to do about it/them?
How will I measure whether I have been successful?

[99] Macan, T. H., Shahani, C., Dipboye, R. L., & Phillips, A. P. (1990). College Students' Time Management: Correlations with Academic Performance and Stress. *Journal of Educational Psychology, 82*(4), 760–768.

[100] Gonzalez, V. M., & Mark, G. (2006). Managing Currents of Work: Multi-tasking Among Multiple Collaborations (pp. 143–162). Presented at the Proceedings of the Ninth European Conference on Computer-Supported Cooperative Work, Paris.

[101] Marulanda Carter, L., & Jackson, T. W. (2012). Effects of e-mail addiction and interruptions on employees. *Journal of Systems and Information Technology, 14*(1), 82–94. http://doi.org/10.1108/13287261211221146

[102] Marulanda Carter, L., & Jackson, T. W. (2012). Op cit

[103] Spira, J. B., & Feintuch, J. B. (2005). *The Cost of Not Paying Attention: How Interruptions Impact Knowledge Worker Productivity. Basex* (pp. 1–21).

[104] Gupta, Ashish & Sharda, Ramesh. (2008). SIMONE: A Simulator for Interruptions and Message Overload in Network Environments. International Journal of Simulation and Process Modelling. 4. 10.1504/IJSPM.2008.023685.

[105] Altmann, E. M., Trafton, J. G., & Hambrick, D. Z. (2014). Momentary interruptions can derail the train of thought. *Journal of Experimental Psychology: General, 143*(1), 215–226. http://doi.org/10.1037/a0030986

[106] Lin, B. C., Kain, J. M., & Fritz, C. (2013). Don't interrupt me! An examination of the relationship between intrusions at work and employee strain. *International Journal of Stress Management, 20*(2), 77–94. http://doi.org/10.1037/a0031637

[107] Oncken, W., & Wass, D. L. (1974). Management Time: Who's Got the Monkey? *Harvard Business Review*, 1–9.

[108] Baumeister, R.F., & Vohs, K.D (2016). Strength Model of Self-Regulation as Limited Resource (Vol. 54, pp. 67-127). Elsevier, http://doi.org/10.1016/bs.aesp.2016.04.001

Chapter 8:

Decision Making

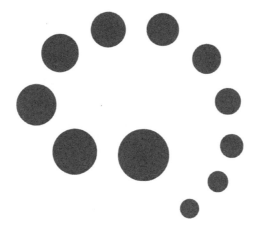

8. Decision Making

General comments

Making decisions is something that we do hundreds, if not thousands of times a day. Yet it is one of the areas that most of us spend little or no time thinking about. Our personal process of decision making. How do we make decisions? What is our own style of decision making? How does the brain impact our decision making? And how successful has our decision making been in the past?

The purpose of this chapter is to pull all those things apart, and help you understand your own decision-making process, determine if it works for you, and, if it doesn't, to develop one that does.

What works

- Understand where you are in your decision-making process. Be honest.
- Where possible, identify the optimum outcome of a decision before attempting to make it
- Evaluate your choices before making a decision (even if one of the choices is do nothing)
- Use a decision matrix
- Understand whether you are a "sufficer" or a "maximizer"
- If possible, identify the biases and past patterns of behavior that you typically bring to the type of decision you are making
- Become aware of the different aspects of yourself that are likely to influence your decision-making processes
- Differentiate between bias driven decisions and evaluation driven decisions
- Explicitly identify what your role is in any given decision-making process
- Speak up – act independently if necessary
- Take decisive action when command and control is appropriate
- Recognize the impact of wicked problems on decision making
- Recognize the influence of timing on your decision making
- Recognize the impact tiredness has on your decision making
- Determine the amount of time you have before a decision needs to made – and use it
- Use appropriate decision-making techniques
- Take breaks, change environments and change the people you surround yourself with when faced with key decisions
- Identify people who consistently add value to your decision-making process – and use them
- Should the decision be based on analysis or insight – recognize the value of each
- Avoid making too many decisions one after another
- Review past decisions – within a week, and then a year later

- Take several stakeholder viewpoints in evaluating a decision
- Be clear about the assumptions you are basing your decision upon – and challenge them
- Be clear about your own emotions (threat state or happiness) when making a decision
- Be clear about, and wary of, feelings of knowing, certainty, correctness, being right and conviction

Brief examples

A recent client of Phil's, a middle-aged woman, was facing a choice of two different futures; one choice was to continue with the company she was with; the other was to branch off with a new company, but, essentially, doing the same job. Not an unusual dilemma – one that many of us have faced. Neither was a perfect solution. The current company had some chronic issues that needed to be resolved; the new company has already solved some of those issues but will involve several years of diminished income. She chose the new horizons. As Phil worked with her, in looking back over her life patterns, it became clear that one of her tendencies was to run away from difficult issues rather than face them. In work and her social life. And she repeated that pattern with this decision. She ran away from the difficult issues that had to be faced in her current company.

The question that needed to be asked was, "What impact do my life patterns have on my decision making?" Not that the decision for a new horizon was a wrong decision; rather, it would have been useful to have recognized that it was yet another repetition of a life pattern.

One of the things that you will see in the "What works" section and the "Discussion" section is to be very clear on where you are in the process of decision-making, whatever the process is that you are using. Be honest. If you have already made up your mind, say so. In doing so, it may cause feedback that will make you review that position but it's better to get it out there. It is very frustrating for other people for you to ask for their opinion about a decision that you are facing only to find that you have already made your mind. It's worse still, if you are the boss or an authority figure to them.

Let's give an example. Some years ago, when Phil was still in IT (and before he knew we even had brains ☺) he was asked to select the next generation of computers upon which his company would run for the foreseeable future. It was a key decision that would set the path of IT strategy for many years to come, and a wrong decision could be costly. He did his data gathering and analysis and decided to give his boss an update.

Sometime before that meeting took place, she and Phil had talked about how people make decisions. Phil had observed a key, time-consuming element of many decision processes – and that was one of justification. He observed that people had often made a decision, sometimes consciously, and sometimes nonconsciously – and yet spent a long time justifying the decision to themselves. Seeking out more and more data, to prove that what they had already decided. We now know it as confirmation bias. Then there was a subsequent phase - the need to justify it to others.

When Phil arrived in the meeting, he presented an analysis of where he was, describing all of the possible choices and the different criteria that would be needed to make the analysis. He knew the level of urgency of making a recommendation (budget time was coming up) but estimated that the process would take another three or four months. His boss made a simple statement. She said that, based on his decision-making hypothesis, it seemed to her that he had already made his mind up and that he was entering into a "personal justification phase." Then she asked a question. If this was true, what would it take to get to the decision?

It became clear that she was right. Phil had made the decision. Other data might have confirmed the decision and may indeed have been necessary for justifying it to the Executive Team, but her statement and question had identified truly where he was in the process. Those few moments saved three or four months of effort.

A few years ago, Scott was working with an executive that had to make a major decision regarding a customer that represented thirty two percent of the company's revenue. Her decision centered around keeping the client or letting them go. The executive explained that, while the revenue was critical, the impact to the business was significant in that the resources she was spending on keeping this client happy were easily over 50 percent of her team's time and resources. Her other clients were much less resource hungry and she suspected that she was leaving more profitable business to her competitors. She further explained that this client had been with her since the founding of the company so there was a loyalty factor that was keeping her from taking the leap. She had learned from her mentors that "There is no price too high for loyalty" and that had stuck with her through the years. This axiom or rule was costing her something and she was refusing to acknowledge it. She further acknowledged that she did not know how fast she could replace the revenue if she were to discontinue the relationship. When Scott asked if she could renegotiate the price for that client which had been established 8 years ago when she was a smaller and less experienced firm, she gasped "I can't do that, they might be offended and leave". "So, you would rather fire them than give them a choice to pay more or leave?" Scott replied. It did not take long for her to see the irony and the potholes of her decision-making process. Thirty days later they renegotiated their price to her satisfaction.

Discussion

As soon as we start to pull the process apart, we find out very rapidly that there are many components to the decision-making process. To start with, most, if not all, of the topics in *UYBFAC* have some role in the decision-making process. First, let's look at the brain principles, as a reminder:

Brain Principle # 1: the brain has one purpose – survival; it reviews its environment for threats and rewards and takes appropriate action. As you are standing on the sidewalk (pavement for the Brits) the brain sees that car speeding down the road and decides to step back from the curb. Just in case.

Some of this is conscious but many times, especially if, for example, you are distracted on your phone or in conversation with another person, it happens at a nonconscious level.

Brain Principle # 2. Our brains are very good at making nonconscious decisions and then coming up with conscious rationale about why we made the decision.

Brain Principle # 4. The things that the brain picks up on will generate internal thoughts and feelings, again some conscious and some nonconscious.

Now let's take a look at the five brain dynamics, in a similar manner fashion:

We are biased. And these biases come roaring out when it comes to decision making. Let's take, for example, our good old friend, confirmation bias. It is built to aid in quick decision making. If a piece of information arrives that confirms what we already know, we take it on face value without giving it much, if any consideration; we then rapidly make a decision and act upon it. A piece of information that arrives that contradicts what we already know, and that is easy. We ignore it and go about our business!

We are irrational. Once again, our irrationality has a major role in decision making. As we pointed out in *UYBFAC*, this irrationality can come from many areas – something is unfair, some specific words or metaphors were used, the issue is being framed a certain way, something has already been anchored in our brain and/or we are being influenced in a certain way. This ranges from buying a certain type of wine in a liquor store through to how we view political candidates.

We are stress driven. How we make decisions, and the choices that we make, are very much driven by the level of stress that you are under. This applies whether you are under acute stress at a specific point in time, or whether you have been operating under chronic stress for a while.

In general, we don't like change. The brain sees change as a threat to be wary of. If we are facing a decision where one choice will lead to the status quo, and the other choice will lead to a need to change, we will tend to want to stay with what we know and avoid the choice that leads to change.

We are driven by brain rhythms. We tend to be able to make clearer decisions in the morning than in the afternoon. [109] And if you are ever in the unfortunate situation where you are coming in front of a parole board, you better hope that you are reviewed in the morning. Yet there is a significant amount of research that suggests if we need to develop some extra choices for our decision, then it might be better to do that in the afternoon. So, the time of the day, and the day of the week, when we think about our decisions, can impact the eventual decision we make. Following this reasoning, the common phrase, "Sleep on it," is good advice.

Let's go back now and look at Brain Principle # 5, the Five Forces of Protection, Participation, Prediction, Purpose and Pleasure. There are a large number of different facets within these driving forces. 59 of them, in fact. Any one of these facets can nonconsciously drive, or at least influence, your decision making. Let's take a look some examples, one from each of the five drivers. (The facets that we refer to here, are all described in more detail in *UYBFAC*.)

We'll look at Protection first. What if one of the facets that drives you, is your need to feel financially secure and avoid financial losses? (Facet #3) Then, without extra thought and attention, your natural instinct, for example, will be to hold on to assets, like stocks, that have lost value and sell those that have gained somewhat. This instinct will be ever present and might override any analysis you might do with regard to the future of the two assets in question. Let's say, in addition, that you have a preference for short-term gain over long-term gain, (Facet #4) then this will compound the problem.

Now we'll take a look at Participation. We'll do this by looking at the example of a person who has a high need to be associated with people with whom they have something in common, with whom they feel they belong and are accepted, and who they like. (Facet # 11) This will tend to lead them to favor their own "in-group" when it comes to decisions about recruitment, bonuses, promotions, etc. You can easily imagine how this might be influenced by other social biases.

On to Prediction, and we will take a look at someone who has a high need to know what's going on (Facet # 27) They will spend a lot of time in attending meetings just for fear of FOMO (Fear of Missing Out) rather than making decisions about which meetings would be useful for them to attend and which will be a waste of time. This need leads to a huge time sink, and probably has a greater impact, for this person, than any time management improvements that could be implemented.

Our fourth driver is Purpose. Let us assume that you are a person who wants to achieve mastery in your field and wants to have an opportunity to practice it on a regular basis. (Facet # 45) This might have a couple of impacts on you. You may sign up for classes or sign up to attend conferences in your domain that, while adding to your knowledge, may not be necessary for the job you do. If we now add in the possibility that you also want to live in accordance with your core values (Facet # 48) you may find out that you are frequently faced with dilemmas. Should you attend that conference or be at your child's rehearsal?

The last, but not least, of our drivers is Pleasure. If one of your drivers in experiencing instant gratification, (Facet # 56) then it is easy to imagine many scenarios where your decision is driven by this need, rather than alternatives that might be available.

Now let's add to all of this your Personal Threat Context i.e. all of the other stressors that might be going on in your life. The greater the number of other stressors, the less chance that your PFC will act as a brake and take control, and the greater the chance that your decisions will be made by your drivers, or other nonconscious factors.

Finally, it would be good for you to take a look at how the various aspects of your Self can impact your decision making. One way to do this is by a series of questions: and them some examples.

"What impact < *fill in the blank* > have on your decision making?"

… does your overall Personal Threat Profile …
… does your current Personal Threat Context …
… does your Brain Profile …
… does your Chronotype …
… does your Grassi 8 Factor profile …
… does your Advocacy/Inquiry profile …
… does your TAPS process …
… does your FFI profile …
… does your Zimbardo Inventory …
… does your Social Style …
… does your Team Profile …
… do your Leadership Profiles …
… do your biases …
… do your habits …
… do your life patterns …
… do your triggers …
… does your world view …
… do Cialdini's Big Six influencers …
… do your other influencers …
… do your personal experiences …
… does your current life cycle …
… do recent events …
… do your future dreams …
… do your values …
… does your environment …
… do your strengths and weaknesses …
… do your various intelligences …
… do your different and multiple characters …
… does your current outlook …

As you can see, between the influences that are coming from our brains, and the influences from the various aspects of our selves, there are many ways that our decision making is driven, much of it at a nonconscious level. Not that this is bad. Or at least, not all bad. Recognizing your overall decision-making tendencies is the important thing here.

At this point, however, we would like to apologize. We have jumped straight into this decision-making topic without giving a definition. What do we mean by decision-making? Some of you might respond by saying "Well, dummy. Isn't it obvious? It's the act of making decisions!" Maybe it's that simple, but let's make sure. As we did on many occasions in the previous book, it might help to have a formal definition.

We can find one such definition from Lee et al. [110]:

> *"Decision making can be defined as the flexible integration and transformation of information from the external world into action."*

i.e. decision making is taking what we see in our external environment, integrating it with what we already know and acting upon it. Hmm. Interesting, but is it useful?

Let's lean on our old source of wisdom Wikipedia [111] which seems to give us a much more useful result. In fact, two of them:

> *"In psychology, decision-making is regarded as the cognitive process resulting in the selection of a belief or a course of action among several alternative possibilities. Every decision-making process produces a final choice, which may or may not prompt action."*

and

> *"Decision-making is the process of identifying and choosing alternatives based on the, preferences and beliefs of the decision-maker."*

So. A cognitive process, alternative possibilities, a selection process, values, preferences and beliefs that may or may not mean action.

Interesting again. But, having researched quite a lot on this topic, we assert that there are several things either incorrect or missing from all of these definitions.

The first incorrect or missing aspect is that the decision-making processes may be "cognitive," but the process is often either fully nonconscious or is influenced by the nonconscious.

The second incorrect or missing aspect, is that the process is influenced by a host of other dynamics such as an individual's Personal Threat Profile, Personal Threat Context, and the totality of the contributions from their Self aspects.

The third incorrect or missing aspect is that the implication here is that the "cognitive process" upon which our decisions are based, is a rational one. The research clearly shows that not only is it not rational, but it is strongly influenced by an emotional component, and an emotional component is actually a requirement.

The fourth incorrect or missing aspect is that our actions are frequently irrational.

While we may not have our formal definition, we propose that we have the components of a formal definition:

"A conscious and nonconscious cognitive process, with alternative possibilities, accompanied by a selection process, which is influenced by our personal make-up, emotions, values, preferences and beliefs, which may or may not mean action, which may be rational or irrational."

Wow. A mouthful indeed.

Let's talk about a number of other things that influence our decision making, and some techniques we can use to improve it:

<u>Where you are in the/your process</u>?

Here's a process of decision-making that we have observed in many people over the past few decades:

It seems that there are several phases or events/milestones that we go through:

1. A recognition that a decision is required. In some cases, it is obvious. To ourselves and to other people. In some cases, it is not obvious, and we have to discover it. Maybe it comes to us as the result of a number of conversations over time. In some cases, we are handed the decision to make, by circumstances that are out of our control.
2. Data gathering. We then do analyses of our options. Once again, sometimes they are clear and sometimes, not so clear. Sometimes the options that we first see are not palatable, so we have to get inventive to find options that we can deal with. Sometimes this process takes a long while, and sometimes it is very quick. We do our best to be objective in this phase, but in many cases, we are not. Nowhere near.
3. We make the decision. Sometimes we are aware of having made the decision and sometimes not. The decision has sometimes been made at a deep, nonconscious level. Nevertheless, it has been made.
4. We realize that we have made the decision. And we make a judgment as to whether we "like" the decision. If we like it, we move to the next phase. If we don't like it, we go back to the data gathering phase in order to find data that will result in a different decision. We rarely do. We can go around this circle many times. ☺
5. We spend some time justifying the decision – first, to ourselves. We find supporting data to show why the decision that we have already made, is the right one. Sometimes we confuse this with the data gathering phase. It is different. Confirmation bias is singing from the rooftops.
6. We move into a phase of testing out our decision. With our friends, close allies and supporters. We are, deep down, hoping and praying that they agree with us. We phrase it that we want their opinion, but often we just want confirmation.
7. We spend some time selling and justifying the decision – this time, to others. We do this in indirect ways. Floating "what if" ideas. And temporarily backing away if we meet too much resistance. But the resistance rarely causes us to change our decisions. We find other ways to justify it … or move around

the resistance, convincing ourselves that any decision and subsequent action will have consequences and occasional collateral damage.

8. We announce our decision. Either explicitly or implicitly.
9. We act upon it. Sometimes the action happens before the announcement or is the implicit action-oriented announcement.

This list of phases is, however, somewhat deceiving. A simple list like this gives the implication that they are all of the phases are equal in weight, time and effort. That isn't true. Each of the phases take a different time – and sometimes we cycle around in them.

But being clear where you are in the process is important.

Decision Matrix

The concept of a decision matrix is to provide a formal method of evaluating alternative choices. First you develop a list of ideal outcomes, independently from thinking about possible choices. Then you develop as many choices as you can. Then plot a matrix to contain your analysis. It works like this:

Develop ideal outcomes. If possible, before embarking on the decision-making process, and before examining your choices or alternatives, generate a list of attributes for an ideal solution or decision. This separates the evaluative criteria of any resulting decision from the process itself, or the choices available. This act starts to eliminate some of the pernicious biases and behavioral patterns that come into play. Not all of the criteria will have equal weight, so assigning a weighting to each of the criteria offers another level of refinement. Indeed, some of the criteria may have such a weighting as to make the criteria binary i.e. any choice which failed to satisfy this criterion would eliminate it as a choice.

If time permits, develop the criteria and then take a break. Go for a walk. Do something different. Sleep on it. Talk with a trusted advisor. Then review the list of criteria. Repeat until satisfied.

(Another method of identifying the criteria for success is to use the Risk Analysis method described below)

Identify your options. Identify all of the possibilities that you think might be available to you. Even the crazy, unlikely or seemingly impossible ones. If you need help in developing some of the more "out-there" options use some of the techniques described in Chapter 9 on Personal Innovation and Insight.

But also remember that the brain can rapidly become overwhelmed if there are too many choices.

Lay the matrix out such that the choices are along the top and the criteria are down the side, as shown in the diagram below. This shows 5 choices and 8 criteria, but clearly the matrix can be any size.

Take each choice one at a time. Evaluate each of the criteria for that choice and give it a score from 1 to 10. Then multiply each of the scores for any given choice/criteria by the weight for that criteria to get a choice result. Then total all of the results for each choice.

	Weight	Choice 1		Choice 2		Choice 3		Choice 4		Choice 5	
		Score	Result	Score	Result	Score	Result	Score	Result	Score	Result
Criterion 1											
Criterion 2											
Criterion 3											
Criterion 4											
Criterion 5											
Criterion 6											
Criterion 7											
Criterion 8											

In the example above, there is a clear winner. Choice 4 at 587. And there is a clear loser. Choice 3 at 439. The difference between choices 2 and 5, however, is only 14 – not a great difference so we would treat them as equal. So, if choice 4 proved not to be feasible, for whatever reason, then either choice 2 or 5 would work.

Some readers will be loving this approach. It appeals to people who have a high degree for detail and prediction in their Personal Threat Profiles. It also appeals to some people who have a high degree of Fairness in their profiles as it tends to eliminate bias towards one choice or another. We say tends, because clearly the results could be manipulated. It also lends itself to multiple evaluators i.e. a complete team doing the evaluation.

Decision Matrix example

	Weight	Choice 1		Choice 2		Choice 3		Choice 4		Choice 5	
		Score	Result	Score	Result	Score	Result	Score	Result	Score	Result
Criterion 1	10	6	60	8	80	5	50	9	90	8	80
Criterion 2	9	4	36	8	72	6	54	8	72	9	81
Criterion 3	8	7	56	9	72	7	56	9	72	9	72
Criterion 4	7	6	42	5	35	7	49	10	70	6	42
Criterion 5	8	8	64	7	56	9	72	8	64	9	72
Criterion 6	6	9	54	7	42	6	36	8	48	7	42
Criterion 7	9	8	72	10	90	8	72	9	81	8	72
Criterion 8	10	6	60	8	80	5	50	9	90	8	80
			444		527		439		587		541

Other readers will inherently dislike the approach. They see it as cumbersome, time consuming and unnecessary. Just remember it is always an option which is available to you.

Although this book is about your brain on its own, it is sometimes useful to consider who else will be reviewing how you made a choice. The level on detail and analysis this approach provides can be useful as back-up material – especially if the person who is reviewing the decision has a high need for detail and prediction.

Decision-making type

Are you a sufficer or a maximizer? Sufficers review options until they find one that satisfies all of their requirements, opt for that and move on to whatever is next on their plate. Maximizers want to take a look at all of the options and get the best possible choice. Neither is inherently good or bad – both have advantages and disadvantages.

Determine what is your normal style – and make a decision as to which is most appropriate for any given decision.

Biases and patterns

Next, assuming that you are the sole decision maker, if time permits, write down the things that might be influencing your decision. Biases? Past patterns of behavior or choices? Other internal and external pressures that you are feeling? Some of them will be obvious. Some won't. Is the interviewee's accent weighing in my decision as to whether to hire them or the other candidate? Is the fact that I can't pronounce their name a factor in my decision? Is the fact that they are good/bad looking influencing my decision?

As we discovered in *UYBFAC*, there are, literally, hundreds of biases and we are not very good at identifying our own. (In fact, we are very bad at it.) Seek help from other trusted advisors.

In his about to published book, Tom Rieger [112] suggest that, by understanding how our brains work, we can move from a biased way of making decisions to a more deliberate and objective manner. While Tom approaches thinking from an organizational perspective, it equally applies to an individual making a decision.

Each decision involves three phases which we see again and again:

1. How do I deal with the quantity and complexity of information available to me?
2. How do I combine disparate inputs and building consensus, knowing that some of those disparate thoughts are from different parts of my own thinking?
3. How do I determine, and convince myself and others, that I am making the right decision?

And our own brains don't help – as they too are divided. The emotional brain (driven primarily by the mammalian brain and limbic system) wants to make rapid decisions. These decisions tend to be bias driven. That's what it has evolved to do. The rational brain (driven primarily by the Pre-Frontal Cortex) wants to take a more deliberative approach.

Rieger uses the following structures to differentiate the two approaches of dealing with the three phases above:

Phase	Emotional approach	Deliberative approach
Dealing with the quantity and complexity of information	Simplify	Evaluate
Combining disparate inputs and building consensus	Unify	Integrate
Convincing myself and others, that I am making the right decision	Justify	Substantiate

He describes the three elements of the emotional approach as organizational blind-spots (we would call them individual habits) and then goes on to examine the underlying biases involved with each one. He continues his argument, and the book, by describing the more rational and preferred approach of Evaluate-Integrate-Substantiate.

Ladder of Inference

The Ladder of Inference was introduced by Chris Argyris [113] in the early 1990's and demonstrates how we take a small piece of data and, mostly nonconsciously, make inferences about people, events and situations. Then we make decisions based upon those inferences. With regard to a person, it goes like this:

1. We observe a person's behavior
2. We summarize that behavior or select certain portions of data from what we have observed
3. If we don't have all the data, or a complete picture, we fill in the gaps
4. We interpret that data through the lens of our own world view and previous experience, either with that person or similar people
5. We summarize, as our brains are not good at keeping all of the detail hanging around
6. We make assumptions about that person and the narrative that we have told ourselves
7. We draw conclusions or inferences about that person.
8. We make decisions, engage in arguments, and choose actions based upon those inferences

This sequence happens very quickly and, mostly, nonconsciously. It gets worse, however. Once we have run up that ladder, our conformation bias tends to ensure that, from then on, we seek out and only entertain data that confirm our conclusions and inferences. This is often accompanied by the, sometimes unspoken, phrase "See. It told you so."

One way to avoid this inference making, is to go back down the ladder, and identify the actual data that you observed that caused these various internal leaps.

So, let's move on to things that you need to take into account in order to leverage your brain when making decisions at work.

The very first thing is a somewhat obvious, but often overlooked process that is always worth addressing. What is your role in the decision-making process? Are you the sole decision maker? If there are several of you, what is the agreed upon process that you are going to use? And what is your role within that group? A useful model for determining your role is that offered by Rogers and Blenko in their paper "Who has the D?" [114] The model is the RAPID model, and it suggests that you have one of the following five roles: Recommend, Agree, Perform, Input, or Decide.

We will address this more when we talk about the processes involved in a group decision. For now, ensure that you are clear. What is your role?

You may choose to make the decision by taking advice from others. In some cases, from other people in the organization. In some cases, from people outside the organization – other colleagues, mentors, or consultants. If you do seek "advice," how do you view it? Do you see it as another piece of data that you can add into your data set or do you see it as a dictum, i.e. something that you have to take into account and act upon? And how do you rank your need for control and self-determination (Facet # 25) and integrate that with an advice-seeking activity? Does your need for control and self-determination prevent you from seeking advice? What about the degree to which you are influenced by authority figures?

We now know that there are many dimensions that are likely to influence our decision making, probably more than we can totally get our arms around and understand. And the longer we are engrossed in the decision-making, the more difficult it can be to sort our objective and rational thoughts out from all of the other influences.

Bottom line summary

We would all love to think that our decision making is done in a cool, calm, and clear manner, and that our decisions are objective and rational. Unfortunately, for the most part that is not the case. Understanding what impacts your own decision making will give you a step in the direction of making better decisions.

What's next?

What one or two things am I going to focus on to improve my decision making?
What I am going to do about it/them?
How will I measure whether I have been successful?

[109] Pink, D. (2018). When: The Scientific Secrets of Perfect Timing. Riverhead Books.
[110] Lee, A. M., Tai, L. H., Zador, A., & Wilbrecht, L. (2015). Between the primate and "reptilian" brain: Rodent models demonstrate the role of corticostriatal circuits in decision making. *Neuroscience, 296*, 66–74. http://doi.org/10.1016/j.neuroscience.2014.12.042
[111] https://en.wikipedia.org/wiki/Decision-making. Accessed on March 22, 2019
[112] Rieger, T. (2020). Curing Organizational Blindness: Three Deadly Blindspots and How to Overcome Them. In final edits.
[113] Argyris, C. (1994). The Fifth Discipline Fieldbook: Strategies and Tools for Building a Learning Organization (1st ed.). Crown Business.
[114] Rogers, P., & Blenko, M. W. (2006). Who Has the D?: How Clear Decision Roles Enhance Organizational Performance. *Harvard Business Review*, 1–17.

Chapter 9:

Personal Innovation and Insight

9. Personal Innovation and Insight

General comments

When do you have your best ideas? For some people it's when they are jogging. For others it's when they are driving the car. Yet others, it's when they are in the shower. About to go to sleep. Immediately upon waking up. While exercising. While walking the dog. Talking with a friend. Or talking to the dog, your best friend, while jogging. ☺

The list goes on, but these are some of the more common themes that we find. Not surprisingly, it's different for all of us. We have asked this question of attendees in classes over decades now. On only one occasion has a person said: "While sitting at my desk." ☺ We're not saying that it's impossible to come up with new ideas at your desk – just that the data suggest that, statistically speaking, it is unlikely.

What works

> Create a safe place for yourself
> Stop thinking about the problem and move onto something else
> Go for a walk
> Go and explain the issue to someone else – and ask them to wait before they give you any ideas
> Describe what would have to happen for the problem/issue to go away
> Think about someone who you know who always comes up with good ideas – how would they tackle it?
> If your organization is big enough, search for someone else in the organization who has already solved the problem. [115]
> Think about what if you never solved the problem – what would you do to get around it?
> If the problem were to arise under different circumstances, what would you do to prevent it next time?
> Think about it first thing the next morning – or last thing in the afternoon.
> Search Google or Google Scholar
> Doodle or paint a picture
> Ask a kid to solve it for you
> If you can't fix it, feature it. [h]
> Can you break the issue into smaller issues? If so, what sequence can you solve them in?
> If you had an unlimited amount of resource, would it make any difference about solving the problem?

---

h That was one of Phil's Father's favorite sayings. If he came across a problem that seemed unsurmountable, he would ask how he could turn it to his favor.

- How will you view the problem in one month's time? One year's time? Five year's time?
- Put yourself in someone else's shoes. How would your significant other approach the problem? Your coach? Your attorney? Your kids?
- What are the assumptions you are making? About the problem? About the solution? What are you hanging on to? Physically, emotionally and psychologically?
- What aspects of your world view are helping? What ones are getting in your way?
- What other problems have you seen that are just like or similar to this problem? How were they solved?

Brief examples

Many years ago, Phil had decided to change the landscape in his garden. He had allocated a budget of twenty thousand dollars but kept getting stuck on exactly what he was trying to achieve and how to achieve it. He went around and around about how to get everything he wanted into the space allocated and keep it within budget.

One evening, while sitting in the garden with a glass of wine, he had the breakthrough. He was sitting on it. He was sitting on an old redwood bench. He was attempting to design everything around an old bench. He was constructing an approach for which he would spend twenty thousand dollars around a ten-dollar bench that was close to falling apart. Once he identified (and removed) the bench everything else fell into place. And the fact that he had been sitting on the problem, and hence not noticing it, was not lost on him.

The context, in all of its manifestations, needs to support innovation. As an example of what not to do, one of our clients had been wanting for at least five years to grow the number of stores they operate but were wondering why it wasn't happening. Upon examination, we found that the bonuses of the regional leaders were based upon the total profits of the stores within their region. Opening a new store, in a new area, would inevitably reduce the profit of the region for the first couple of years – and hence the leaders were not inclined to spend any time looking into new and (to their mind) risky expansions. Hence no expansion.

As an aviation executive for many years, Scott often found the term "innovation" thrown around the industry. One of the stories often told was when Arthur Young was commissioned by Lawrence Dale Bell in the early 1940s to complete the design of a helicopter rotor system that would allow for a safe landing when the engine quits. Aircraft Engine technology was still emerging in the early 1940s and the risk associated with a new technology like a helicopter was even greater due to its unconventional design. Mr. Bell told Arthur Young, "If you can demonstrate for me that a helicopter can have an engine quit and land safely, I will pay you and use your design for the first Bell Helicopter produced." This was a huge challenge and Mr. Bell knew it. Mr. Young was certain he could create the right design but testing it and proving that it would be safe was another story. The story goes that Mr. Young created a model design, strapped an egg where the pilot would sit and after two attempts was able to land the model to the ground without breaking the egg. Bell Helicopter was born. Perhaps we miss the power of innovation and insight when we are blind to the limitations of application we put on many things in our daily life. Even if that answer is right at our breakfast table! Mr. Young was able to see the egg beyond just a breakfast food when he most needed to. Perhaps it's true that "Necessity is the mother of all invention"!

Discussion

In many of the chapters in this book and in *UYBFAC*, we have spent much time in getting to a useful working definition of the subject in hand; originally, we had intended to do so here as well. What we discovered, however, is that, while there is a lot of discussion in the academic literature about the definition of innovation, and the distinction between creativity, problem-solving and innovation, the relevance of all that discussion to the real world (or to a field guide) is about as useful as the discussion of how many angels can dance on the head of a pin.

So, we won't be including a definition here. What we did discover, however, was some really useful suggestions by Dyer et al. [116] concerning the dynamics and components of innovative people and processes. We offer this as one of the better summaries that we have found in the field and a great starting point for looking at how our brains facilitate (or get in the way of) innovation and personal insight.

First of all, like many other researchers and authors, they put to rest the myth that creativity is all about genetics. The concept that you are either born with creativity or forget about ever having it, is not how it works. They cite several studies where it has been shown that only about 30% of creativity could be ascribed to genetics. So, most of it can be learned. They summarize it by saying that you need to understand the skill, practice it and then gain confidence in your capacity to be creative.

On page 27, of their book, they offer the diagram shown below. They suggest that there are three sets of attributes (our word, not theirs) – the courage to innovate, some behavioral skills and some cognitive skills.

We will take a look at each of these attributes in more detail

Let's start with the courage to innovate, which they subsequently divide into two, the ability to challenge the status quo and the ability to take risks. These abilities are not binary, in that you either have them or you don't. Before we even take into account the proclivities of your brain, your world view, background and mindset, together with the context that you are operating within, will all impact the degree to which you have the ability to challenge the status quo, and the willingness that you have to exercise it.

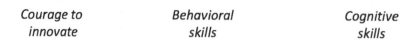

| Courage to innovate | Behavioral skills | Cognitive skills |

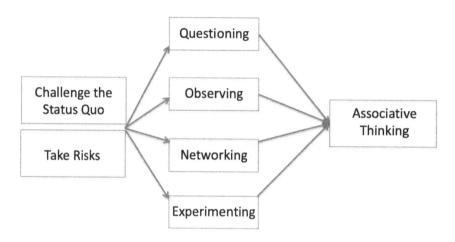

Dyer, Gregersen, & Christensen (2011)

With regard to your world view and background, let's say for example that you grew up, using in their words, "in a society that promoted community over individualism and hierarchy over merit," you are probably less likely to exhibit the courage to challenge the status quo or take risks. Not that your brain cannot do it; it's just less likely to. What about if you grew up in an environment which, for whatever reason, didn't feel safe? Or how about if your teachers slapped your wrist if you even considered painting outside of the lines or painting trees purple? How would having those dynamics in your background, impact your ability to challenge the status quo?

As to your current context, what about if you just don't feel safe in the environment you are currently working in? Maybe you have an over-bearing, micro-managing, take-all-the-credit boss. Or maybe the reward systems don't support taking risks. Or maybe someone was fired for taking a risk. Or maybe risky projects were seen as likely to have their funding withdrawn. Or maybe you are newly married with a young family and have just taken on your first mortgage? Any or all of these dynamics, and indeed many more, make it less likely that you will "have the courage to innovate" by taking risks or challenging the status quo. Reviewing your Personal Threat Profile and Personal Threat Context might help to illustrate where you might be reluctant or vulnerable.

We will address the whole topic of Courage in more detail in chapter 14 but for now let's take a look at two aspects with regard to the brain; the general reaction of the brain to new ideas and your own Personal Threat Profile. We learned in chapter 4, that the brain evaluates new ideas in three ways – feasibility, appeal, and the degree of change. And this happens immediately and nonconsciously. Unless we have been trained otherwise, we tend to "allow" new, and possibly innovative, ideas to come into the light of day only if we can see some chance of them being feasible and we don't have to change that much. In many instances, the idea is stifled at birth.

Now let's consider just a couple of facets from the PTP, one from each of the three threat P's. Let's start with Facet #3 ... feeling financially safe. If you score high on this facet, you might not be willing to step out of the box and develop a crazy idea for fear of not being successful and putting your financial security at risk.

How about #15 .... knowing that we have approval from people that are important to us? If you have a high need for your team-mates to like and approve of what you do, you might be reluctant to stand apart from them by having the breakthrough ideas.

Or number 32 ... the ability to tolerate ambiguity? New and breakthrough ideas are often full of ambiguity in the first instance. Living with that ambiguity may be very uncomfortable until the idea has been fleshed out.

Behavioral skills – questioning

Let's now turn to the second of Dyer and team's list of attributes – the behavioral skills of questioning, observing, networking and experimenting. Let's look at them in that sequence. Most people think that they ask a lot of questions. Not surprisingly, when we dig deeper, we find that most people:

> don't ask nearly as many questions as they think they do,
> don't necessarily ask good, let alone great questions,
> rarely dig deeper than the answer to the first question
> often have their mind up before they hear the answer to the question, and hence do not listen.

In *UYBFAC* we introduced the concept of "your conversational style" and gave three models upon which to look at your style. All three involved the degree to which you asked questions. The first model, the Grassi model, offered 8 general topic areas to investigate:

> What are the opportunities?
> What are the constraints?
> How is this similar to what we have seen in the past?
> How is it dissimilar?
> How do we want people to see us?
> How do we want to feel?
> What should we start/stop doing?
> What should we continue to do?

The second, the advocacy/inquiry matrix examined the degree to which you asked questions versus the degree to which you took an advocacy position. It is very difficult to learn anything if you are advocating a position. Know when to flex back and forth between the two.

The third, the TAPS model, expanded upon the advocacy/inquiry matrix and suggested the focus of questioning or advocacy could be either around the solution or the problem, and that questions about the solution were much more brain-friendly than any of the other three combinations.

Using any of these to understand your questioning style, is a good starting point. To break through, however, we need some better questioning "technology." Here's some elements of that technology:

> Use open-ended questions ("What did you do next?" or "How did that approach work?") rather than closed ended ("Did you do < ...> next?")

> Leverage the journalistic questions - what, how, who, when, where, and why appropriately (What and how – best open-ended questions; who, when, and where – closed ended questions; why – open-ended but can create defensiveness in the respondent – use only with extreme care)

> Use one question at a time – and allow the respondent to answer.

> Allow time for the answer – don't fill in the silences.

> Avoid leading questions – which tend to be satisfying but rarely lead to insight.

> Consciously distinguish between expanding (what else could we do) and layering questions (how would we go about achieving that?)

> Avoid "should" based questions (or could you, will you etc.)

> Keep questions simple - avoid multi-layer, multi-topic, rambling, complex questions

> Avoid interpretive questions ("Don't you think that ….?")

> Avoid answering your own questions.

> Remain in curiosity, regardless of what you hear and learn.

> Leverage positive directional questioning (What would have to happen in order for us to achieve this?)

> Don't take no, for an answer (I understand that you don't know how to do that, but if you did know, how would you go about it?)

> Reference others (How do you think so-and-so would have approached that?)

We recommend that you start by developing a set of questions that resonate with you and practice them, so that you become comfortable asking with them. Practice not interrupting; wait and probe or expand.

Now, if we take a step back, and look at what is going on in our brains, we might get a few more insights into our questioning process. Facet 41 is all about curiosity … and if you score low on this, it might be highly important for you to focus on developing a few questions that work for you. Facet 42 is the degree to which you want your opinions heard and be taken into account. The higher you score on this facet, the greater the difficulty you might have in remaining in questioning mode, without offering your own opinion. A high need for conformity, number 36, might in some situations, make it uncomfortable for you to ask a string of questions, or ask out-of-the-box questions.

Observing

Let's talk about speed-dating for a moment. We are going to bet that's not a line you that would have predicted that you would read in a chapter entitled personal innovation. But hang on in there, and you will see the connection. We are all built for observation. Visual circuitry occupies maybe 60 – 70% of the brain. Visual stimulus is one of the senses that the brain uses for survival. Small details and small changes are brought to the brain's nonconscious attention. Researchers at MIT's media lab did some research using speed-dating. (Ah. Here's the connection) They changed the speed-dating process. After each speed-dating encounter [i], under the normal paradigm, each participant would be asked to fill out a card indicating whether they are interested in knowing more about their putative partner. What the Media Lab's researchers did was to turn the paradigm on its head – and ask each participant whether they thought that their putative partner was interested in them. Their answers showed that they were over 90% accurate. Obviously in some cases, they had picked up clear signals, but in many cases the signals were not so obvious – a partial smile, an inclination of the head or the slight lean in.

The bottom line of all this? We are actually very good observers. If we choose to be. If we choose to spend some time looking at the detail and if we remain in curiosity. Noticing. And noticing what we notice. And asking why? Why did that mold grow? Why did that circuit fire when we didn't expect it too? What is the optimum diameter for a CD? And often we need to go back and recall what we notice …. wait a minute. Didn't we learn yesterday that …. and now what we are learning today seems to be in contradiction to that.

Networking

Get out of your box. Your personal box of people that you know and regularly turn to. If breakthrough ideas were going to occur with those people, they would probably have done so already. In a somewhat dated, but still highly relevant article, Granovetter [117] points out that if we step one node further into our network of contacts, we are more likely to engage in conversations which challenge our thinking – which in turn leads to new thoughts and ideas. It turns out that this approach also tends to lead us to our new jobs and turns out to improve our sense of well-being.

Of course, there are many informal and unstructured ways of going about this. Join local clubs, or on-line groups, or listen in to webinars, podcasts etc. This works to a

---

[i] Both of us wish to state clearly that this data is second-hand knowledge. Neither of us have actually experienced speed-dating ☺

large degree, but our experience has shown that a more formal and structured approach can be even more effective. The approach goes like this:

Ask someone for fifteen minutes of their time. When you get with them, mentally break the time into three five-minute parts. During the first five minutes, let them know your situation, what you are attempting to do, what you are facing etc. Just the relevant parts so as not to overwhelm them with your life story, no matter how interesting. ☺ Then, for the next five-minutes ask them what they would do if they were in your situation. Listen carefully to what they say and make notes. Just listen! Ask questions if you don't understand, but don't debate or disagree. Their brains will not be limited by the same background, context, threat profiles etc. as yours – and they may push you out of your thinking box. That is not to say that everything they say will be relevant to what you are doing, or even useful. But they may trigger off some other ideas. Use the final five minutes to ask them what other three people you should talk with, and would they please make an introduction. The process then starts again with each of the next people.

Read and research. Read magazines and books that have apparently little or nothing to do with your field. Research topics that are on the periphery of what you are working on. It is often at the edges and boundaries where links are made, and breakthrough ideas occur.

Contact your local universities, incubators or start-ups. What are other people working on? If you were going to buy a company in an adjacent field of endeavor, who would it be and why? What do they offer? How could you offer it better, cheaper, faster … whatever your metric is!

Experimenting

Be willing to try new things – and throw them away if they don't work. Many years ago, we used to call it Rapid Prototyping. Mock-up an idea to test its viability. In the new Agile oriented world, it is referred to as creating the MVP – the Minimum Viable Product; try it and listen very carefully to customer feedback. Try lots of variants – not just one or two.
Experimenting will involve failure. Possibly lots of it, so if fear of failure is one of your drivers, this may be more difficult for you. But if you understand your brain, and the fact that a single failure will not mean that you are going to die, or that you are a failure, then it becomes easier to adopt this approach.

Now for the third of Dyer and team's attributes – the cognitive skill of associative thinking.

Associative Thinking

At its simplest level, associative thinking is the ability to link two or more apparently unconnected ideas, thoughts or concepts. Examples of associative thinking range from linkages between simple unidimensional aspects through to associations of complex theories. A simple example might be that you think of a past colleague whenever you hear a certain song played. A complex combination might be where you draw a correlation between change failures and lack of leadership.

The ability to draw new linkages between disparate objects or activities is one of the keys to breakthrough thinking. Associative thinking can often be driven by positive directional, open-ended questions, for example:

> What would have to happen in order to ….?
> What if we …?
> In what way could …?
> How could you imagine …?
> What would it take …?

And creating these new linkages can be facilitated by exploring things, ideas, words and symbols. Our conscious brains tend to work with words; our nonconscious brains use concepts, ideas, pictures and symbols. For example, place an object in front of you and then invent uses for the object, other than what it was originally designed for.

Additional attributes

When working with clients, we like to add in three more attributes to Dyer's list: habit formation, multi-cultural sensitivity and evaluation.

Habit formation

You will recall from *UYBFAC* that the Pre-Frontal Cortex is an energy hog. It takes a lot more energy to use the PFC to think about new things; the more that you can build up the habit of all of these attributes, the easier it will be to come up with new ideas. Whether it be questioning, observation, idea generation, associative thinking, curiosity, networking, experimenting – or indeed, anything to do with the innovative process, the more you practice it, the more the process gets embedded as a habit in your brain. You can do this habit building all of the time. When you see something new, imagine what else it could be used for. When you see something you don't recognize, invent uses for it. When you see a picture, be curious about what went through the person's mind as they were painting it.

Multi-cultural sensitivity

While this book is intended to be oriented towards your brain on its own, no person is an island. We are always around other people. As you will have read many times in this and *UYBFAC*, we are all different. That is equally true across cultures. What works and is readily acceptable in one culture, may not be so in another. Asking for someone to give you feedback about an idea you have is perfectly legitimate in some cultures – but not in others. Giving someone feedback about their idea works in some cultures, but not in others. Be sensitive to the culture that you are operating within.

Evaluation.

At the end of the day, turning an idea into reality means putting it to the ultimate test. Does it work? Will it fly? Does it have legs? It is easy to get carried away with one's ideas … only to run into the brick wall of feasibility at a later stage. Earlier on we described how we tend to throw out ideas too early based upon their feasibility and cautioned you not to fall into this trap. There is, however, a time to test the idea. Not too early. Ideas tend to be delicate and need care and feeding when they are first being formed. But at some time, they need to be vetted.

Many people have leveraged the "green team/red team" concept in moving from ideation to implementation. The concept works like this. Choose a number of people from your circle who seem to have the natural ability to take an idea, support it, run with it and enhance it … they are your green team. Use them to develop what you have come up with. Choose another set of people who always seem to have the ability to tell you what might be wrong with your idea or where it is deficient. This is your red team. Additional qualities that your red team needs to have – you need to trust them, and they need to have your best interests at heart. Then let them loose with your idea. You don't have to take what they say into account … but it might stimulate some more thoughts for you to improve your idea or approach.

Idea generation

As you will have gathered by now, in all situations, one of our strong recommendations is to find out what works for you. Take a moment and look back at those times when you have had breakthrough ideas. What were you doing? What were you facing? What was going on around you? How did you feel? If you are able to identify a number of times when you have had breakthrough ideas, what was the pattern? It seems reasonable to assume that if that is what has worked for you in the past, then that might be the most likely source of future ideas.

So, the next question might be: "How can I best leverage those moments?" What are the conditions that cause us to have these new ideas … these "aha" moments? It turns out that there are a number of them:

> The most common condition for breakthrough ideas, for many people, is when they are not thinking about the problem, situation or solution. The ideas come, supposedly, out of the blue. While from a brain perspective this may not be the case, it certainly appears that way at first glance.
> When you have loaded your brain with data. The theory here is that, if you get to the point where the conscious mode of your brain becomes overloaded, your nonconscious brain is still working away. It might need time to sort a

few things out, but it will, working away in the background. That's what it is good at.

> When you are not too aroused. We mean that in the scientific sense. ☺ Not too happy and not too stressed. Ideas often come creeping up very quietly and give subtle signals. If there is too much going on in your brain, then you may well miss the ideas as they gently fly by.

> Following on from that, when you are quiet. If there is a lot of noise around you, then it is difficult to either concentrate or let your mind wander. This can be specially so for people who are more on the introverted end of the scale.

> When you are slightly inwardly focused. It might be as a result of exercise, as a result of meditation, as a result of some deep-breathing or just as a result of taking a moment to stop and smell the coffee.

So, the more we can create these conditions, the greater the chance of coming up with new ideas. These conditions are different for different people. For many people, these are created as they wake up or as they drop off to sleep. For others it is when they are walking, jogging or exercising. For others it is when they are in the shower. Yet for others, it is when they are daydreaming over a cup of coffee. Explore what works for you – if you don't already know. And, in order to leverage the ability to implement your new idea, there is another requirement: the opportunity to capture the idea in the moment. It is very tempting to tell yourself that it is such a good idea, of course you won't forget it. But, as you know, the PFC, which has now got ahold of the idea, gets easily distracted and can wander off very easily. The result is that you forget the very idea you just had! But what you do remember is that it was such a breakthrough idea! A small piece of paper and pen/pencil will suffice. We know, it is an old-fashioned approach, but it rarely runs out of batteries. ☺ A smartphone with a recorder. A telephone call to your own answering machine. Lots of ways to capture it – but please don't rely on your PFC and memory. There are too many occasions when we are frustrated trying to remember that brilliant idea we had just a short while ago.

Fix it or feature it?

As we mentioned earlier, Phil's father had an overall approach to life. If you can't fix it, feature it. When you are faced with a problem that you cannot solve, how can you turn it around so that you can leverage it as an advantage or to your benefit? This often involves the process of reframing – but often generated a completely different way of looking at solutions to a particular problem.

Attitude

The suggestions outlined so far are some of the real-time or event driven aspects of innovation.

But what about attitudinally or behaviorally? What can we do in our brains to increase the chances of a new idea? It turns out, a lot; some of the concepts that we outlined earlier will appeal to some of you, and yet will leave others cold. If the concept appeals to you, we would challenge you as to why? Is it an approach you know and use? If so, has it generated useful ideas in the past, especially in the recent past? Is it just your "go to" approach when faced with challenges? Or does it appeal because it is different? What about concepts that don't appeal? Again, the challenge, why? Something new? Or something you have tried before which didn't get you anywhere?

Now let's go back to your Personal Threat Profile (PTP) and Personal Threat Context. First review your PTP. Are there any of your major threats that are getting in the way of coming up with innovative approaches? Either in any specific instance, or in general? What about the other things that are going on in your life at the moment? Are you attempting to come up with breakthrough ideas, when there is so much going on around you that your brain wants some stability?

Bottom line summary

There are a lot of ways in which we can develop our own abilities to come up with innovative solutions. Experiment over a period of months, if not years, as to what works best for you.

What's next?

What one or two things am I going to focus on to increase my personal innovation?
What I am going to do about it/them?
How will I measure whether I have been successful?

---

[115] Marsh, D. R., Schroeder, D. G., Dearden, K. A., Sternin, J., & Sternin, M. (2004). The power of positive deviance. *British Medical Journal*, *329*, 1177–1179.
[116] Dyer, J., Gregersen, H., & Christensen, C. M. (2011). The Innovator's DNA. Harvard Business Review Press.
[117] Granovetter, M. S. (1973). The strength of weak ties. *American Journal of Sociology*, *78*(6), 1360–1380.

Chapter 10:

Presence

10. Presence

General comments

Once again, this topic, also known as "leadership presence" or "executive presence" in the leadership literature, like many of them we have been addressing in *UYBFAC* and this book, is difficult to define. One paper stated that it is "intuitive and difficult to pin down" and this is fairly representative of what is out there. In many instances, publications side-step the issue by referring to it by other names, such as charisma or transformational leadership, although these seem to be different in our minds. Maybe by looking at a list of phrases of "what works" we can come up with some descriptors rather than a definition.

Before we do so, however, a few more general words. What might be seen as "presence" in one culture may not be so in another. There would be a large difference in how we would describe presence in, for example, the UK, the United States, Japan and Saudi Arabia. So, there's probably no one definition or list of descriptors which would suffice. In addition, we could now complicate the issue if we attempt to take into account gender and racial identity. Any definition now starts to get increasingly confused and blurry. Now if we add to the complexity with the question of, "What does it take to have presence in both a 'virtual' and a global environment?", it gets even worse. Now if we complicate it even more by taking context into account, for example by looking at the difference of "presence" in a company like Google versus what it might mean at a company like Chase bank, it might become impossible.

The introduction to Gumbrecht's recent book [118] even states that it might, indeed, be impossible:

> "Interpretation alone cannot do justice to the dimension of "presence," a dimension in which cultural phenomena and cultural events become tangible and have an impact on our sense and our bodies."

Indeed, in a recent Master's thesis Dunnink [119] offers this:

> "Currently, practitioners in the field of executive presence development and coaching for executive presence are operating in the absence of a solid theoretical foundation, and this may detract from good practice or even impact negatively on the credibility of the coaching profession."

Nevertheless, we are going to give it a try!!!

Some of the very elements of presence that are frequently used and assumed to be desirable, can, if they are incorrectly or overly used, prove to have a negative rather than a positive impact. For example, in his book, Chamorro-Premuzic [120] suggests that we often confuse self-confidence, one of the many components of presence, with competence, and that gets us into trouble. For example, there is a tendency to promote, especially men, based upon a view of their "confidence" only to find out later that their "competence" was in serious doubt.

What works [j]

- ➤ The ability to project mature self-confidence
- ➤ The ability to make tough choices or decisions in a timely manner
- ➤ The ability to remain calm
- ➤ The ability to leverage humor to defuse difficult situations
- ➤ The ability to interact in a manner which fully engages the other stakeholders
- ➤ The ability to instruct as and when needed
- ➤ The ability to stimulate and motivate
- ➤ The ability to remain silent if appropriate
- ➤ The ability to hold your own with other talented and/or strong-willed members of a team
- ➤ The ability to demonstrate wisdom
- ➤ The ability to show compassion
- ➤ The ability to make sense of a wide variety of situations
- ➤ The ability to give credit where credit was due
- ➤ The ability to influence others
- ➤ The focus on others
- ➤ Illustrating an even demeanor even in the face of other people's emotional responses
- ➤ Having outstanding listening skills
- ➤ Having a positive posture
- ➤ Having an appropriate energy level
- ➤ Demonstrating an acute sense of knowing when to enter a conversation and when not to
- ➤ Demonstrating that you can take control of difficult and unpredictable situations
- ➤ Demonstrating body language that shows comfort in all situations
- ➤ Being appropriately succinct, focused and on-point
- ➤ Being unruffled, unflappable and unhurried
- ➤ Being appropriately dressed and groomed
- ➤ Being organized
- ➤ Being unrushed and on time
- ➤ Being appropriately deferential
- ➤ Being sure-footed in your approach
- ➤ Being authentic
- ➤ Having empathy
- ➤ Being appropriately vulnerable and open
- ➤ Having powerful speaking and presentation skills
- ➤ Being able to read an audience
- ➤ Knowing what you are talking about – or admit otherwise

---

j This list is an amalgam of many sources, so no specific citations are made

It is worth noting a few things that don't come up on this list, or at least hasn't come up in all of the research that we have done:

- o Being charismatic
- o Having a dramatic flair
- o Pushing the limits
- o Being visionary
- o Being colorful
- o Being bold
- o Being mischievous
- o Being overly assertive
- o Being overly loud
- o Being overbearing
- o Being manipulating
- o Being controlling
- o Being condescending
- o Being intimidating
- o Being rich
- o Overreacting
- o Taking things (too) personally – and showing it
- o Assuming a defensive response (that you will later regret)

Some of other things that have been shown to improve presence are:

- ➢ Attendance at Toastmasters
- ➢ Presence coaching
- ➢ Video coaching
- ➢ Mentoring
- ➢ Action learning
- ➢ Team development
- ➢ Leadership programs

If you consider these lists, when we meet someone in real life, it doesn't take much for our nonconscious brains to pick up on small cues that either project these traits or project the absence of them. And we are pretty accurate in interpreting these cues.

Brief examples or case studies

One of the characteristics that comes up again under the topic of executive presence is authenticity. Phil has an example which could have been placed under Self-Awareness or here, under, Presence. It involves the visit of the VP of Customer Service of a Silicon Valley high tech company to their offices in Europe. We will call her Vera. She hadn't been with the company very long, and this was her first visit to the location. Everyone wanted her to have a successful and enjoyable visit, so they invited her out to dinner, suggesting that they all go to a Japanese restaurant that had just opened nearby.

The following morning, as the previous night's dinner was being discussed, Vera asked them a question. What was that green vegetable that had been served along with the sushi and sashimi the previous evening? They told her that it was called wasabi and was the equivalent of Japanese horseradish. Very, very hot. It turned out that Vera, not knowing what she was about to do, had eaten a whole mouthful of wasabi. But hadn't wanted to complain about the fiery explosion in her mouth, so covered up her difficulties and didn't mention a thing.

After she had finished her short visit, and had returned to Silicon Valley, the group started to talk about her, and decided that they would never be able to trust her. One of the dinner participants summed it up by saying "If she had been authentic, it would have been obvious to us all last night. If she can hide her emotions that well, who knows what else she will hide from us."

Maybe they over-reacted, but it is a good example of the negative result of not behaving authentically. She did not survive long in the organization.

In 2007 Scott met a very successful entrepreneur from Wichita Falls, Texas named Fred Lowder. Fred had made several million dollars through the acquisition and modification of convenience stores throughout west Texas from the early 1970s through the mid-1990s. He had a reputation for being a very savvy, but tough businessman and he was well known in the community. A towering man in stature, he had the ability to intimidate without saying a word. In the late 1990's he reportedly realized that he did not have everything he wanted in life. He had money, he had a home, he had family. What was missing? It was "Peace". Fred told Scott in 2012 that his life with money was meaningless if he could not use it to create lasting and positive impact on those around him. It was then that he went into several months of self-reflection and, with the help of some very influential people he discovered his true purpose. He proudly stated: "My purpose is to instill self-worth in every person I encounter." From that point he founded a 501(c)3 and over a period of about 15 years he impacted thousands of lives by giving people a chance, through weekends of self-discovery, to better understand their own presence and their influence. He turned his presence into a force that changed lives for the better.

Discussion

Once again, Executive or Leadership Presence presents us with a topic that is clearly important, but as of the time of writing, continues to defy an adequate definition. With regard to its importance, for example, in 2019, Dalavai [121] writes:

> "Scholars and academic practitioners generally agree that executive presence can increase leadership effectiveness, widen leaders' spheres of influence, and can be a career "game changer"

Yet he adds a word of caution:

> "As fascinating as the concept appears to be, there remains much confusion as to the nature of what executive presence truly represents."

He expands this by saying:

> *"While some experts feel that executive presence relates to character, substance and style, others contend that it is connected to appearance, communication and "gravitas."*

And many other authors and researchers make very similar comments with regard to both its importance and lack of definitional clarity. Dalavai, however, does step into the breach and helps us understand some of the concepts by providing us with a meta-review of other researcher's definitions according to three (relatively) practical themes – whether something is trainable, non-trainable and intangible.

Trainable	Appearance
	Communication
	Style, substance
	Impression -based (physical features, reputation, status)
	Seriousness of purpose
	Focused awareness
	Personal connection
	Relationship building
Non-trainable	Charisma
	Character
	Evaluation-based (values-in-action, intellect, expertise)
Intangible	Aura
	Self-confidence, self-esteem
	Gravitas
	"Je ne sais quoi" (I don't know what)

Let's dig into a few of the researchers behind this meta-review.

Hewlett et al. [122] identified three main characteristics as:

Gravitas	Identified as most important by 67% of respondents
Communication	Identified as most important by 28% of respondents
Appearance	Identified as most important by 5% of respondents

This is a good example of why it is important to know the details about some of this research; although three characteristics were identified (and often get reported upon) it is clear that two of three are way more important than the third, which, while it cannot be ignored, is clearly not given the same level of import.

Using Hewlett's words:

> *" ... style expands into appearance, intentionality, inclusiveness, interactivity, and assertiveness, whereas substance includes executive essentials like composure, confidence, resonance, and vision."*

One useful definition is given to us by Dagley and Gaskin [123]:

" … we suggest that a person with executive presence is someone who, by virtue of how he or she is perceived by audience members at any given point in time, exerts influence beyond that conferred through formal authority."

They go on to give us a helpful summary of their findings:

5 main findings emerged:

(a) executive presence is based on audience perceptions of the characteristics of particular people
(b) perceptions are based on impressions made during initial contacts and on evaluations made over time
(c) 10 core characteristics affect executive presence
     5 made during initial contact
        o   status and reputation
        o   physical appearance
        o   projected confidence
        o   communication ability
        o   engagement skills
     5 made over time
        o   interpersonal integrity
        o   values-in-action
        o   intellect and expertise
        o   outcome delivery ability
        o   coercive power use
(d) the characteristics combine in different ways to form 4 presence archetypes
        o   positive presence
        o   unexpected presence
        o   unsustainable presence
        o   dark presence
(e) the majority of the executives described as having presence were men.

Phil once had the pleasure of attending a workshop with Richard Olivier [124] who demonstrated the leadership presence of Henry V in the Shakespeare play of that name, by single handedly acting all of the roles. Olivier described the approach taken by Henry in his famous "Once more unto the breach, dear friends." Faced with terrible odds, and with a significant part of his army sick, he focused instead on his own troops, and used his powerful oratory skills to motivate them. But not at 3.00 p.m. in the afternoon, via a teleconference call. He was right there, in their midst, even in the early hours of the morning. Olivier contrasted that with how the average Chief Financial Officer would have made the same "presentation" focusing on the ratio between the number of French soldiers and the number of English soldiers, and the fact that a good percentage of the English army was unable to fight. Henry inspired them. It is a famous speech. If you haven't read it or listened to it, it is worthwhile doing so.

But can we all do that? Can we all develop presence like that. Our contention is that, even we can't get to that level, we can considerably improve from what most of us are today.

We have a partnership with a company that focuses on teaching how to come across better on video [125]. Ryan, the owner of the company, offers one-on-one training to help people become more comfortable in front of the video camera, and hence produce better videos that get their message across in a much-improved manner. It is amazing what he can do in a couple of hours. As he was working with people in this process, he noticed a number of side benefits, the biggest one being that it seemed to increase their presence in the rest of their life! No kidding. It seemed to give them more confidence and presence even when they were not in front of the camera. For some reason, whatever he was doing, brought out an ability that they didn't know they had. We are still investigating the brain aspects of this change.

Let's go back for a moment to a one of the characteristics that we mentioned earlier, "Appearance."

While "Appearance" is only rated at 5%, any mistakes in appearance (baggy clothes, dirty clothes, stains etc.) can be severely detrimental to a sense of Executive Presence for men or women. And what about your appearance? What should you look like? Well, it depends. Showing up in t-shirt and jeans at a Banker's conference might not establish great Executive Presence. On the other hand, dressing in a suit and buttoned-down shirt with a red power tie, might get you thrown out of most Silicon Valley start-ups. So, it is a blend or balance … between you and the expectations of your audience. And when you add authenticity into the mix, it has to be you – not someone you are trying to emulate.

Last of all, can we measure executive presence? The answer is yes, but probably not directly. We have to measure it in totality by measuring each of the probable component parts, but this should give us a good start. We include a sample list of the types of questions that you might ask yourself (or others) to get a handle on your Leadership Presence Quotient in Appendix C.

Meanwhile, what's going on in our brains and how does all of this tie in with Your Personal Threat Profile? Take another look at your PTP and see what connections you make.

Bottom line summary

We probably don't know what "presence" is and we cannot define it exactly; we can come up with some descriptors but we know that the list will never be comprehensive and not all elements will always be applicable; on the other hand we know that great leaders demonstrate presence and we know that we want to see it in our leaders.

What's next?

What one or two things am I going to focus on to increase my presence?
What I am going to do about it/them?
How will I measure whether I have been successful?

[118] Gumbrecht, H. U. (2020). Production of Presence: What Meaning Cannot Convey. Stanford University Press.

[119] Dunnink, J. S. (2017). *Coaching for Executive Presence: A Descriptive Account*. Faculty of Commerce, Law and Management, University of the Witwatersrand.

[120] Chamorro-Premuzic, T. (2019). Why do so many incompetent men become leaders? Harvard Business Review Press.

[121] Dalavai, Emmanuel, Executive Presence: Myth, Meaningful or Mastery? (September 5, 2019). Proceedings of the Ninth International Conference on Engaged Management Scholarship (2019). Available at SSRN: https://ssrn.com/abstract=3454084 or http://dx.doi.org/10.2139/ssrn.3454084

[122] Hewlett, S. A., Leader-Chivee, L., Sherbin, L., Gordon, J., & Dieudonne, F. (2012). *Executive Presence* (pp. 1–4). Center for Talent Innovation.

[123] Dagley, G. R., & Gaskin, C. J. (2014). Understanding executive presence: Perspectives of business professionals. *Consulting Psychology Journal: Practice and Research, 66*(3), 197–211. https://doi.org/10.1037/cpb0000011

[124] https://www.oliviermythodrama.com/

[125] https://betteron.video

Chapter 11:

Happiness and Resilience

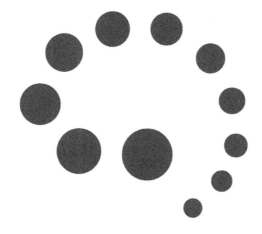

11. Happiness and Resilience

"We make a living by what we get; we make a life by what we give."
Winston Churchill

"Plan as though you will live forever; live as though you will die tomorrow."
Chinese proverb

General comments

So, you think you know what makes you happy? Not so fast. Most of the 'experts' tell us that we are not very good judges of what makes us happy. This section is intended to help you take a look at understanding what makes you happy – and why reaching that understanding might not be as easy as you think.

Before we delve too deeply, however, we are once again faced with a definitional crisis. Not really a crisis, but it could be seen as such. What do we mean by "happiness"? Rather than go into a lot of detail, we propose to take an approach from a couple of the researchers on the subject:

> " … the evidence suggests that positive affect—the hallmark of well-being—may be the cause of many of the desirable characteristics, resources, and successes correlated with happiness." [126]

So – positive affect, well-being and happiness seem to be inextricably linked; so, we will be using them all in our investigation.

By way of caution, there are, as in many cases where research is concerned, a wide range of conclusions with regard to happiness, the pursuit of happiness and whether or not there is much point in pursuing it; one paper even concluded that "trying to become happier may be as futile as trying to become taller" [127]. Putting that downer to one side ….

What works: The happiest people: [128] and [129]

- ➢ Are comfortable expressing gratitude for all they have
- ➢ Practice optimism when imagining their futures
- ➢ Avoid overthinking and social comparisons
- ➢ Practice acts of kindness
- ➢ Are often the first to offer helping hands to coworkers and passersby
- ➢ Nurture social relationships – they prioritize and devote a great amount of time to family and friends, nurturing and enjoying those relationships
- ➢ Develop strategies for coping – they focus on solutions to their problems and manage their negative emotions
- ➢ Learn to forgive
- ➢ Increase "flow" experiences – activities where they are totally absorbed in what they are doing
- ➢ Savor life's pleasures and live in the present moment

- Are deeply committed to lifelong goals and ambitions
- Set meaningful short-term goals and monitor progress
- Make physical exercise a weekly and even daily habit (at least 30 minutes daily)
- Practice some form of religion or spirituality
- Get involved with outside activities
- Learn the art of likeability
- Focus on the happiness of others
- Do one unusual, kind thing every day
- Make a best friend at work
- Monitor their health
- Live with someone – but choose the right spouse
- At the end of every day, practice recalling three things that they are grateful that happened during the day
- Voluntarily, go and help someone else

We also have included many, many other suggestions under the discussion portion of this chapter.

The fact that many, if not all, of these practices are extremely healthy for the brain was not lost on us.

Brief examples

In the movie, "The Story of Us" the couple, Bruce Willis and Michelle Pfeiffer, use a weekly practice to ensure that they celebrate their own and each other's successes and, at the same time, ensure that if things are going wrong, they know about it in a timely manner. As the story goes, as they have dinner on a Friday evening, they review their week and share their "highs" and "lows" for the week. We have recommended that couples (and teams) do this practice on a regular basis, and many people have reported that it has made them, and their relationships, happier.

Taking this one step further, Phil and his wife Cathy, do something more long-term on a yearly basis. On January 1st every year, they do their review/preview process. They review what they committed to in the prior year; and then they write down what they are going to commit to for the following year. The goals can be around anything – as large and long-term as where they will retire to, and as short and immediate, as getting the credit cards under control. The process (always accompanied by a glass of wine) has proven to help develop and monitor those much longer-term goals that we all tend to forget in our daily living.

In discussing this with a long-standing friend and ex-colleague [130] recently, she added another layer that she and her significant other do. They select a challenge each year that will take them out of their comfort zone. The examples she gave was that one of them was learning to play ice-hockey (she) and one of them was learning to play the violin (he)

Clearly, the COVID-19 pandemic compelled CEOs across the country to find their "center" through the abrupt halt of business that torpedoed their profit and loss statements in 2020. As both of us are in the Executive Coaching space, we found it remarkable the number of CEOs that went into triage mode vs those that saw this as the opportunity to reshape the business for its ultimate resurgence on the other side of the pandemic. March of 2020 served as a brick wall for an economy that was roaring on all cylinders just 30 days prior. There seemed to be a polarity of CEO responses from our experience of coaching others through those days. There were CEOs who decided to "cut" their way to success by laying off workers, shuttering doors, and, in many cases, simply shutting down the business. Then there were those that took this as the opportunity to adapt and reshape the business. One of them said to us:

> *"It is in these moments of ambiguity that I am most terrified and invigorated. One of the things I have found to be true in my life is that, as the CEO, I am compelled to see what might be rather than focus on what I have lost. My customers, employees and my family all expect that.....and they should. When armed with the knowledge that the fear, in most leaders, is tied to the loss they have suffered and the future consequences of that loss, I have a bolt of energy that goes through me which says: While they stand in shock, I am breaking ground in a new direction. Never is there a better time to position myself and my company in a place of competitive advantage than now. This is really an exciting time for us."*

Resilience is not about how much you have in resources, but the ability to be resourceful with what you have at your disposal. Happiness is often highlighted after we have reframed the situation away from the loss and focused more on what we want for our future. Creating a compelling future is key for our brain and our energy management.

Scott was part of a coaching and mentoring program that involved working with prison inmates in Texas that were scheduled for release in the coming months. In this program, Prisoners are given access to entrepreneurs who critique business plans, marketing ideas, and simple financial models that will help them when their release comes through. One month in 2019, Scott met Dan. Dan was a 58-year old inmate who had been sent to prison when he was 25 years old. He had never seen a cell phone, a computer or used the internet. Scott was surprised when Dan confided in him that he was concerned about leaving prison. Dan had learned to be happy in prison because he knew the rules, he knew his place, he had friends and there was a level of comfort in the community he had adapted to in prison. When he reflected on the changes the world had experienced since his incarceration, it stressed him out.

About 6 months after his release, Scott received an email from Dan. It was clear from the email that Dan had not mastered the skill of typing, but he had discovered something important and wanted to share it with Scott. Upon his release, it took about three months for him to learn patterns, create a few friends and access the internet. He admitted it was a rough start at first, but through his ability to focus on what he wanted vs what he feared, it gave him a great platform for adjustment. Dan is now running a small, but successful package delivery company. He still struggles with how to use a cell phone.

Discussion

It turns out that many of the things that we think will make us happy, don't. At least, they don't produce long-term lasting happiness. Take money for example:

> " ... we think money will bring lots of happiness for a long time, and actually it brings a little happiness for a short-time." [131]

It also turns out not to be found in our typical pursuits. At least, once again, not for long term happiness. Fame, bonuses, promotions, recognition, an evening with a good-looking date, birthday celebrations; while they might lift spirits for a short term, none of them work for long-term happiness.

Sonja Lyubomirsky is one of the expert researchers in this area. She and two colleagues presented a model for thinking about improving our happiness [132] and it boils down to three things:

> " a genetically-determined set point for happiness, happiness-relevant circumstantial factors, and happiness-relevant activities and practices."

i.e. you are born with a certain tendency towards being happy (or not), some external factors can have some influence and there are some things that you can do about it. They even put percentage points against all three, as follows:

- ➢ genetically-determined set point   50%
- ➢ circumstantial factors   10%
- ➢ activities and practices   40%

Take a look at those numbers for a moment. All three have something remarkable about them.

50% is predetermined. In her book, Lyubomirsky states it as follows:

> " ... a baseline or potential for happiness to which we are bound to return, even after major setbacks or triumphs."

10% is based upon your circumstances. So, forget about blaming the rest of the world or your bad (or good) luck. Again, she summarizes it well:

> " ... accept that life circumstances are not the key to happiness, we'll be greatly empowered to pursue happiness for ourselves."

The remaining 40% is controlled by what we do and how we think.

At the end of Buettner's book [133] he includes some recommendations from experts in the field of happiness. We have extracted some of them here:

- Gain control over your life – lacking control can lead to all sorts of bad things including a reduction in the quality of the immune system
- Recognize that you might not have much insight into what makes you happy, so experiment
- Get more education
- Avoid negative habits such as drinking and gambling
- Develop financial security
- Mentor others
- Do things for others
- Learn good relationship skills
- "Don't seek happiness – live it"
- Embrace curiosity
- Engage in activities that challenge you
- Give both money and time
- Find a job that you believe contributes something worthwhile as well as providing an income
- Maintain a strong, close romantic relationship
- Find an engaging hobby
- Eat a healthy diet especially more fruit and vegetables
- Keep active – paid or unpaid
- Get sufficient sleep
- Buy your house – don't rent
- Reduce commuting time
- Dare to change
- Stay out of debt
- Focus on intrinsic motivation rather than extrinsic
- Leverage your strengths and what you are good at
- Do something that improves the community that you live in

One of the experts, [134] was so much more prolific with her recommendations than the others, that we pass on all twenty-four of them, even though there is some repetition:

- Consider writing gratitude letters
- Count your blessings
- Practice savoring …
- Share personal positive experiences with a partner on a regular basis
- Perform kind or pro-social acts (including spending on others)
- Try to make someone else happier
- Live this month like it's your last
- Write about an intensely positive experience
- Write a forgiveness letter
- Practice loving-kindness meditation

- ➢ Visualize your best-possible self
- ➢ Identify signature strengths and then use them
- ➢ Set goals and monitor them
- ➢ Laugh and use humor on a regular basis
- ➢ Engage in physical exercise on a regular basis
- ➢ Act extroverted (even if you aren't)
- ➢ Seek activities with the right balance of challenge for your skill
- ➢ Practice religion and spirituality (in a way that works for you)
- ➢ Maintain an attitude of self-compassion
- ➢ Prioritize close and fulfilling social relationships
- ➢ Regularly go out into nature
- ➢ Establish routines that promote adequate sleep
- ➢ Spend money on experiences rather that material possessions
- ➢ Engage in activities that promote feelings of competence, connectedness and autonomy

Let's examine one of the items in the above list. Something that you can take specific action on: "Identify signature strengths and then use them." This is a two-part process. The first is to identify your signature strengths. The second is to use them. So, for example, if you think that creativity is one of your signature strengths, then be creative in one or two ways every day. This may simply be by choosing to go to work a different way or choosing to cook a different dish in the evening or starting on that book that you have been thinking about for years. If you don't know what your signature strengths are then go on to the Values in Action Signature Strengths website and take their survey. [135]

We are compelled to include some of the research by Martin Seligman who, according to the cover of his latest book, [136] "works on positive psychology, learned helplessness, depression, ethnopolitical conflict, and optimism" and has published numerous books and papers on these topics. He is recognized as an expert in the field of happiness. In Flourish, he describes how he took a change of tack in researching Happiness … and instead, looked at Well-being, developing the theory of Well-being en route.

He defines the elements of Well-being as:

- Positive Emotion: a subjective measure of happiness and life satisfaction using aspects such as pleasure, warmth, ecstasy, comfort etc.
- Engagement: once again a subjective measure, reflecting on the degree to which one was engrossed, absorbed, involved in a task or tasks
- Positive Relationships: the positive interaction with, and helping of, others
- Meaning (or Purpose): as covered in Chapter 4 of this book
- Achievement: the pursuit of success, accomplishment, winning, and mastery over something

He provides us, not only with some definitions and descriptions of each of these five elements, but also some attributes that each of them must have in order to qualify as elements:

- It contributes to well-being
- Many people pursue it for its own sake, not merely to get to any of the other elements
- It is defined and measured independently of the other elements

Going back for a moment just to "Happiness," if you are interested in measuring your own happiness level, there is an assessment to do that: the Oxford Happiness Inventory which we have included in Appendix C.

Let's turn our attention to Resilience. We debated whether the topic of resilience should go along with Stress Mastery or Happiness; we reached the conclusion that it could go with either. We landed on putting it here, as it seemed to us that many of the attributes that contribute to resilience, seem also to be those that make one happy.

One of the best descriptions of resilience that we found in our research was written by Connor and Davidson, [137] so we lean heavily on a summary of their work. One of the factors that makes it such a useful paper is that they clearly delineate the "salient features" of resilience which we adapt here. People who are resilient:

- View change or stress as a challenge or opportunity
- Have or make commitments
- Recognize the limits of their control
- Engage the support of others
- Create close, secure attachments to others
- Create personal or collective goals
- Have high self-efficacy
- Recognize the strengthening effect of stress
- Leverage past successes
- Have a sense of humor
- Have a realistic view of what they can control and the choices they have
- Take an action-oriented approach
- Have patience
- Have tolerance for negative affect
- Have a great adaptability to change
- Have optimism
- Have faith

For those of you that have an interest in taking a self-assessment on your own resilience level, we have included the Connor-Davidson Resilience Scale in Appendix C.

Bottom line summary

Although we may not know what actually makes us happy, and there is certainly no one 'magic bullet', there are many avenues to explore to see what actually works for each one of us individually.

What's next?

What one or two things am I going to focus on to increase my happiness and resilience?
What I am going to do about it/them?
How will I measure whether I have been successful?

[126] Lyubomirsky, S., King, L., & Diener, E. (2005). The Benefits of Frequent Positive Affect: Does Happiness Lead to Success? *Psychological Bulletin, 131*(6), 803–855. http://doi.org/10.1037/0033-2909.131.6.803

[127] Lykken, D., & Tellegen, A. (1996). Happiness is a stochastic phenomenon. *Psychological Science, 7,* 186–189.

[128] Lyubomirsky, S. (2008). The How of Happiness. Penguin Press – citing Dan Gilbert.

[129] Buettner, D. (2017). The Blue Zones of Happiness: Lessons from the World's Happiest People. National Geographic.

[130] Thank you, Robin Pitman

[131] Lyubomirsky, S. (2008). Op cit

[132] Lyubomirsky, S., Sheldon, K., & Schkade, D. (2005). Pursuing Happiness: The Architecture of Sustainable Change. *Review of General Psychology, 9,* 111–131.

[133] Buettner, D. (2017). Op cit

[134] Kristin Layous, California State University, Hayward, California

[135] https://www.viacharacter.org

[136] Seligman, M. E. P. (2011). Flourish. Simon and Schuster.

[137] Connor, K. M., & Davidson, J. R. T. (2003). Development of a new resilience scale: The Connor-Davidson Resilience Scale (CD-RISC). *Depression and Anxiety, 18*(2), 76–82. http://doi.org/10.1002/da.10113

Chapter 12:

Focus, Attention and Will-Power

12. Focus, Attention and Will-Power

"Of all the balls that you are juggling in the air, only a few are made of glass"

Lieutenant Colonel Joe Black

General comments

If we turn, once again, to our dear friend Wikipedia, we find that the entry on 'focus'

" .... selectively concentrating on one aspect of the environment while ignoring other things"

refers us directly to 'attention' which provides us with a reasonable basis upon which to focus on the subject (pun intended):

"Attention is the behavioral and cognitive process of selectively concentrating on a discrete aspect of information, whether deemed subjective or objective, while ignoring other perceivable information."

and

"It is the taking possession by the mind in clear and vivid form of one out of what seem several simultaneous objects or trains of thought. Focalization, the concentration of consciousness, is of its essence. Attention has also been described as the allocation of limited cognitive processing resources."

This is a useful beginning, but it does seem to miss out on a few important aspects:

1. It doesn't reference much about time frames; the description defaults to real-time. One of the aspects of focus that is important in the workplace, is the ability to maintain focus on something over long periods of time - hours, days, weeks, months and for many projects, even years.
2. It doesn't seem to differentiate between the ability to focus and not be distracted by external cues versus not being distracted by one's own competing thoughts.
3. The manner in which we focus, and the focus of our focus. It seems that there might be cultural differences on how we focus: [138]

"The Mayan caregivers and their toddlers were more likely to attend simultaneously to spontaneously occurring competing events than were the U.S. caregivers and their toddlers, who were more likely to alternate their attention between competing events and, in the case of the caregivers, to focus attention on one event at a time."

What about will-power? The Wikipedia entry for will-power leads us directly to self-control:

"Self-control, an aspect of inhibition, is the ability to regulate one's emotions, thoughts, and behavior in the face of temptations and impulses. As an executive function, self-control is a cognitive process that is necessary for regulating one's behavior in order to achieve specific goals."

"A related concept in psychology is emotional self-regulation. Self-control is like a muscle. According to studies, self-regulation, whether emotional or behavioral, was proven to be a limited resource which functions like energy. In the short term, overuse of self-control will lead to depletion. However, in the long term, the use of self-control can strengthen and improve over time."

So, they are sort of connected, but will-power is the longer-term related attribute, while focus and attention are in the service of real-time or short-term activities. That seems to give us a useable, working definition.

What works

- Identify systems that work for you – don't automatically assume that what works for someone else will work for you
- Develop personal mechanisms of self-control; if you seem not to be very good at it, take some brain-training exercises
- Exercise regularly
- Focus on one task at a time
- Find situations/environments that work for you
- Find the length of time that you can concentrate/focus for
- Turn off distractions for that period of time
- Get organized
- Start!
- Listen to music – maybe?
- Nap – maybe?

Brief examples

When it came to examples of what had worked and what had not worked in terms of focus, attention and will-power, it didn't take us long to find some. Right under our noses, as it were. Since we are writing a book about the application of brain principles, we do our best to practice what we preach. In this instance, that means determining how good we are at focus and attention and what causes us to get distracted.

One of us, Phil, gets distracted during his investigation of brain-based topics, by other fascinating discoveries, theories or research. One day during the investigation of the topic of focus, attention and will-power, Phil 'stepped back' and realized he had spent nearly an entire day, reading articles about the topic of whether there are differences between the brains of men and women. An important topic, and one that we have included in this book, but not an activity that moved the topic under investigation forward.

Like many of these topics about the brain, they all interact with each other. Phil states that he was certainly in Flow mode, but it wasn't helping this specific investigation. It would have helped if he had engaged in more real-time self-awareness, a topic that we addressed earlier.

In 2019 Scott was working with a newly promoted executive who had taken on a role outside of her particular mastery as part of the executive development program at the company. The executive, we will call Lisa, was bewildered by the limitation she was facing when trying to read the new regulations associated with the new role. The material was dry and hardly easy reading. She found herself jumping in on conversations and emails associated with her previous role simply to keep her sanity. As they discussed the patterns, she noted that she was putting off these "stimulating" reads until the late afternoon and putting her energy into other things more familiar earlier in the day. There were two things going on in her behavior that was not serving her. First, she was waiting until the late afternoon to read complex topics and her brain was already exhausted from the activities done earlier in the day. She was a lark when it came to energy management. Second, she left her phone open and in sight secretly hoping that someone would rescue her from this draining task and, of course, she took every call, every time. She had to make some distinct changes in her patterns.

After identifying that she was inadvertently sabotaging herself, she created a map of her day using a blank piece of paper which illustrated when she usually felt the highest energy levels and then she put some basic boundaries in place to protect those time frames. She reported three weeks later that she had completed the regulation marathon and was much more encouraged to understand the new role she was in.

Discussion

So, what about the brain? As a reminder, it is the Pre-Frontal Cortex that is involved in concentration, prioritization, self-control, executive functions etc. We learned in *UYBFAC* that the PFC gets 'tired' or depleted, and is it does so, it starts to 'lose' the struggle with the Amygdala and is less able to act as the brake against biases, habits and fear responses.

But there are a number of questions that immediately come up:

- ➢ How can we increase our focus and attention?
- ➢ How do we minimize distractions?
- ➢ How do we increase our self-control?

Let's start with focus and attention and that will inevitably lead us on to distractions.

To take an obvious approach, clearly one of the starting points could be to avoid decreasing attention and focus. We covered a number of these issues in *UYBFAC* – getting enough sleep, reducing stress, practice mindfulness, eating well, exercising and many other such activities can put our brains into a more ready state to pay attention and stay focused.

Einstein (no, not that one) et al. [139] published their results in a paper which might be seen as a blinding flash of the obvious – that *"maintaining intentions over brief delays is not a trivial task for the human cognitive system."* They report:

> *"Demanding conditions as well as interruptions revealed rapid forgetting of intentions at levels that would be considered significant in applied settings. (Experiments 2 and 3) showed that this rapid forgetting was not reduced by strategic rehearsal and implementation intention strategies."*

Avoiding these "demanding conditions" and distracting environments, situations, and people is an obvious strategy. In the last decade or so, in Silicon Valley 'open-office' environments have almost become the norm. It has become noticeable, however, that in order to focus in those environments, many people choose to use headphones. This reduces the impact of these environments and situations on focus and attention. On the other hand, it also decreases the amount of interaction – ironically, exactly the dynamic that these environments were designed to increase! But taking oneself out of these environments is a legitimate strategy for increasing focus and attention and being less distracted.

This strategy might be especially useful for those people who consider themselves as introverts. It might not work as well for people who consider themselves as extroverts. Many extroverts seem to thrive in environments where there is a lot of background activity.

Barbara Frederickson has spent much of her career studying positivity and has published many papers on the subject; one such paper showed how positive emotions broaden our scope of attention and negative ones narrow our scope of attention. [140]

So, one way of increasing our focus and attention, is to attend to our own positivity.

O'Connor et al. [141], give us some hope with regard to increasing our ability to focus. They report that regular brain-training exercises improved self-regulation by 14% in 30 days.

Now let's turn to self-control. One of the giants in the field of willpower is Roy Baumeister; he has published over 500 articles and written many books and book chapters about the field. In their book, *Willpower*, [142] he and John Tierney give us a wide-ranging description of many aspects of willpower. Their view of the importance of self-control (willpower) is well-summarized on page 13:

> *"The results couldn't be clearer: Self-control is a vital strength and key to success in life."*

The underlying theory that was proposed by Baumeister is that our willpower or ability for self-control acts like a muscle. [143] It gradually loses its strength, or in the jargon, "gets depleted" during the day. And many, many things, big and small, cause it to get depleted. In a now-famous experiment, even:

" … people who forced themselves to eat radishes instead of tempting chocolates subsequently quit faster on unsolvable puzzles than people who had not had to exert self-control overeating."

So, that's the first takeaway. Our ability to self-regulate gets worse and worse as we are forced to self-regulate. If you have a task to do, which will involve some aspect of self-regulation, do it in the beginning of the day rather than the end. Before you have made other choices, which will deplete your ability to self-regulate.

How about training for it? This is where there have been some surprising results. Let's look at a paper by Muraven et al. [144] as written up in Baumeister's book (He was also a coauthor of the paper):

"Unexpectedly, the best results came from the group working on posture."

and

"By overriding their habit of slouching, the students strengthened their willpower and did better at tasks that had nothing to do with posture. The improvement was most pronounced among the students who had followed the advice most diligently."

And it's not just about posture:

"The key is to concentrate on changing a habitual behavior."

A focus on changing a habit, for example using your left hand instead of your right, or changing your speech patterns, can result in an increase in self-control.

Oaten and Cheng published a series of papers, [145, 146, 147] showing that almost any activity practiced diligently had collateral effects on other aspects of self-control. Once again, from Willpower:

"But – and here was a truly pleasant surprise – they also got better at other things. The students who did the study-discipline program reported doing physical workouts a bit more often and cut down on impulsive spending. Those in the fitness and money-management programs said they studied more diligently."

and from Oaten and Cheng:

" … participants (who were in the exercise regime) reported significant decreases in perceived stress, emotional distress, smoking, alcohol and caffeine consumption, and an increase in healthy eating, emotional control, maintenance of household chores, attendance to commitments, monitoring of spending and an improvement of study habits."

What's not to like? Exercise impacts not only your physical health and your brain health but releases a whole bunch of self-control.

Before we move on, let's take one last cut at these topics, by examining them together. If one is constantly having to pay attention to maintain focus and avoid being distracted, then this too increases the issue of depletion of self-control.

If you were paying attention, ☺ you will have noticed that we side-stepped the topic of distractions. Daniel Levitin has written a wonderful book [148] which addresses distractions, focus, attention and many other related topics. The list that follows contains many of his suggestions from this book, together with many of our own additions:

➤ Get physically organized and/or structured using a system that works for you; organization and structure makes things easier on the brain – we are better able to predict and have less ambiguity. As a colleague of Phil's at Apple once said "There's nothing wrong with structure. It's stupid structure that you have to avoid."
➤ Get mentally organized using a system that works for you
➤ Develop a system for making decisions that works for you – what things have to be just 'good enough' vs the things that need to be 'as good as they can be'
➤ Develop a system for dealing with tasks that works for you e.g. from Getting Things Done [149] - Do it, Defer it, Delegate it, Dump it.
➤ If you can do something in under two minutes, do it.
➤ Break large tasks into smaller tasks and make the first task of the sequence something that you have control over – i.e. you can decide or act upon it.
➤ When you review your to do list or task list ask yourself the following: what do I need to do, or what information do I need to obtain, in order to move this task forward
➤ Catch yourself in the mind-wandering or rehearsal modes … label what's happening, smile and move back to focus
➤ When an extraneous thought pops into your mind, write it down – then get back to focus
➤ Carry a small notebook, or a number of 3 x 5 cards, to write these things down
➤ Focus on one thing at a time – do not multi-task. Multi-tasking depletes the brain's energy and interferes with memory
➤ Distinguish between what information or knowledge is useful vs what is distracting (no matter how interesting it might be)
➤ Make lists – the fear of forgetting something can trigger off your mind-wandering mode or your rehearsal mode
➤ Develop a system for putting things in place so that you know where everything is – sunglasses, keys, cell phone – and place them there before doing anything else
➤ Name and file things in the same way on all of your devices
➤ Remove clutter from your desk-top
➤ Make visible the things you need on a regular basis – and hide the rest
➤ Throw away what you won't use
➤ Turn your phone off. Better yet, put it another room.
➤ Turn your e-mail system off and give yourself specific times to respond
➤ When you respond to e-mail, recognize the addictive, dopamine driven mini-reward system of sending each one ☺

- Be aware of the brain's novelty bias - we are attracted to, and distracted by, new things
- Color code or otherwise differentiate major projects – helps the brain focus on what you need to
- Develop a protocol of engagement for e-mail, text or phone for people with whom you regularly communicate e.g. 911 at the beginning of the title line for something urgent
- Box your day - protect the beginning of the day when you are at your most productive and use the latter part of the day for more rote functions or activities
- Take rests during the day, every 45 – 60 minutes if possible – change location, go outside into nature
- Build rhythms or patterns into your day
- Exercise
- Eat breakfast and lunch
- Drink water and protein drinks rather than sugar-filled sodas

Let's review a couple of these, some from Levitin's work and some others which we have found useful from our coaching practices.

One of the five elements of the NEO-FFI which we spoke about in *UYBFAC* is conscientiousness. Early on in the book, Levitin points out:

> *"The trait of being organized is most highly associated with conscientiousness …."*

and

> *And it, (conscientiousness) in turn, is the best predictor of many human outcomes, including mortality, longevity, educational attainment, and a host of criteria related to career success. Conscientiousness is associated with better recovery outcomes following surgery and transplants. Conscientiousness in early childhood is associated with positive outcomes decades later."*

So, if being organized and conscientiousness go hand in hand, it seems to make sense that getting organized is a good thing to do.

Without being too simplistic, getting organized has three parts to it; getting started, developing and executing a plan, and finishing. In terms of planning, from Phil's IT background, he recalls IT projects always having two bullet points from the very beginning for developing and executing a plan: 1. Produce Plan. 2. Proceed according to Plan. We add the issue about getting started and getting finished as there are some people who seem to become paralyzed by one or other or both of these.

Getting started can be difficult for some people. They want to analyze the issues, acquire and examine every aspect of every factor, work out risk likelihoods and develop all sorts of contingency plans before they will even take the first step. Others dive straight in. Let's take a look at a few issues that can get in the way of getting started.

Which task to start on first? There are a number of dimensions to be considered. Categorizing into emergency/critical, urgent, or important can be useful. Clearly, emergency/critical situations need to be dealt with. Then the debate comes up: urgent vs. important. If something is urgent, but unimportant then 'classic' management training would say, put it to one side. If, however, we take our brains, and our Personal Threat Profiles into account, then an urgent issue hanging over our head may make it almost impossible to focus on anything else. Stepping back and, with your current Personal Threat Profile (PTP) and Personal Threat Context clearly in your brain, deciding what are the optimum priorities and best sequence for you to address your tasks, is worth spending some time on at the beginning of every day.

Another dimension to be considered in thinking about what to do first, is whether the tasks that you face are those that you like doing and are suited to your PTP and skillset, or not. Do you get the unpleasant tasks over with or do the things you like? We are all different on this. Working out what is optimum for you is the key. And it might change, both from situation to situation, and over time. From a brain perspective, working on something you enjoy, are good at and can succeed at, especially if it is not too time consuming, can give the brain a great reward and put you in good stead for tackling those more 'yucky' tasks! Scott had a client who would make a list of all the mundane things that they did not enjoy doing at work and would put an appointment on their calendar to complete the list. As they completed things, his client took great joy in "crossing" things off the list. This person's profile leaned heavily toward the prediction category so by making the list they enjoyed the task of marking things off which seemed to help.

Katherine Benziger, [150, 151] one of the early writers about the whole brain, recommended that you take the following simple approach. Start with a positive task. One that makes you feel good. So now your brain's 'ledger' is positive. If you now have to do a 'negative' task, your brain's ledger is now back to zero. But at least you have been in the positive. If you start with a negative task, then your ledger is negative. If you now do the positive task, your ledger is again back to zero, but you have been in the negative the whole time. Being in the negative puts your brain in less than an optimum mode.

But again, depending on your PTP, having a negative task hanging out there, may put you under stress, that you would prefer to deal with it and get it out of the way. As we have said many times, we are all different. The regime that works for one person, may well not work for the next. What works for you, at this moment in time, is what is important.

Once you have decided on priorities and sequence, some people still have difficulty getting started. As coaches, we have both seen this tendency on many occasions, even from really smart people. How, for example, do I go about writing this report or developing this project plan? This is where our brains get themselves hung up and start to spin in circles. Our process and background conversations tend to go something like this:

There are lots of things to consider when starting a project, and we need to want to make sure we don't miss anything. So, we think we had better start writing. As soon as we start writing (or keying in) our brain wants to apply some logic. Oh, that activity will need to be before that one, or that topic needs to be a subset of that one. We try and organize at the same time as we are coming up with thoughts, capturing our ideas or inventing. Our PFC is playing with us at this point. We know that the PFC is not very good at staying focused, and it is in fact, starting to multitask – without even asking for our permission or guidance to do so ☺ It rocks back and forth between coming up with ideas, evaluating them, discarding them, trying to remember several that have come up all at once, sorting them and thinking about what we might make for dinner! Before we know it, our thinking has gone all over the place.

This only has to happen to us once or twice, and we then tend to shy away from the whole process. We will put the task off, saying that we know it is going to be difficult … and adding all sorts of other judgments about ourselves.

There are a couple of approaches to this. Tony Buzan [152] is credited with introducing the concept of Mind-Mapping and has written many books on the subject. It is an extremely useful way of capturing, in a visual format, ideas, concepts thoughts etc. and linking them into a usable structure. It still, however, involves the brain doing at least two things – coming up with thoughts, and determining where they fit into the map or structure. Once again, we are back to doing something the brain is not good at. In order for the brain to be optimized, we need to pull the process apart even further.

We call it the Spider Diagram, because by the time you are finished, it looks like a spider has made its web all over the paper. The process goes as follows. Take the largest sheet of paper you can find. We recommend an unlined sheet of flip-chart paper, laid in landscape orientation. Pick up your pencil or pen or crayon and start writing. Write down any words that come to your head about the topic, report, plan – whatever task you are facing. Write down all of the words that come to mind, regardless of their importance or relevance. That part will get sorted out later. Have your brain do nothing but come up with any words that it can about the topic. Write them down anywhere on the sheet of paper. Yes anywhere. No sorting. Nor organizing. Nor changing color of writing instruments to try and categorize. Yes, your brain will want to do all of these things, and others, but resist.

Most people run out of ideas after about ten, fifteen or twenty minutes. Don't push it much beyond that as you will start to get diminishing returns on your time. Take a break and go back to it if you are of a mind to. Avoid the temptation to start organizing.

Once you have completed the "coming up with words" phase, we can now go into the first step of the "organizing" phase. Look at all of the words, and see which words have some sort of linkage to other words. The words may be synonyms, or relate to each by being in similar categories, or are subsets of one another. The exact relationship between the words doesn't matter at this stage. Just the fact that they are related is important. Now draw a line between them. It doesn't matter that they may be at opposite sides of the page, and that the line may go across other words. Connect the two words with a line. Then look for other connections. As many as possible. By the time you have finished your paper will look like the proverbial spider's web.

This is where the magic starts. You now step away from the sheet of paper. Yes, physically draw back from the sheet of paper. As you draw away, in most instances, you will see various words on the paper that have become 'nodes.' They have more lines going to them than the other words. Circle those words. If you have a different color pen, pencil or marker, now is the time to use it. These circled words become your chapter or subject headings for the report. Or the main tasks or activities for your project plan.

Now is the time, to take your words and put them into something more structured, like a mind-map, or mind-mapping software, or a text outliner.

What we have described here is a brain-friendly way of tackling what can otherwise be a daunting task. We have addressed it by focusing our brains on one activity or task at a time.

Barbara Minto [153] has a slightly different approach to essentially the same issue, in that she suggests imagining everything being organized in a pyramid structure. The top of the pyramid is a single statement about the topic, report, project, etc. Subsequent "layers" expand upon the layer above them, until the lowest layer contains all of the detail. Other book-writing techniques suggest a similar imaginary visual approach, but often add the visualization of a diamond. The bottom part of the diamond is a summary, which can be chapter by chapter or the complete book.

The advantage of this, from a brain perspective is two-fold; it is visual which the brain likes, and it adds in an element of predictability. The disadvantage is the same as before; you are asking your brain to do more than one processes at a time.

A discussion of focus and attention would not be complete without a discussion about the topic of FLOW! We mentioned it in one of the case-study examples we wrote about earlier. The concept was introduced by Mihály Csíkszentmihályi [k] – and he has written about it many times since 1975. [154] [155] He looks at the relationship between the task difficulty that you are faced with and the skills that you bring to that task. The concept has since been developed further and many books and papers have been written on the subject. The bottom line of the concept is that if your skill set is aligned with the challenge that you are facing, then the brain gets into a flow state, sometimes known as the Zone. If the task is too much for your skill set, that brings on Anxiety; if the task is not hard enough for your skill-set that brings on Boredom. Like the story of Goldilocks, the challenge of the task has to be just right. ☺

---

k Don't even try pronouncing this at home!!!

In diagrammatic form, it looks like this:

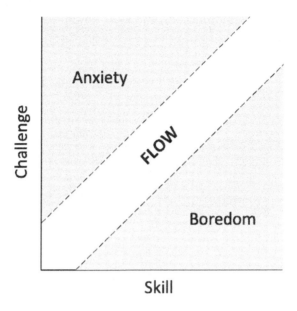

The original simple model has been adapted and now looks as follows:

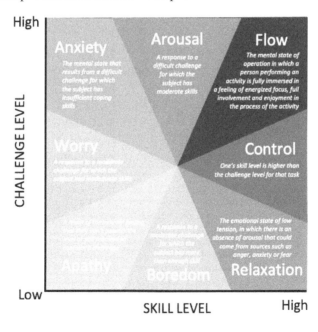

Note that this is not the only reason for the state of boredom; habituation i.e. doing the same thing again and again, can lead to the same state.

So, when faced with a task, a quick review of where it sits in relation to your own skill level, might cast some light on how to go about tackling it.

Let's pick up on the issue of multitasking and look at it in more detail. Here's a few things that Levitin has to say:

> " ... our brains are not wired to multitask well ... When people think they're multitasking, they're actually just switching from one task to another very rapidly. And every time they do, there's a cognitive cost in doing so."

> "Multitasking has been found to increase the production of the stress hormone cortisol as well as the fight-or-flight hormone adrenaline, which can overstimulate your brain and cause mental fog or scrambled thinking. Multitasking creates a dopamine-addiction feedback loop, effectively rewarding the brain for losing focus and for constantly searching for external bias"

> "To make matters worse, the PFC has a novelty bias, meaning that its attention can easily be hijacked by something new – the proverbial shiny objects we use to entice infants, puppies, and kittens. The irony here for those of us who are trying to focus amid competing activities is clear: the very brain region we need to rely on for staying on focus, is easily distracted. We answer the phone, look up something on the Internet, check our e-mail, send an SMS, and each of these things tweaks the novelty-seeking, reward-seeking centers of the brain, causing a burst of endogenous opioids (no wonder it feels so good), all to the detriment of our staying on task."

> " ... showed that the cognitive losses from multitasking are even greater than the cognitive losses from pot smoking."

> " ... found that learning information while multitasking causes the new information to go to the wrong part of the brain" (making it a lot harder to later retrieve.)

So. Forget it. Multitasking is a delusion. Much better to stay focused on one task at a time.

Let's finish this discussion with one last topic that we have been putting off – procrastination. ☺

Levitin, as you will have surmised by now, has some things to say about it. He cites Piers Steel, one of the world's foremost authorities on procrastination, saying that there are two underlying factors that lead us to procrastinate:

> "Humans have a low tolerance for frustration. Moment by moment, when choosing what tasks to undertake or activities to pursue, we tend to choose not the most rewarding action but the easiest. This means that unpleasant or difficult tasks get put off."

> "We tend to evaluate our self-worth in terms of our achievements. Whether we lack self-confidence in general – or confidence that this particular project will turn out well – we procrastinate because that allows us to delay putting our reputations on the line until later. (This is what psychologists call an ego-protective maneuver.)

These two factors, according to Steel, are based upon two false beliefs:

> "First, that life should be easy, and second, that our self-worth is dependent upon our success."

As mentioned in *UYBFAC*, the brain has many internal struggles. Levitin gives us yet another, in explaining the neural underpinnings of our low tolerance for frustration:

"Our limbic system and the parts of the brain that are seeking immediate rewards, come into conflict with our PFC, which all too well understands the consequences of falling behind. Both regions run on dopamine, but the dopamine has different actions in each. Dopamine in the PFC causes us to focus and stay on task; dopamine in the limbic system, along with the brain's own endogenous opioids, causes us to feel pleasure. We put things off whenever the desire for immediate pleasure wins out over our ability delay gratification, depending on which dopamine system is in control."

Levitin (based upon Steel) also gives us an equation to quantify the likelihood of procrastination, as follows:

Procrastination likelihood = (time to complete task x distractability x delay) / (self-confidence x task value)

➢ Time to complete task is obvious – the longer the task, the greater the chance of putting it off
➢ Distractibility is the combination of our need for immediate gratification, our level of impulsivity, and our ability to exercise self- control
➢ Delay is the time one has to wait to receive positive feedback for completion of the task

If these elements of the equation are large, then the chances of procrastination are increased.

➢ Self-confidence
➢ The value of completing the task

If these elements of the equation are large, then the chances of procrastination are decreased.

Now we are going to expand on a topic that we included in UYBFAC; the question of whether music helps you focus. The answer appears to be yes and no – depending on, guess what, you and the make-up of your brain. The founder and researchers at Focus@Will [156] suggest that there are certain types of music that enhance your ability to focus and certain types that detract from your ability to focus. In general, they suggest that music that contains the human voice, and music made by instruments that replicate the tonal range of the human voice, will detract from your ability to focus. The reasoning is that the nonconscious brain is constantly looking for threat or reward – and something like the human voice is likely to be a source of that threat or reward, therefore it gets our attention.

They create music designed for your brain, based on what keeps your attention, and changes sufficiently that you don't get bored with it.

In a recent test using streamlined music, Mossbridge [157] found the following:

"Overall the results suggest that at least for individuals who enjoy using streamlined music as a focus tool, streamlined music can have a beneficial impact on cognition without any obvious costs, while at the same time it may potentially boost mood."

Does it work for everyone? Probably not. There are indications that people who score higher on the "Openness" scale of the NEO-FFI are more likely to see positive outcomes. Are there downsides to trying it? Again, other than the time spent to create an account, determine your type of music and explore, probably not.

Baumeister, an eminent researcher in this field, in a couple of seminal papers, [158, 159] and a more recent book [160] introduced us to the concept that our self-control is a limited resource. The concept goes something like this: As we get "more cognitively tired" we are less able to exercise self-control. The process of becoming cognitively tired, can be caused by many things including feeling tired, feeling stressed and even prior acts of self-control. One of his premises is that the more you exercise self-control, then as you go through the day, the less able you are to exercise further acts of self-control.

He and a couple of researchers continue to publish on this and related topics and in a recent paper [161] they report on what desires are likely to cause us to get distracted and hence lose self-control. To some degree, they are the "usual suspects":

"Desires for sleep and sex were experienced most intensively, whereas desires for tobacco and alcohol had the lowest average strength, despite the fact that these substances are thought of as addictive. Desires for leisure and sleep conflicted the most with other goals, and desires for media use and work brought about the most self-control failure."

What about sleep and naps? It has long been known that lack of sleep causes many negative issues, reduced ability focus being just one of them. But what about if you have had a reasonable amount of sleep. Will an extra nap help? Probably. Goldschmied et al. [162] found that people who took a 60-minute nap were more able to deal with frustration and less inclined to be impulsive that those who didn't. Will it work for you? We don't know. Try it.

How about brain-training? Once again, the answer is somewhat in dispute. If you train your brain with certain brain-training exercises, then your brain will indeed get trained at becoming more efficient and focused on doing the exercises that you train in. The unresolved question is whether that training transcends into a wider set of applications. Our sense, as we stated in *UYBFAC*, is that training your brain won't do any harm – and depending on your make-up, may help out.

Bottom Line summary

Take a moment and reflect upon these factors for yourself. How well do you do in managing distractions? How are you at focusing your attention? How often do you put off doing something that you know needs to be done? What about starting projects? How do these factors relate to your Personal Threat Profile? What would have to happen for you to increase your aptitude in all of these areas?

What's next?

What one or two things am I going to do to increase my ability to focus?
What I am going to do about it/them?
How will I measure whether I have been successful?

[a] Chavajay, P., & Rogoff, B. (1999). Cultural variation in management of attention by children and their caregivers. *Developmental Psychology, 35*(4), 1079–1090.

[a] Einstein, G. O., McDaniel, M. A., Williford, C. L., Pagan, J. L., & Dismukes, R. K. (2003). Forgetting of intentions in demanding situations is rapid. *Journal of Experimental Psychology: Applied, 9*(3), 147–162. http://doi.org/10.1037/1076-898X.9.3.147

[a] Fredrickson, B. L., & Branigan, C. (2005). Positive emotions broaden the scope of attention and thought-action repertoires. *Cognition & Emotion, 19*(3), 313–332. http://doi.org/10.1080/02699930441000238

[a] OConnor, M., Cooper, N. J., Cooper, N., Williams, L. M., DeVarney, S., & Gordon, E. (2010). NeuroLeadership and the Productive Brain. *Neuroleadership Journal.*

[a] Baumeister, R. F., & Tierney, J. (2011). Willpower. Penguin Press.

[a] Baumeister, R. F., Bratslavsky, E., Muraven, M., & Tice, D. M. (1998). Ego Depletion: Is the Active Self a Limited Resource? *Journal of Personality and Social Psychology, 74*(5), 1252–1265.

[a] Muraven, M., Baumeister, R. F., & Tice, D. M. (1999). Longitudinal Improvement of Self-Regulation Through Practice: Building Self-Control Strength Through Repeated Exercise. *Journal of Social Psychology, 139*(4), 446–457.

[a] Oaten, M., & Cheng, K. (2006). Improved Self-Control: The Benefits of a Regular Program of Academic Study. *Basic and Applied Social Psychology, 28*(1), 1–16.

[a] Oaten, M., & Cheng, K. (2007). Improvements in self-control from financial monitoring. Journal of Economic Psychology, 28(4), 487–501.

[a] Oaten, M., & Cheng, K. (2010). Longitudinal gains in self-regulation from regular physical exercise. *British Journal of Health Psychology, 11*, 717–733.

[a] Levitin, D. J. (2014). The Organized Mind. Dutton.

[a] Allen, D. (2015). Getting Things Done: (Revised Edition). Penguin Books.

[a] Benziger, K., & Sohn, A. (1989). The Art of Using Your Whole Brain. KBA Publishing.

[a] Benziger, K. (2006). Thriving in Mind. KBA Publishing.

[a] Buzan, T. (2018). Mind Map Mastery: The Complete Guide to Learning and Using the Most Powerful Thinking Tool in the Universe. Watkins Publishing.

[a] Minto, B. (2002). Pyramid Principle: Present Your Thinking So Clearly That the Ideas Jump Off the Page and into the Reader's Mind (Third). Pearson Education Ltd. Prentice Hall.

[a] Csíkszentmihályi – Beyond Boredom and Anxiety (1975)

[a] Csíkszentmihályi – FLOW (1990)

[a] https://www.focusatwill.com/?mul0mufb=focus_at_will_total_brain

[a] Mossbridge, J. (2016). The Influence of Streamlined Music on Cognition and Mood. *Quantitative Biology.*

[a] Baumeister, R. F., Bratslavsky, E., Muraven, M., & Tice, D. M. (1998). Ego Depletion: Is the Active Self a Limited Resource? *Journal of Personality and Social Psychology, 74*(5), 1252–1265.

[a] Ego Depletion and Self-Control Failure: An Energy Model of the Self's Executive Function. (2002). Ego Depletion and Self-Control Failure: An Energy Model of the Self's Executive Function, 1–9.

[a] Baumeister, R. F., & Tierney, J. (2011). Willpower. Penguin Press.

[a] Hofmann, W., Vohs, K. D., & Baumeister, R. F. (2012). What People Desire, Feel Conflicted About, and Try to Resist in Everyday Life. *Psychological Science, 23*(6), 582–588. http://doi.org/10.1177/0956797612437426

[a] Goldschmied, J. R., Cheng, P., Kemp, K., Caccamo, L., Roberts, J., & Deldin, P. J. (2015). Napping to modulate frustration and impulsivity: A pilot study. *Personality and Individual Differences, 86*, 164–167. http://doi.org/10.1016/j.paid.2015.06.013

214

Chapter 13:

Accountability

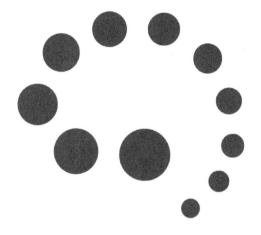

13. Accountability

General comments

We placed this topic close to the end for one main reason. While many of the other topics build upon each other, in many ways, accountability requires most, if not all, of the others. It is trivial to say that accountability is "Say what you will do and do what you say;" in order to do the things that you say, you need several of the other literacies in order to maximize the chances of achieving what you commit to. You need to understand yourself in order to know your own wishes, goals, tendencies and patterns. You need to be intentional about what you are going to do or say. You will need to be self-aware – at least enough to know whether you are, indeed, going to do what you say. In order to be accountable, you have to be clear about what you are going to do, focus on it, be resilient to the resistances you will inevitably face, possibly go through some personal change, experience some stress … and so on. Accountability depends upon most, if not all, of the other literacies.

What works

- Be very clear about what you intend to do.
- Be clear about why you are doing it – what does it lead to in the short term, and what does it lead to in the long term
- Be sure that whatever you are about to do is in alignment with your longer-term goals or vision
- Be clear what it takes to do what you say you are going to do
- Be public about your intentions
- Pick a thinking model which works for you
- Use that model to assist in your decisions
- Measure yourself against that model
- Learn how to recognize success – and mistakes
- Be willing to take ownership, own up and apologize
- Learn how to forgive – yourself and others
- Improve your ability to self-analyze
- Learn how you learn
- Be aware of your reactions to internal and external events in terms of your Personal Threat Profile
- Practice being accountable – start with the little things
- Use accountable language
- Step out of your comfort zone – sometimes that takes considerable courage
- Stand up for what you believe in – sometimes that takes even more courage

Brief examples or case studies

First, an example at a local level. Many years ago, Phil was teaching an evening class at a local community college. The program was called Business & Society and, as part of the program, students were grouped together, assigned a real company, and had to develop a five-year business plan for that company, using what they learned during the program. At the end of the semester, the group was expected to deliver a presentation of the business plan to a "board" – made up of people that Phil had invited in specifically for that purpose. The plan and the presentation became part of the student's final grade.

On one occasion, the presentation was not going well. In fact, it was going very badly. It seemed unclear, was disjointed and had no major theme to it. After ten minutes, one of the students in the presenting team, stood up, clearly surprising her fellow team members. She strode to the front of the class, picked up one of the company's brochures and spent the next three minutes delivering a perfect speech about the new vision of the company, the new tag-line, the strategy that they would adopt and the parameters by which the management team would define success.

Her action was all the more astounding because she had never said anything aloud in class during the prior fifteen weeks. Partly this was because she was very shy, and partly it was because she was Brazilian and was working in her third language – Portuguese and German being the first two. So spontaneously moving to the front of the group, and the room, was totally out of character. She received a rapturous round of applause, whereupon she burst into tears.

In speaking to her afterwards, she described how she could see that the presentation was going badly but couldn't see any of her teammates stepping up and taking control. So, even though she had never done so before, she decided to. She knew that they had done good work during their discussions and didn't want to see their hard work all be for nothing. She literally stepped out of her comfort zone and stood up for something she believed in – her team and the work they had done. She took accountability, not only for her own part, but for the whole team. It also took courage to do what she did, and we will come to that in the next chapter.

The next example was at a much wider and way more public level. As we were writing this book in 2019, and while we don't wish for this book to be political, we couldn't help but notice so many examples of lack of accountability in the political arena. So, when we saw an example of a group taking accountability, we thought it worth pointing out. In early September 2019, a group of 21 Tory politicians in the UK rebelled against Prime Minister Boris Johnson in order to stop a no-deal Brexit. We are not making a comment about their political position, but that fact that they stood up for, and took action for, something they believed in. And they paid the price. The Tory party withdrew their support. In many cases, this will be the end of their career.

In a parallel process and parallel timeframe, in the US political arena, as most of us are aware, there has been a whistleblower. Someone, who at the time of writing remains anonymous, but who took the accountability to bring to the attention of the US congress something that she or he believed was wrong. This is another example of someone taking accountability and acting to influence what they could.

On a more humorous note, one of Phil's favorite movies is The Jungle Book (the original 1967 Disney version). OK you may be asking, so what? What's this got to do with accountability? There's a part in the movie where Mowgli is lost. Lost in the jungle. And Shere Kahn, the tiger, his sworn enemy, is searching for him in order to kill him. Mowgli's new friend, the baby elephant pleads with his father, Colonel Hathi, the leader of the elephant troop to abandon what they are doing and attempt to find Mowgli before he is killed. Colonel Hathi haughtily dismisses the little elephant's pleas. Then Colonel Hathi's wife, Winifred, steps out of ranks, walks up to the Colonel, muttering to herself "This has gone far enough." She walks up to the Colonel and states "Now listen hear, you pompous old windbag. Unless you do something to find that child, then I am taking over command of this herd."

Now that's accountability! ☺

Discussion

Let's do what we have done many times and start with a definition. What do we mean by accountability? The first definitions that we found were not that helpful: But then we find something that actually assists:

> " ... an obligation or willingness to accept responsibility or to account for one's actions."

This helps a little but maybe a model is more useful than a simple definition. This model has been around for some time; it has various names but is most commonly known as the victim-accountability model and is usually represented as follows: [163]

The model works as follows:

1. We have an intention to do or say something. Once we see the results of our actions or statements, we have a choice. We can either go into the "victim loop" or we can elect to go around the accountability loop.
2. If we choose the victim loop, we go through one or more of the stages identified above. In addition, we often add a few more ... like getting defensive or deflecting legitimate responses from others, or repeatedly justifying our actions. As we look around, it is not difficult to find examples of this behavior.
3. On the other hand, we can choose to adopt the accountability loop. The first steps in this loop are to honestly recognize the consequences of our actions, assess the impact, label it (and our own emotions) in some way for ourselves and "own" our component of that. The next step is to forgive ourselves (and others if they played a contributing role), examine what we could have done differently, learn from it, and determine what action we might take next.

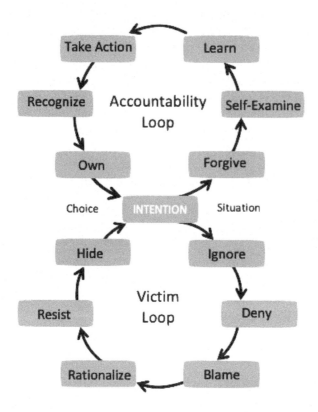

In the cold light of day, or the relatively cool calmness of reading this book, it might be easy to assume that we all, most often, "take the high road" i.e. choose the accountability loop. Unfortunately, that is not the case. Why? The lower loop is often easier. At least in the short term. Ignoring or denying what happened is quicker and easier than examining what happened, determining our own part in it, owning up and repairing any damage that might have been done. Blaming others is so much easier. Somehow, we get comfort in wallowing in self-righteousness. The brain loves to be right, and if we never examine what went wrong, then the brain can convince itself that it was right. Furthermore, if we think and feel like we are right, then our brain gets a quick boost of dopamine which feels good. We feel rewarded. And we are more likely to repeat this behavior.

Initially, it is far more difficult to do self-reflection and admit that what you did was either wrong or far from perfect. This self-reflection also might mean that we bump right into some of our fears hidden in our Personal Threat Profiles. The narrative goes something like this "I got it wrong or made a mistake. People might think less of me. I am an imposter after all. I don't know how to do this." Depending on your Personal Threat Profile, this thinking could put your brain into a threat state.

Sometimes, during progress through the accountability loop, as part of recognition and ownership, it also becomes important to apologize. Effectively apologize. It's part of being accountable. Randy Pausch [164] suggests that good apologies consist of three parts:

1) What I did was wrong.
2) I feel bad that I hurt you.
3) How do I make this better?

Sometimes the impact is not "hurt" … it could be "sorry I misled you", "Sorry I didn't live up to your expectations", etc. You fill in the impact.

Let's move on and talk about language for a while. The language we (and others) use can often be an indicator of whether we are being accountable or not. Let's look at our language in three ways: the statements we make, the words we use and the ownership we take.

Here's some of the statements that we often hear in our workshops [165]:

> - I didn't get the resources to get it done …
> - There was no buy-in for this decision …
> - I wasn't given all the information I needed to be successful …
> - People didn't show up at the meetings …
> - I left you a voicemail …
> - I wasn't kept in the loop …
> - It wasn't my job …
> - Lots of things went wrong on this …

Take a look and identify which of these represent taking accountability … and in which of them is the speaker traveling around the victim loop?

We can start to see this trend of blaming others when we listen to kids:

What happened to your toy?	It broke
What happened to your drink?	It spilled
How did the exam go?	They failed me

Unfortunately, however, we see the same lack of accountability at every level in the workplace:

How come you always answer your cell phone in meetings?	It might be important
How come you are late?	Too much traffic
Where's the document?	It got lost

Take a moment and reflect. Where do you naturally hang out? What are some of the phrases that you use to hide from taking accountability?

Let's examine our use of language a little more by looking at some specific words. Some words, even though they are small, are immensely powerful – especially to our brains; we illustrated that in some detail in *UYBFAC*. As we stated there, words such as "try," "can't," and "should" have great impact – on us and on other people. For example, if you say to someone, "I will try and get it done today" it has impacts on your brain and their brain. The impact on your brain is that "I only committed to try". Therefore, there is nothing wrong if I don't succeed. There's nothing inconsistent there, and the brain loves consistency. The impact to the other person's brain is that they are left in a state of ambiguity. Will it get done or won't it? Being clear about what you will do and what you won't is one of the first steps on the road to accountability. For everyone's sake.

Finally, the language around ownership. We mentioned this in *UYBFAC*, but the principle is so powerful, that it is worth repeating. It concerns the usage of the words "you" and "I." Now, you might be saying to yourself, what can be simpler than those two words? In general, you would be correct. Nothing could be simpler. Except how and when we use them. We gave a couple of examples in UYBFAC, but here's another one.

Imagine the following scenario. A person was going to a meeting with a potential client. As they arrived, they realized that they had not remembered the time correctly and that they were, in fact, an hour late. Later that day, they had to give a report back to their boss.

> *"Well. It was like this. I was doing so well. I left in plenty of time to get ahead of the traffic across town and was fully prepared. I had done my research and was sure that we would have a good solution for them. It turns out that I knew one of the people that would be at the meeting, so had a spring in my step as I left my car."*

> *"Since I thought I was twenty minutes early, I thought I would just check e-mail to see whether there was anything urgent. It was then that I saw the text from them asking where I was."*

> *"You know that feeling you get when you know that something has gone drastically wrong. You rapidly start thinking of what you should do."*

In his (or her) description, when everything is going well, he (or she) uses the word "I," taking full ownership of the situation. When things turn out not to go so well, he (or she) changes usage to the word "you." At a nonconscious level he (or she) is deflecting the internal feeling – and not taking full ownership. We all do it. When something feels wrong, uncomfortable, inconsistent with our values, we use the technique as an emotional relief valve. Look for it in other people. After you see it once or twice, it will be difficult to not see it. Then look for when you use it. See if there are any patterns for you.

One of the "What works" statements from above is:

> Be clear what it takes to do what you say you are going to do

Here's a simple thinking model that helps in that process – it's known as OMR [166] and looks like this:

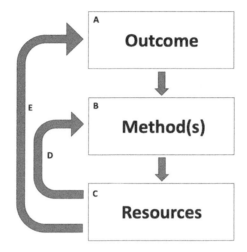

It works like this. Whatever outcome (A) (or goal) you desire, then the next thing to think about is the method (B) (or manner, or strategy) that you are going to use to get it done. Next is to think about the resources (C) (time, money, skill, willingness, support etc.) that will be required to achieve the end-result. If you don't have all of these resources, then you cannot achieve the desired outcome using that method. You have to go back, pathway D, and rethink the method that you are using and come up with a different one. If you can develop a different approach for which you have all of the resources, then you are home and dry. If not, and you exhaust the method-resources loop, then you have to "go back to the drawing board," pathway E, and change your outcome.

This is a simple technique for helping you, in advance, to not promise something that you cannot deliver. The first couple of times through, it might take a while, but after you have used the model a few times, it becomes fairly quick to follow the process.

The final aspect of this discussion is courage. Courage comes in many different flavors. It takes courage to admit that we are wrong, or we didn't do something we promised to do, or we simply failed. The brain loves to be right and admitting to our failures does take courage. Sometimes it takes courage to take the accountability loop and not play the victim. We will dig into this in more detail in the final chapter.

Bottom line summary

If we look ahead to working with others, leading teams or leading organizations, then one of the key factors in each of these areas is trust. One component of earing trust is reliability. Becoming accountable in the manner described in this chapter, is a foundation stone for reliability.

What's next?

What one or two things am I going to focus on to increase my accountability?
What I am going to do about it/them?
How will I measure whether I have been successful?

[138] Chavajay, P., & Rogoff, B. (1999). Cultural variation in management of attention by children and their caregivers. *Developmental Psychology, 35*(4), 1079–1090.

[139] Einstein, G. O., McDaniel, M. A., Williford, C. L., Pagan, J. L., & Dismukes, R. K. (2003). Forgetting of intentions in demanding situations is rapid. *Journal of Experimental Psychology: Applied, 9*(3), 147–162. http://doi.org/10.1037/1076-898X.9.3.147

[140] Fredrickson, B. L., & Branigan, C. (2005). Positive emotions broaden the scope of attention and thought-action repertoires. *Cognition & Emotion, 19*(3), 313–332. http://doi.org/10.1080/02699930441000238

[141] OConnor, M., Cooper, N. J., Cooper, N., Williams, L. M., DeVarney, S., & Gordon, E. (2010). NeuroLeadership and the Productive Brain. *Neuroleadership Journal.*

[142] Baumeister, R. F., & Tierney, J. (2011). Willpower. Penguin Press.

[143] Baumeister, R. F., Bratslavsky, E., Muraven, M., & Tice, D. M. (1998). Ego Depletion: Is the Active Self a Limited Resource? *Journal of Personality and Social Psychology, 74*(5), 1252–1265.

[144] Muraven, M., Baumeister, R. F., & Tice, D. M. (1999). Longitudinal Improvement of Self-Regulation Through Practice: Building Self-Control Strength Through Repeated Exercise. *Journal of Social Psychology*, *139*(4), 446–457.

[145] Oaten, M., & Cheng, K. (2006). Improved Self-Control: The Benefits of a Regular Program of Academic Study. *Basic and Applied Social Psychology*, *28*(1), 1–16.

[146] Oaten, M., & Cheng, K. (2007). Improvements in self-control from financial monitoring. Journal of Economic Psychology, 28(4), 487–501.

[147] Oaten, M., & Cheng, K. (2010). Longitudinal gains in self-regulation from regular physical exercise. *British Journal of Health Psychology*, *11*, 717–733.

[148] Levitin, D. J. (2014). The Organized Mind. Dutton.

[149] Allen, D. (2015). Getting Things Done: (Revised Edition). Penguin Books.

[150] Benziger, K., & Sohn, A. (1989). The Art of Using Your Whole Brain. KBA Publishing.

[151] Benziger, K. (2006). Thriving in Mind. KBA Publishing.

[152] Buzan, T. (2018). Mind Map Mastery: The Complete Guide to Learning and Using the Most Powerful Thinking Tool in the Universe. Watkins Publishing.

[153] Minto, B. (2002). Pyramid Principle: Present Your Thinking So Clearly That the Ideas Jump Off the Page and into the Reader's Mind (Third). Pearson Education Ltd. Prentice Hall.

[154] Csíkszentmihályi – Beyond Boredomand Anxiety (1975)

[155] Csíkszentmihályi – FLOW (1990)

[156] https://www.focusatwill.com/?mul0mufb=focus_at_will_total_brain

[157] Mossbridge, J. (2016). The Influence of Streamlined Music on Cognition and Mood. *Quantitative Biology*.

[158] Baumeister, R. F., Bratslavsky, E., Muraven, M., & Tice, D. M. (1998). Ego Depletion: Is the Active Self a Limited Resource? *Journal of Personality and Social Psychology*, *74*(5), 1252–1265.

[159] Ego Depletion and Self-Control Failure: An Energy Model of the Self's Executive Function. (2002). Ego Depletion and Self-Control Failure: An Energy Model of the Self's Executive Function, 1–9.

[160] Baumeister, R. F., & Tierney, J. (2011). Willpower. Penguin Press.

[161] Hofmann, W., Vohs, K. D., & Baumeister, R. F. (2012). What People Desire, Feel Conflicted About, and Try to Resist in Everyday Life. *Psychological Science*, *23*(6), 582–588. http://doi.org/10.1177/0956797612437426

[162] Goldschmied, J. R., Cheng, P., Kemp, K., Caccamo, L., Roberts, J., & Deldin, P. J. (2015). Napping to modulate frustration and impulsivity: A pilot study. *Personality and Individual Differences*, *86*, 164–167. http://doi.org/10.1016/j.paid.2015.06.013

[163] This model is in wide-spread use, has been replicated, amended and/or simplified many times by many different authors and practitioners, but its origins are difficult to determine. If anyone can tell us the true source, please do so.

[164] Pausch, R. (2008). The Last Lecture. Hyperion.

[165] These are from a variety of workshops and we don't cite them here for reasons of confidentiality

[166] This model came from Lieutenant Colonel Joe Black. Phil's agreement with him was that every time Phil used it in his teaching, he would pay Joe 25 cents. ☺ Now that Joe is longer with us, we would love to increase the royalty!

Chapter 14:

Courage

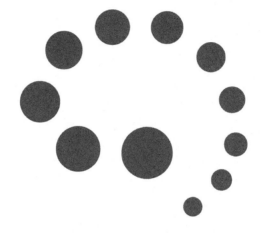

14. Courage

General comments

We left this topic to the very end for one main reason. While many of the other topics build upon each other, in many ways, in order to execute many of the others, you will require courage.

> *"Courage is viewed as the most universally admired virtue because it is grounded in self-sacrifice, serves the needs of others, <u>and is needed to enact all of the other virtues</u>."*[(167)]

As you will see from our discussion below, courage manifests itself in many ways and comes from a variety of underlying reasons.

Courage, in its various invocations, has been studied for several thousand years, perhaps even longer, and ranges from obvious physical courage to moral courage with many different types in between. Most leadership discussions include the need for courage as a vital arrow in the quiver of leadership attributes.

In some ways, the topic of courage brings us back to our initial topics i.e. those of self-awareness and self-understanding. Many of the acts of courage that people describe are people taking action (or resisting taking action) because something they believed in, or personal values that they held, were being violated. Knowing what it is you stand for, therefore, seems to be an important foundational factor in courage.

In this chapter, we will be focusing on "workplace courage;" it might be argued that it is not possible to exhibit workplace courage when you are on your own, and therefore the topic does not qualify to be included in a book entitled "Your Brain On Its Own." We believe, however, that the fundamental personal dynamics that cause a person to exhibit courage, will be best explored and laid down, when you are on your own. Hence our decision to address the topic here.

One final comment before we plunge ahead. In the literature, there is some debate as to whether courage, in its broadest context, is either a "trait" or an act/behavior. In other words, is courage something that is inherent to some degree or other in all of us, and/or is it something that we choose – either consciously or nonconsciously. The resolution of this seems to be summarized as:

> *" … a person that repeatedly performs these (courageous) behaviors is then considered to possess trait courage"*

What works [l]

> ➤ Be fully self-aware, understand who you are and what you stand for
> ➤ Take the initiative to challenge powerful individuals in one's own organization in order to remedy a problematic situation
> ➤ Confront one's own peers (for example if they commit an unethical act, are abusive, create a hostile work environment etc.)
> ➤ Call (whistle-blow) unethical or illegal behavior
> ➤ Take the lead on unpopular, but necessary, actions
> ➤ Address personal fears, biases and phobias
> ➤ Express moral or ethical views despite possible (real or perceived) sanctions
> ➤ Express the necessity for change even when it means confrontation and might be considered as insubordination
> ➤ Refuse to participate in unethical or immoral acts sanctioned by one's own organization
> ➤ Act when faced with injustice, unfairness, or violations of human rights
> ➤ Take accountability to act outside one's own direct sphere
> ➤ Leave organizations that are unethical, resistant to change or foster turbulent and hostile environments [m]
> ➤ Foster an adaptable and positive mission-oriented culture within your own domain of influence
> ➤ Act as a courageous role-model for others
> ➤ Imagine yourself doing courageous acts or taking on courageous roles
> ➤ Be aware of the thin line between courage and foolhardiness

Brief examples or case studies

Phil left England to take up a position as an IT consultant in a small but growing consultancy in Holland. At that time, his expertise was in the application of the latest computing technology to commercial transaction processing. Upon arriving on his first day, he learned that he had been assigned to a project for the Dutch army – the technology for which he knew absolutely nothing about. It was not only futile for him to engage in the project, but it was dishonest to charge for his services. He brought this to the attention of his manager, and the owner of the company, both of whom stated that it was too bad, but they couldn't go back on the composition of the team. Asking around, he found that this was common practice at the company. He went back and had a further conversation with his manager, who told him that being as Phil hadn't been with the company very long, and he was no longer in his own country, he should not rock the boat. Phil resigned one week later.

---

[l] Please note that many of these examples are taken from the paper by Detert & Bruno that we reference in our discussion

[m] Please note that there is an argument to be made that staying in such environments also takes courage; it is a question of judgment about which will be more effective; it is likely that both actions will take courage

Phil had been with another company for nearly six months when a new manager was brought in. He and his two colleagues would be reporting to the new manager. In the first week, they attended a one-week technology workshop together. On the evening that they all arrived, they all went out to dinner – and didn't finish talking shop until ten thirty at night – five and half hours later. This lengthy discussion was repeated on the second evening – until eleven. At the end of the third afternoon, it was again suggested that the team get together for dinner for a business discussion. Phil replied that he would be happy to do so, but would be leaving the discussion at nine, as he intended to get to sleep. At nine, the discussion was not finished, so Phil made his apologies and left. On the fourth evening, when the team sat down for dinner, the manager looked at her watch and said that they had better make the discussion quick as she knew that Phil would be leaving at nine. By taking a stand, Phil had established boundaries with regard to healthy sleep practices.

A few years ago, Scott was the senior sales executive of a helicopter company that provided firefighting helicopter services as well as specific parts manufacturing for certain types of helicopters. This company was unique in that they also had the ability to build brand new helicopters. Most operators only operate aircraft, but this company had the ability to operate and manufacture aircraft. As part of the five-year strategic growth plan Scott was asked to present a comprehensive sales plan that would support the strategic direction of the company at the time. The strategic plan centered on aircraft sales as the catalyst for growth in an already crowded market. As Scott prepared for this meeting, he was conflicted. He knew that the strategic plan had made a fatal assumption. That assumption was that there was enough demand in the market for new aircraft with a very specific niche, at a very high price point to open the future on new aircraft sales. After much reflection and homework, Scott stood in front of his fellow executives and outlined a case that reflected the true competitive advantage of the company was not going to be fulfilled with aircraft sales but with expanding aircraft services which would allow the customer to simply contract his company on an as needed basis. The irony in this story is that he was hired specifically for his aircraft sales skills. He knew that by bringing this conversation to the table he was risking his very role with the company. His decision came after realizing that if he did not have this conversation with his fellow leadership, he would be set up to fail within the prevailing strategy. As you might imagine, there was quite a bit of hand wringing after his presentation. The other executives were, not surprisingly, upset; after some honest and respectful conversations, however, a decision was taken to reshape the value proposition of the company portfolio and two years later, they accomplished a very successful public offering based on the true value of the company.

Phil had been promoted to Acting Director of IT and, in his first week in his new position, he was due to give a presentation on the $25 million IT budget to the Executive team. This team consisted of many type A personalities who felt no remorse in pulling apart any presentation that wasn't perfect – and in the immediate past they had a reputation for not approving the IT budget. From discussions with members of the Executive team, Phil learned that some of their past frustrations with IT had been that they didn't know what was going on and, even when they did, they felt that they did not have say in the direction IT was taking. It was in the old days of slides and foils. Phil presented all of the main budget items on one slide, in sequence … the most expensive first. He told them that if there wasn't a champion for any given item, he would remove it from the list. That would mean that they would know what was going on – and would be in control. The first budget item was a $2 million item … and no-one was willing to champion it. He drew a thick red line across it. The second was a $1 million item – and again no champion. This process was repeated for the next three items before the CEO stopped the meeting and suggested to the executive team that they had to get real and take ownership. Four hours later all but one of the budget items was approved – and each had a champion. Phil had given the CEO a chance to spot the patterns and lead his team, once it was obvious that ownership was a challenge.

Recently Scott was working with a senior executive who had expressed some concerns about one of the divisions and its performance. Though a series of discussions, it was decided that Scott should go and sit down with the senior team at that location and hear firsthand the challenges the team were facing. After a week of interviews and other interactions, Scott reported back to the CEO his findings. He recalled the words from the CEO as he presented his findings and that was that he needed to replace the president. The CEO was faced with a difficult decision. The president of that division was extremely talented and had a great pedigree. On top of that, the investors loved him. Nine months ago, he was hired to turn things around. His presence was part of a key initiative to create profitability in that division which had not turned a profit in a couple of years. The challenge for the CEO was that the president did not represent the values of the company nor of the CEO when it came to the way employees were treated. This showed up in the culture survey and interviews. The CEO was faced with one of the most difficult decisions he could make. If he kept him in place, he stood to lose the leadership team working for him. If he made the change, he stood to lose the support of his investors. After spending some time discussing the options the CEO made the courageous decision to do what was right for the employees and take the chance that his investors would stick with him. By no means did this make his job easier but he knew deep inside that by remaining true to what was right in the face of risk he stood a much better chance of a longer and lasting success in that division.

Discussion

Once again, our initial foray into the subject indicated that there were wide range of different focuses for the term "courage" and that a simple definition might not be easy to find. Fortunately, Tkachenko et al. [168] give us seven different recent definitions of courage given by people who focus on the topic. Since those experts chose not to attempt to find a single common definition, we have chosen not to either ☺ and we offer, in full, the table that they use:

Van Eynde (1998)	Managerial courage is the willingness to do what is right in the face of risk. In practice, managerial courage includes such actions as: (a) confronting the status quo (b) embracing change in the face of resistance (c) opposing a popular but unhealthy idea.
Klein and Napier (2003)	Courage involves five factors: (a) candor (speak and hear the truth), (b) purpose (pursue lofty and audacious goals), (c) rigor (invent disciplines and make them stick) (d) risk (empower, trust, and invest in relationships) (e) will (inspire optimism, spirit, and promise)
Rate and Sternberg (2007)	We describe courage as: (a) an intentional act executed after willful deliberation (b) involving the acknowledgment and endurance of substantial risk to the actor (c) attempting to bring about a noble good or worthy purpose (d) persisting, perhaps, despite the presence of personal fear
Kilmann, O'Hara, and Strauss (2010)	We define a courageous act in an organization as including five essential properties: (1) free choice in deciding whether to act (vs. being coerced) (2) significant risk of being harmed (3) assessment that the risk is reasonable, and the contemplated act is considered justifiable (not foolhardy) (4) pursuit of worthy aims (5) proceeding with mindful action despite fear
Schilpzand, Hekman, and Mitchell (2014)	Courageous action is a 'voluntarily pursuing a socially worthy goal despite the risk that accompanies and the fear produced by a challenging event.' Four types of courage: (a) standing up to authority (b) uncovering mistakes (c) structuring uncertainty (d) protecting those in need
Koerner (2014)	Three components of courage: (a) morally worthy goals (b) risks, threats, or obstacles (c) intentional actions that interact and result in several forms of courageous behavior at work Four different forms of courage-based identity work: (a) endurance (b) reaction (c) opposition (d) creation.
Detert and Bruno (2017)	Workplace courage is a work domain-relevant act done for a worthy cause despite significant risks perceivable in the moment to the actor

Even with their working definition, however, Detert & Bruno [169] acknowledge the difficulty of getting to the next level of specificity as to what workplace courage actually is:

"How, for example, workplace courage overlaps with prosocial rule breaking, positive or constructive deviance, voice, risk-taking, internal social activism, or tempered radicalism cannot be established without valid assessments."

By way of illustration, they point out that workplace courage might be viewed differently if it is a single act as compared to an act or process that needs to be repeated continually.

Howard et al. [170] give us an, albeit simple, model of different types of courage, which we have adapted:

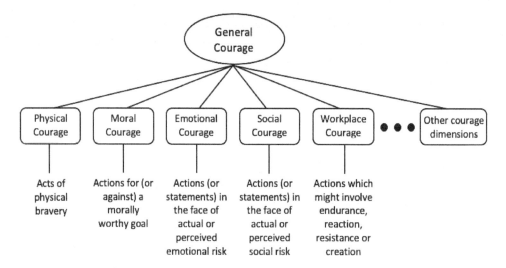

As we do more and more research, it is clear that there is no single definition of courage; it might turn out to be like "intelligence" where research is indicating that there are multiple intelligences. We also want to point out that the dimensions outlined above are not necessarily independent; any one act in the workplace might require social, emotional and moral courage.

The 2014 paper by Koener [171] gives three reasons why looking at workplace courage is important:

"First, complex organizations require people with different backgrounds and perspectives to cooperate, which inevitably leads to power struggles and conflict. In work organizations, courage is routinely required to raise issues, advocate minority positions, and oppose individuals and groups, as well as to combat significant organizational maladies such as corruption, catastrophic failure, and organizational decline. Second, courage is at the heart of the collaboration required for the innovative and entrepreneurial endeavors that allow organizations to thrive, particularly endeavors that involve high levels of risk and the possibility of significant financial loss. Third, work is a central feature in the lives of most adults, and it fulfills a host of instrumental, psychological, and social needs. The perceived risks of courageous acts in the workplace can

therefore be far-reaching, threatening people's livelihood, friendships, reputation, career, and personal identity."

Howard [172] goes even further by hypothesizing:

"We expect social courage to have a positive relationship with organizational citizenship behaviors (OCBs) and voice, while we expect it to have a negative relationship with counterproductive work behaviors (CWBs)."

and

"Therefore, we expect social courage to have a negative relationship with stress, depression, and anxiety, while having a positive relationship with life satisfaction."

Wait. What? If people exhibit workplace or social courage, then they will be better able to:

- ➢ address power struggles
- ➢ address conflict
- ➢ raise issues
- ➢ advocate minority positions
- ➢ oppose individuals and groups
- ➢ combat significant organizational maladies
- ➢ better collaborate for innovative and entrepreneurial endeavors
- ➢ positively impact organizational citizenship behaviors
- ➢ reduce counterproductive work behaviors
- ➢ decrease stress, depression, and anxiety
- ➢ positively impact life satisfaction

Shouldn't we be trying to bottle this?

His results show that these hypotheses are mostly true:

"Those with higher levels of social courage were less depressed and had higher life satisfaction, suggesting that the benefits of social courage outweigh the consequences. As mentioned, working through situations that require social courage may result in professional benefits, such as being recognized for exceptional performance, but these instances may also provide a personal sense of fulfillment. For this reason, social courage has the potential to influence many different aspects of personal"

Social courage, however, did not have a direct impact on stress and anxiety.

He adds:

"The current results suggest that courageous individuals may be more goal-oriented because they are more approach motivated, and thereby these individuals may be more motivated to achieve their goals in general."

In addition to her definition of courage, Koener gives us four different "storylines" (or themes) of courageous workplace acts, together with a "no courage" motif. She also cites with frequency of their occurrence within her research:

- Endurance   4%
- Reaction   19%
- Opposition   55%
- Creation   5%
- No courage   17%

and combines these into the following summary table:

Storyline	Morally worthy goal(s)	Risk, threat or obstacle	Intentional Action
Endurance	Courageous actor endures significant hardship and perseveres to reach goal.		
	To accomplish important outcome. To retain valued job. To provide income for family.	Unreasonable workload Distasteful tasks Fatigue	Sacrifice Perseverance Fortitude
	Moral: It is honorable to withstand adversity to achieve a goal; suffer with dignity.		

Reaction	Courageous actor is faced with a threatening or risky situation caused by an error, problem, or crisis and chooses to address the problem		
	To be honest. To be altruistic. To be fair. To prevent harm to others.	Guilt Embarrassment Physical harm Job loss	Responding decisively Admitting fault Correcting problem
	Moral: Respond decisively to problems or crises that your expertise can address, even at the risk of personal harm.		

Opposition	Courageous actor takes initiative to confront powerful individuals in his/her organization in order to remedy a problematic situation.		
	To maintain integrity. To be fair. To show respect. To prevent harm to self, others, or organization.	Job loss Career derailment Social isolation Retaliation	Voicing opinion Reporting misconduct Disobedience Circumvention
	Moral: Where important principles are concerned, stand up constructively to those in power even if the personal impact is likely to be negative.		

Creation	Courageous actor seizes challenging, risky opportunities in order to innovate, grow, and improve		
	To achieve meaningful goal. To grow and improve. To create new enterprise.	Financial loss Damage to reputation Failure to reach goals	Enthusiasm Concerted effort Determination Creative thinking Optimism
	Moral: Pursue opportunities for growth, innovation, and improvement, even if they are risky.		

No courage	Actor has an opportunity to behave courageously and chooses not to.		
	All of the above	All of the above	All of the above
	Moral: Don't be a coward		

Koener also identifies four separate aspects of a "courageous act" namely:

- *the tension that precedes action*
- *the choice to behave courageously*
- *the act itself*
- *the reflection that follows the act.*

The tension that precedes the action can take many forms; Koener explicitly cites uncertainty, dissonance, anxiety, distress, and excitement, but it is easy to imagine it taking other forms such as confusion, hesitancy, a sense of exclusion etc., - in fact anything that might trigger your Personal Threat Profile. And you might only be able to label that tension if you self-aware enough of your own feelings and are contextually aware of what is going on around you.

With regard to reflection after the act, Koener again explicitly identifies some feelings … integrity, pride, joy, relief and confidence. Again, it is easy to imagine many other personal outcomes depending on what is important to you. Simply having done the right thing is often enough for most people.

In chapter 2, "Peeling the Layers of Your Personal Onion" we introduced the concept of identities. Koener makes the case that exhibiting workplace courage is one of those times when we, either explicitly or implicitly, take stock of our identities and, frequently, find that, in executing a courageous act, we have created a new identity or brought one out that we didn't know existed or only existed weakly.

With regard to the creation storyline, in his thesis Hardy [173] reports that both latent/nascent entrepreneurs and actual entrepreneurs thought that courage was highly important in starting a business; where latent/nascent entrepreneurs and actual entrepreneurs differed was:

> *"… actual entrepreneurs reported significantly higher levels of commitment to their entrepreneurial goals than latent/nascent entrepreneurs."*

and

> *" … actual entrepreneurs reported having experienced a point of no return significantly more often than did latent/nascent entrepreneurs."*

Can we measure workplace courage? It seems likely that we might be able to do. Howard et al. [174] provide us with a series of validated questions specifically oriented to workplace courage, which we include in Appendix C. Their original list consisted of 49 items, but their desire was simply to measure "social courage" – so they removed anything that didn't address social courage, reducing the final list to 17. Since we are looking for practical application in the workplace, we include all 49.

Now we can look broadly across various aspects of courage, can we say anything about what is happening in the brain when courageous acts are carried out or contemplated? Yes, we can. Let's take just one of our earlier definitions [175] and review the phrases that it contains:

(1) free choice in deciding whether to act (vs. being coerced)

(2) significant risk of being harmed

(3) assessment that the risk is reasonable, and the contemplated act is considered justifiable (not foolhardy)

(4) pursuit of worthy aims

(5) proceeding with mindful action, despite fear

It is reasonable to assume that most, if not all, of these aspects are engaging one of more parts of the PFC. "Assessment", "mindful action", "reasonable risk", "contemplated acts" and "justifiable" are all words that we would use to describe the Executive Functions of the PFC, rather than something coming from the Limbic System.

This differentiation leads us to suggest that we might want to change our approach to training in leadership courage. Over the past three or four decades, many leadership programs have included a "courage" component, for example a ropes course where participants face the fear of walking across a 60-foot ravine. The fundamental assumption is that addressing and increasing "physical courage" will lead to an increase in, for example, "social courage" ; i.e. if we have leaders face their fear of heights, then that will develop a willingness to stand up and be counted when it comes to speaking out for a point of view in a meeting or challenging an aggressive boss. We contend that the two involve different brain circuitry and improving one set of neural circuits won't necessarily result in an improvement in the other set.

Howard [176] makes reference to this distinction:

> " ... people may habitually perform courageous behaviors with certain types of associated risk, such as the risk of bodily harm, but the same people may habitually retreat from courageous behaviors with other types of associated risk, such as the risk of damaging social relationships."

In a recent HBR article, [177] Detert introduces us to the term "competently courageous." He suggests that being competently courageous:

> " ... rests upon a set of attitudes and behaviors that can be learned rather than on innate characteristics."

This is good news for us writing about becoming courageous!!! The behaviors required can be learned!

He gives us a brief list of activities that they carry out or the conditions they create and/or ensure are in place, by:

- ➢ Laying the groundwork - by establishing a strong internal reputation
- ➢ Improving their fallback options in case things go poorly
- ➢ Carefully choosing their battles
- ➢ Discerning whether a given opportunity to act makes sense in light of their values, the timing, and their broader objectives
- ➢ Maximizing the odds of in-the-moment success by managing the messaging and emotions

> ➢ Following up to preserve relationships and marshal commitment

What about learning to be courageous, as Detert suggests we can? Marching into the CEO's office and telling her the way to run her business might not be a good first step. ☺ There are several approaches that we have found work. Explicitly embracing the four of the approaches outlined by Detert would be a good start; we will dig into his approach slightly more deeply, and add to it:

Laying the groundwork:
- by establishing a strong internal reputation
- being seen as invested in the success of the organization
- playing things even handedly
- accumulating a stock of goodwill and trust from other stakeholders
- engaging with, listening to, and empathizing with other people
- helping other people develop

Carefully choosing their battles:
- discerning whether a given opportunity to act makes sense in light of their values, the timing, and their broader objectives
- performing a risk-reward assessment (See Chapter 8 on Decision making)
- obtaining a good answer to the "Why this? Why now?" questions
- being aware of personal emotional triggers, biases and patterns
- being aware of other people's emotional triggers, biases and patterns
- balancing short term wins with competing longer-term wins
- being acutely aware of timing and what else is going on
- acting when potential support is above a minimal threshold

Maximizing the odds of in-the-moment success by managing the messaging and emotions:
- focusing on framing the issue in terms that the audience will relate to (remember, the brain is strongly influenced by framing)
- making effective use of data, information and knowledge that is available
- managing the emotions in the room – your own and others
- connecting their agenda to the organization's priorities, values, direction and culture
- explaining how your idea addresses critical areas of concern for all stakeholders.
- ensuring that other decision makers feel included—not attacked or pushed aside
- divide and conquer – work one on one beforehand to get some support in the room

Following up to preserve relationships and marshal commitment.
- following up after they take action, no matter how things turned out
- thanking supporters and sharing credit.
- addressing lingering emotions
- repairing relationships with those who might be hurt or angry.
- taking a one-size-fits-one approach to each stakeholder
- recognizing that every stakeholder has a different Personal Threat Profile

Other aspects that are paramount:
- tackling small issues in order to practice and gain experience

- imagining – imagining yourself in a given situation and how you would ideally respond; this gives the brain the sense that "we've been here before" when a real-life situation arrives
- explore the boundaries: what's the best-case outcome? What's the worst? Do I have plans to take the next steps in either case?
- recognizing that courage is not a 'stand-alone' attribute – it is highly related to who you are, what you stand for, how you make decisions, your tolerance for risk-taking, your tolerance for ambiguity .... and many other facets.

In a recent paper, Howard & Cogswell [178] explored other factors that might contribute to a greater sense of social courage and found that five factors seemed to increase social courage:

Personality	High-grit (perseverance and passion) and/or proactive individuals may be more likely to judge their psychological resources sufficient to withstand any adverse consequences of courageous action.
Social support	An employee with many supportive relationships may believe that their social support can withstand short-term conflicts. Also, employees with ample social support may believe that their strong social networks can alleviate any damage to their 'esteem in the eyes of others.'
Empowering leadership	Positive aspects of leadership, such as ethical and empowering styles, have both been suggested to influence follower proactive and prosocial behaviors
Culture	Cultures with a humane orientation reward each other for fair and altruistic treatment. In these cultures, members may feel that retaliation for social courage behaviors is unfair, as these behaviors have a prosocial intent – thereby promoting the performance of such behaviors. Likewise, members of these cultures particularly value the prosocial treatment of others, and social courage may be actively promoted due to the helping nature of this type of behavior.
Demographics	Gender will probably have an impact on social courage; also, employees may grow bolder and become more courageous as they spend more time in an organization, causing age and/or tenure to also relate to behavioral courage.

Interestingly they found that "perceived courage benefits and risks did not impact the effect of these factors."

All of these positive attributes of social courage sound wonderful. But what about the downsides? Can we have too much of a good thing? Is too much courage dangerous? Once again, Howard offers some advice:

"At the same time, it is possible that some courageous individuals may be excessively goal driven. In this case, these individuals may be unable to effectively disengage from fruitless goals, and courage may thereby produce some negative outcomes"

"Those high in courage may need to be continuously conscientious of their tendency to perform (these) foolhardy and/or unsafe behaviors."

Let's now explicitly look at how courage ties back to the brain. Clearly, courage has its roots firmly in the fear-based behaviors which tie to the five P's as we have described them, specially the threat-based ones of Protection, Participation and

Prediction. While much of courage comes via the form of one's immediate action in crisis, such as those actions of a first responder, we find courage also finds its impact in less acute situations where the brain will run all kinds of scenarios that lead to an over amplification or simplification of a specific fear or group of fears. When courage impacts our sense of our psychological Protection we will often have to stop, assess the situation and acknowledge that our brain will default, at first, to the direst of outcomes given its primary mission of survival. The same is true if Participation or Prediction are the more sensitive of our threats. In all these cases there are opportunities to manage the threat and take action that is rational. Courage then becomes the label we provide to the introduction of a more rational and reasonable response to a situation that, without intervention, is likely to excite our limbic response to nonconscious fears.

Take a step back for a moment and return to your Personal Threat Profile. This will make you more aware of the things that are likely to trigger you and cause you to take notice. Facets that are the most and least important to you, will be those things that cause you to identify what, to you, is a morally worthy goal, to focus on a specific risk, threat or obstacle and decide to take intentional action. These things will alert you to those areas where you may require workplace or social courage.

Bottom line summary

Whenever we make a decision or take an action, we are, almost by definition, taking a position or making a stand. Many times, these are relatively easy and do not require us to reflect on our personal values or make value judgments regarding whether the impact of what we do will have serious consequences. Occasionally, we are required to take actions that require us to dig a little deeper – and act in line with our value system. This sometimes means that we have to bring forth that part of us which will make the courageous act.

One final thought; like many emotions, courage tends to be contagious ☺

What's next?

What one or two things am I going to do to increase my courage?

What I am going to do about it/them?

How will I measure whether I have been successful?

---

[167] Comte-Sponville, A. (2002). A small treatise on the great virtues: The uses of philosophy in everyday life. Picador.

[168] Tkachenko, O., Quast, L. N., Song, W., & Jang, S. (2018). Courage in the workplace: The effects of organizational level and gender on the relationship between behavioral courage and job performance. *Journal of Management Organization*, 1–17. http://doi.org/10.1017/jmo.2018.12

[169] Detert, J. R., & Bruno, E. A. (2017). Workplace Courage: Review, Synthesis, and Future Agenda for a Complex Construct. *Academy of Management Annals*, 11(2), 593–639. http://doi.org/10.5465/annals.2015.0155

[170] Howard, M. C., Farr, J. L., Grandey, A. A., & Gutworth, M. B. (2016). The Creation of the Workplace Social Courage Scale (WSCS): An Investigation of Internal Consistency, Psychometric Properties, Validity, and Utility. *Journal of Business and Psychology*, 1–19. http://doi.org/10.1007/s10869-016-9463-8

[171] Koerner, M. M. (2014). Op cit

[172] Howard, M. C. (2018). Applying the approach/avoidance framework to understand the relationships between social courage, workplace outcomes, and well-being outcomes. *The Journal of Positive Psychology*, 00(00), 1–15. http://doi.org/10.1080/17439760.2018.1545043

[173] Hardy, Benjamin, "Does It Take Courage to Start a Business?" (2016). All Theses. 2585. https://tigerprints.clemson.edu/all_theses/2585

[174] Howard et al. (2016) Op cit

[175] Kilmann, R. H., O'Hara, L. A., & Strauss, J. P. (2010). Developing and validating a quantitative measure of organizational courage. Journal of Business and Psychology, 25(1), 15–23. https://doi.org/10.1007/s10869-009-9125-1

[176] Howard, M. C. (2018). Op cit

[177] Detert, J. R. (2018). Cultivating Everyday Courage *Harvard Business Review*, 1–10.

[178] Howard, M. C., & Cogswell, J. E. (2018). The left side of courage: Three exploratory studies on the antecedents of social courage. *The Journal of Positive Psychology*, 1–17. http://doi.org/10.1080/17439760.2018.1426780

Appendices

Appendices

Appendix A: Additional Brain Information
Appendix B: Bibliography
Appendix C: Other Useful Items

Appendix A: Additional Brain Information

In this appendix, we introduce some more information about the brain which has relevance to the topics covered in the book, and/or expands upon the information that was in *UYBFAC*. We have organized the new information into the same structure as *UYBFAC*. All of the new information applies to section B of *UYBFAC*.

Part 2a: Five Brain Principles

In Brain Principle # 2 we covered the two modes of the brain – the conscious and the nonconscious mode. We also talked about the amount of information that the brain processes per second, and the amount that is handled by each of these two modes of the brain: 11 million bits of information per second in total, but only 40 handled by the conscious mode.

We have been asked a couple of questions – what does a "bit" mean, and can we put the numbers in perspective? To start with a "bit" is a piece of terminology taken from the computer science field and it is short for "binary digit." It is the smallest piece of information that can be represented in a computer – either as a "0" or as a "1." To put this in perspective, most characters that you see on this page are represented by 8 bits. So, as a rule of thumb, one character = 8 bits. There are additional bits used to determine the color of the character and whether, for example, it is regular or italic, bold or normal and so on.

We had suggested that the number 40 bits per second could, based upon different researchers, be as low as 15 or as high as 100. In his book, Levitin [179] suggests that the conscious brain processes 120 bits per second. By way of illustration, he cites that normal speech is delivered at 60 bits per second.

Section B – Part 2c: Five Driving Forces

Under Participation we included a facet (# 14) for self-respect and self-esteem and reported upon the impact of low self-esteem. Since then, we have discovered that the topic of self-esteem is the focus of much debate in the research literature. We thought it would be a failure on our part if we did not include some of the discussion about this debate.

For many decades, it has been assumed and taught that an increase in self-esteem is associated with an improvement in lots of other wonderful attributes. Let's call this the self-esteem movement. To this day, there are many members of the movement and proponents of its approach; the two of us have been part of that wave. There is much research, however, that indicates there is no such correlation between self-esteem and various consequences or influences it may have. Tasha Euric in her book *Insight*, [180] describes one of the earlier reports [181] where this correlation was challenged:

> " … *the associations between self-esteem and its expected consequences are mixed, insignificant, or absent.*"

Roy Baumeister, at Florida State University, is a well-known and respected researcher; he and his colleagues decided to do a multi-decade review of the research. Initially a supporter of the self-esteem movement, he became disenchanted over time. Together, [182] they severely rain on the parade of the self-esteem movement. It is difficult to summarize the comments that they make; their summary is nearly a page long but, given the apparent widely accepted view of the importance of self-esteem we thought it was worth including in its entirety. We underlined certain sections for emphasis:

> "Appraisal of the effects of self-esteem is complicated by several factors. Because many people with high self-esteem exaggerate their successes and good traits, we emphasize objective measures of outcomes. High self-esteem is also a heterogeneous category, encompassing people who frankly accept their good qualities along with narcissistic, defensive, and conceited individuals."

> The modest correlations between self-esteem and school performance do not indicate that high self-esteem leads to good performance. Instead, high self-esteem is partly the result of good school performance. _Efforts to boost the self-esteem of pupils have not been shown to improve academic performance and may sometimes be counterproductive._

> Job performance in adults is sometimes related to self-esteem, although the correlations vary widely, and the direction of causality has not been established. Occupational success may boost self-esteem rather than the reverse. Alternatively, self-esteem may be helpful only in some job contexts. _Laboratory studies have generally failed to find that self-esteem causes good task performance, with the important exception that high self-esteem facilitates persistence after failure._

> People high in self-esteem claim to be more likable and attractive, to have better relationships, and to make better impressions on others than people with low self-esteem, but objective measures disconfirm most of these beliefs. Narcissists are charming at first but tend to alienate others eventually. _Self-esteem has not been shown to predict the quality or duration of relationships._

> High self-esteem makes people more willing to speak up in groups and to criticize the group's approach. Leadership does not stem directly from self-esteem, but self-esteem may have indirect effects. _Relative to people with low self-esteem, those with high self-esteem show stronger in-group favoritism, which may increase prejudice and discrimination._

> Neither high nor low self-esteem is a direct cause of violence. Narcissism leads to increased aggression in retaliation for wounded pride. Low self-esteem may contribute to externalizing behavior and delinquency, although some studies have found that there are no effects or that the effect of self-esteem vanishes when other variables are controlled. _The highest and lowest rates of cheating and bullying are found in different subcategories of high self-esteem._

> _Self-esteem has a strong relation to happiness._ Although the research has not clearly established causation, we are persuaded that high self-esteem does lead to greater happiness. Low self-esteem is more likely than high to lead to depression under some circumstances. Some studies support the buffer hypothesis, which is that high self-esteem mitigates the effects of stress, but other studies come to the opposite conclusion, indicating that the negative effects of low self-esteem are mainly felt in good times. Still others find that high self-esteem leads to happier outcomes regardless of stress or other circumstances.

> High self-esteem does not prevent children from smoking, drinking, taking drugs, or engaging in early sex. If anything, high self-esteem fosters experimentation, which may increase early sexual activity or drinking, but in general effects of self-esteem are negligible. _One important exception is that high self-esteem reduces the chances of bulimia in females._

> Overall, the benefits of high self-esteem fall into two categories: enhanced initiative and pleasant feelings. We have not found evidence that boosting self-esteem (by therapeutic interventions or

school programs) causes benefits. <u>Our findings do not support continued widespread efforts to boost self-esteem in the hope that it will by itself foster improved outcomes.</u>

In view of the heterogeneity of high self-esteem, indiscriminate praise might just as easily promote narcissism, with its less-desirable consequences. Instead, we recommend using praise to boost self-esteem as a reward for socially desirable behavior and self-improvement."

Wow. Who would have thought? During the past three decades or so, the extant thought was that an increase in self-esteem would result in a similar positive increase in a whole set of other things. But, apparently, that is not necessarily the case.

Part of the issue is that there is only a slight difference between high self-esteem and self-absorption. Eurich again:

" … research has shown that in general, there is an inverse relationship between how special we feel and how self-aware we are."

and

" … an intense self-focus not only obscures our vision of those around us; it distorts our ability to see ourselves for what we really are."

Although we are convinced that this debate about the value of self-esteem will rage for some time to come, we could probably add the advantages of high self-esteem to our ongoing list of myths!

Section B – Part 3: Facts and Myths.

In *UYBFAC* we included a chapter on "Facts and Myths" about the brain. The bad news is that some of the myths are as strong as ever. One of these persistent myths is that there are major differences between the Female and Male brains.

We wrote our summary of that myth as follows:

"There are some minor differences, but in general, female and male brains are very similar. The myth of major gender differences in the brain is not supported by the research."

Unfortunately, this myth is proving very difficult to stop, in spite of a plethora [n] of books having been written to disprove it. We thought we would add our voice to an ever-growing number that are attempting to counteract this myth.

In the "new to us" realm we recently read Fine's 2010 book, *Delusions of Gender* [183], and Saini's 2017 book, *Inferior* [184] and in the "new to the world" realm, we read Rippon's 2019 book, *The Gendered Brain* [185]. All of them have similar messages, which loudly refute the myth, and in all three cases, they call for a re- interpretation of the existing data. In addition, we read a paper entitled *"Eight Things You Need to Know About Sex, Gender, Brains, and Behavior"* by Fine, Joel and Rippon [186] which gives some background on what is happening in this aspect of the field, why the great debate still

---

[n] We are curious … how many does there have to be to qualify as a plethora?

rages, and how to read and interpret papers that are being published. Hot stuff, indeed! In summary, from all these works, we can deduce that there are numerous reasons for the persistence of the myth:

> It's been around for a long, long time – and hence has a lot of momentum
> It has been supported by many scientists, philosophers, etc., together with <u>men</u> of note
> Much of the 18th, 19th and early 20th century "research" was anecdotal, opinion-based or used to justify a position
> Some of the more recent research has been based upon flimsy or unreliable data, small sample sets and has, in many instances, been wrongly interpreted
> Much of the research has set out to 'prove' a previously held opinion – and, as expected in such cases, it does.
> There are many, many relatively readable books that have made a plausible case about the major differences between the male and female brains e.g. John Gray [(187)], Louanne Brizendine [(188,189)], and Simon-Baron-Cohen [(190)] - each with catchy titles that emphasize the difference.
> Availability bias – the more people hear about an issue or position, the more they believe it to be true – and there's lots of newspaper, magazine and podcast articles that, right or wrong, make the case for the difference
> Differences 'sell' better than similarities

The publications from Fine, Joel, Rippon and Saini, and probably many more, bring to the fore many good, objective, scientifically based arguments to indicate that the myth is wrong.

On the other hand, there are still many current articles that suggest, with "scientific proof," that there are indeed differences between the male and female brains. For example, Voskuhl and Klein's [(191)] April 2019 correspondence to Nature states:

"We also disagree that sex differences in behaviour are due to cultural effects on newborns, not to biological effects. In our view, these are not mutually exclusive. Sex disparities occur in animal models that are not subject to cultural bias. The brain, like many organs, shows differences attributable to sex, both during health and during disease. Two-thirds of people with Alzheimer's disease are women; twice as many men as women have Parkinson's disease. And multiple sclerosis affects three times more women than men, although men with the condition develop neurological disability more quickly."

The debate seems to focus around three areas:

> Are there major differences in the structure of the male and female brains?
> Are there major differences in the behavior of males and females?
> Are the two linked?

We would propose to add an additional question. Does it make a difference when it comes to Using Your Brain at Work? In a leadership role?

As an example of the debate, let's take a look at the corpus callosum. We are willing to take a bet that that is not a phrase you have said to yourself recently ☺. The corpus callosum is an important bundle of fibers that connects the two halves of the brain.

In 1982, a couple of researchers, an anthropologist and a cell biologist, published what became a pivotal paper describing the difference in size between the corpus callosum of males and females. A summary of the data from that paper was used by many of us, including Phil, in the late 80's and since, to explain some of the differences in behavior between males and females.

Later reviewers, however, began to criticize the research. The main criticisms are a) that it was a very small sample size (fourteen males and five females) and b) that the differences in size that were found were statistically insignificant. [o]

Some researchers e.g. Holloway [192] describe the on-going, and sometimes vitriolic, arguments while others continue to provide research which supports one side or the other. On the pro-difference side, for example we have Ardekani et al. [193] who tell us:

> *"These results provide strong additional evidence that the CCA is larger in females after correcting for the confounding effect of brain size."*

and on the no-difference side we have Luders et al. [194] who state that the differences are to do with the size of the brain in question:

> *"That is, the larger the discrepancy in brain size between men and women, the more pronounced the sex difference in callosal thickness, with hardly any callosal differences remaining between brain-size matched men and women. Altogether, these findings suggest that individual differences in brain size account for apparent sex differences in the anatomy of the corpus callosum."*

Forgetting size for the moment, and turning to behavior, Zhang et al. [195] suggest that there is a brain-based behavioral difference between males and females:

> *"Results suggest that males may primarily depend on non-social cognitive ability to make a risky decision in a social interaction, while females will use both social and non-social abilities."*

So, which is it? Is there a major difference between the female and male brain? Sorry to say, but it's not clear. This debate has been raging for some time – and looks like it will continue as furious as ever for the foreseeable future. Some people say that it is a purely scientific debate, and others are declaring that it has become an ideological and/or political/feminist debate. [196]

At this stage of the 'state of the art' of brain science, our sense is that the differences we see in male and female behavior probably has more to do with psychological, social and cultural influences than with major differences in brain structure. We could be wrong. Regardless, for the time being, we are keeping with our statement that there is no major difference between the two genders in terms of the brain.

---

[o] Interestingly, by the time the "information" had reached Phil, the magnitude of the difference in the size of the corpus callosum was quoted as 33% larger in women.

There is, however, another movement happening that may make the debate become moot. (Let's hope so.) The movement is best described by Hyde et al. [197] in their abstract: [p]

"The view that humans comprise only two types of beings, women and men, a framework that is sometimes referred to as the "gender binary," played a profound role in shaping the history of psychological science. In recent years, serious challenges to the gender binary have arisen from both academic research and social activism. This review describes 5 sets of empirical findings, spanning multiple disciplines, that fundamentally undermine the gender binary. These sources of evidence include:

- *neuroscience findings that refute sexual dimorphism of the human brain;*
- *behavioral neuroendocrinology findings that challenge the notion of genetically fixed, nonoverlapping, sexually dimorphic hormonal systems;*
- *psychological findings that highlight the similarities between men and women;*
- *psychological research on transgender and nonbinary individuals' identities and experiences;*
- *developmental research suggesting that the tendency to view gender/sex as a meaningful, binary category is culturally determined and malleable."*

Our guess is that the myth will continue but will become less and less relevant as times and opinions progress; unfortunately, it may take several more decades or longer before that happens.

Part 4: Care and Feeding of the Brain

In this chapter, we included a variety of overviews of some of the areas that are currently being researched and that have an impact on our overall brain health. Since the publication of *UYBFAC*, we have received a number of questions and suggestions about other topic areas. So, we offer new information about some and have added new topic areas:

a. The brain and the gut.

This is not so much about new information, but a reinforcement of the importance of fairly recent learnings about the interaction between the gut and the brain. In their 2018 article Martin et al. [198] report:

"The past decade has seen a paradigm shift in our understanding of the brain-gut axis. The exponential growth of evidence detailing the bi-directional interactions between the gut-microbiome and the brain supports a comprehensive model that integrates the central nervous, gastrointestinal and immune systems with this newly discovered organ. Data from preclinical and clinical studies have shown remarkable potential for novel treatment targets not only in functional gastrointestinal disorders but in a wide range of psychiatric and neurological disorders, including Parkinson's disease, autism spectrum disorders, anxiety, and depression, among many others."

There are many more such articles being published. Watch this space!

---

[p] The decision to show these as bullet points is ours for the sake of clarity; in the original they were in one sentence.

c. The brain and sleep.

While we did comment about the impact of sleep (or lack of it) on the brain, we didn't include any reference to sleep apps or wearable devices, of which there are many. We don't propose to give a rigorous analysis of the pros and cons of each – this would become a technical review book if we did. Our purpose is simply to bring these apps and devices to your attention. The good part of these apps is that they can monitor your sleep, via a variety of different mechanisms and report to you, the following morning, the amount and quality of your sleep. The last time we looked, the downside of most of these apps is they cannot tell you why you had the quality of sleep that you had, and what you can do about it. But, we figure, being made aware of it is a good first step.

What about the research concerning these apps and devices, and their usefulness? The results are somewhat mixed and vary widely between not accurate and hence not useful, to pretty good - and all of this with a high dose of caution from the American Academy of Sleep Medicine. [q]

As a caveat, we have to add here that the combination of the rapid changes in the technology in smartphones that can be leveraged for these types of apps, together with the time it takes to execute these studies and get them published, could mean that older studies may be irrelevant. For this reason, we have not included any studies prior to 2015. Here's some examples, however, of the results of some more recent studies:

Bhat et al. (2015): [199]

> *"Our study shows that the absolute parameters and sleep staging reported by the Sleep Time app (Azumio, Inc.) for iPhones correlate poorly with PSG."* [r]

Shin et al. (2017): [200]

> *"We found evidence to support the use of mobile phone interventions to address sleep disorders and to improve sleep quality."*

Khosla et al. for the American Academy of Sleep Medicine Board of Directors: (2018) [201]

> *"Given the lack of validation and United States Food and Drug Administration (FDA) clearance, CSTs ([s]) cannot be utilized for the diagnosis and/or treatment of sleep disorders at this time. However, CSTs may be utilized to enhance the patient-clinician interaction when presented in the context of an appropriate clinical evaluation. The ubiquitous nature of CSTs may further sleep research and practice. However, future validation, access to raw data and algorithms, and FDA oversight are needed."*

---

[q] "The American Academy of Sleep Medicine (AASM) is the leading clinical professional society dedicated to promotion of sleep health" – from their 2018 position paper on "Consumer Sleep Technologies."
[r] PSG = Polysomnography – the gold standard for measuring sleep quantity and quality
[s] CST = Consumer Sleep Technologies

Choi et al. (2018): [202]

> *"The findings suggest that few apps meet prespecified criteria for quality, content, and functionality for sleep self-management. Despite the rapid evolution of sleep self-management apps, lack of validation studies is a significant concern that limits the clinical value of these apps."* [t]

Conclusion? Many of the studies say that the use of them is promising, but most of the measurement activities (e.g. noise and movement) and associated algorithms have not been validated scientifically and there is little or no clinical oversight. Some studies suggest that the actual act of having a smartphone and/or other such device where you are sleeping could have detrimental effects. We suggest that, given that sleep is such an important factor for a healthy brain, anything that might bring awareness about the quality and quantity of your sleep is probably a good thing – just don't rely upon it as a source of diagnosis.

j. The Brain and Meditation/Mindfulness

In *UYBFAC* we reported on the beneficial results of meditation/mindfulness practices. A recent large (over 1200 regular meditators) study [203], however, also adds a voice of caution:

> *"However, a growing number of reports indicate that psychologically unpleasant experiences can occur in the context of meditation practice."*

and

> *"A total of 25.6%, reported having had particularly unpleasant meditation-related experiences, which they thought may have been caused by their meditation practice. Logistic regression models indicated that unpleasant meditation-related experiences were less likely to occur in female participants and religious participants. Participants with higher levels of repetitive negative thinking, those who only engaged in deconstructive types of meditation (e.g., vipassana/insight meditation), and those who had attended a meditation retreat at any point in their life were more likely to report unpleasant meditation-related experiences. The high prevalence of particularly unpleasant meditation-related experiences reported here points to the importance of expanding the scientific conception of meditation beyond that of a (mental) health-promoting and self-regulating technique."*

On a different tack, again in *UYBFAC* we didn't include any reference to meditation and mindfulness apps of which there are many. What were we thinking?! Once again, our purpose here is to draw your attention to the fact that they are available, often free or very inexpensive, and seem to have some added value for many people. You will need to research and find the one(s) that work for you.

There have been numerous recent studies with regard to the use and efficacy of mobile phone-based apps for mindfulness. In general, the studies say that while mobile apps are an effective method, they are not as good as face-to-face interventions for some people. The apps can work for children but, as with most things, have some limitations. Some example conclusions:

---

[t] This is a very readable paper for anyone who wants to start reading more

Tunney et al. (2017) [204]

"These results indicate that mindfulness delivered via technology can offer a rich experience."

Economides et al. (2018) [205]

"These results suggest that brief mindfulness training has a beneficial impact on several aspects of psychosocial well-being and that smartphone apps are an effective delivery medium for mindfulness training."

Mrazek et al. (2018): [206]

"Smartphone applications and web-based platforms can offer potential advantages over traditional face-to-face formats through enhanced accessibility, standardization, personalization, and efficacy of mindfulness training."

"A growing body of research has documented that a digital approach to teaching mindfulness can improve measures of attention, stress, depression, and anxiety."

"Effective digital mindfulness instruction must overcome a variety of challenges, including the possibility of low engagement, shallow learning, and unaddressed obstacles or frustrations."

Flett et al. (2018): [207]

"Thus, brief mobile mindfulness meditation practice can improve some aspects of negative mental health in the short term and may strengthen positive mental health when used regularly. Further research is required to examine the long-term effects of these apps."

Bottom line? Do some research, try some out and find out which ones work best for you.

p. The Brain and Art

In *UYBFAC*, we did include a section on the brain and music, but we didn't include anything on the brain and art, clearly an oversight. Let's correct that omission right now. At least partially. To be specific, this section will focus on the brain and the visual arts … or neuro-aesthetics … or visual aesthetic experiences. We apologize to the practitioners of all of the other forms of art that we are omitting.

And immediately, we are plunged into the morass of a huge topic, and we will only be able to scrape the surface here. Once again, this is a topic that has attracted much attention over the past two or three decades, both from both artists and neuroscientists. While we were wading through it all it became clear that the research divides it into three sub-topics: Looking at art, Producing art and Art as therapy. For the purposes of this section, we decided to focus on the first of these, although clearly the other two will have some impact on the brain.

The first thing we want to point out is that different brain circuitry is coopted for different types of 'art.' For example, Markey et al. [208] report that the brain responds differently to a painting, a picture of a painting and the actual scene itself.

We mentioned Robert Solso [209] in the introduction to this book. He captured our writing style. He also offers some tentative conclusions that different parts of the brain become engaged with different styles of paintings. He suggests that abstract art:

> " … engages higher-order parts of the cortex (such as the frontal regions) for processing that supplies greater imagination and interpretation from the observer."

whereas

> "Realistic art, on the other hand, seems to engage parts of the brain that seek associations in one's memory systems, which may be distributed widely."

Some additional good news is that he also added a model on how we might look at art and how it impacts us from a brain perspective.

Sensory (perceptual) characteristics	What are the physical attributes of the piece?	Visual, Gestalt Color
	… and what other senses get triggered?	Auditory, Tactile, Gustatory, Olfactory
Psychological characteristics:	What are the psychological aspects of the art?	Tension/harmony, Emotional, Personal meaning
Schema-story relationships:	How do I understand this piece through my own point of view?	Theme, Story, History, Intellectual/cognitive
"Level 3" comprehension of art:	Does this piece touch me in some profound way?	One's own highly personal, if not emotional, reaction to art.

He points out that in each of these levels, we have a primary and a secondary response.

Finally, a quick note on negative responses to art. Not all art resonates with everyone; in many cases a specific item of art causes significant negative emotional response. Silvia and Brown [210] describe two differences in our negative reactions to art:

> " … anger was associated with appraising a picture as incongruent with one's values and as intentionally offensive, and disgust was associated with appraising a picture as incongruent with one's values and as unpleasant."

So, the big difference? If it was intentionally offensive, we get angry. If it was just unpleasant, we feel disgusted.

And talking of raised emotions, what about the contextual description that is associated with art? Does it make a difference? We know for example, that if we place a higher price tag on a bottle of wine then the drinker has a perception that it tastes better. Does that contextual impact have a carry-over in the art world? It turns out that it doesn't. [211] A brief description or a detailed description, makes no difference to the viewers aesthetic experience. But the content of the art does have an impact on our heart rate, heart rate variability, skin conductance, and skin conductance variability.

q. The Brain and Pets

Once again, we didn't include anything on this topic. As soon as we start talking of pets, however, the immediate question comes up ... well, which pets? As of 2012, 62% of American households have at least one pet. [212] Since dogs and cats are very commonplace, and are the most studied, (although there are 10 times as many articles about dogs as there are about cats) we decided to limit our research to those two.

It was also almost impossible to enter into this research without a bias, based on commonly understood mores. These mores are statements or questions such as "Of course dogs bring happiness into your life", "All kids should grow up with a cat and/or a dog", and "Are you a cat person or a dog person?"

It doesn't take a lot of research, however, to realize that few, if any, of these statements hold up very well under the harsh light of scientific based studies. Does owning a dog improve mental well-being? It turns out that there are almost as many studies that show that having a dog as a pet reduces your mental well-being, as there are studies that conclude it increases your mental well-being. What about owning a cat? Is that better than owning a dog? Turns out that it depends on which study you look at! What about dogs in the workplace? Good idea or bad idea? How about the impact of dogs or cats in the bedroom? Is there an impact on the amount and quality of sleep?

Let's take a look at a few of the studies, looking at those "for", those "against" and those that are mixed or undecided. Once again, we decided to focus on recent studies. We'll start with the pros.

Pro pet ownership

Study 1, 2016, [213]

"Results indicate that pet owners were more satisfied with their lives than non-owners."

and

"Dog owners scored higher on all aspects of well-being compared with cat owners."

and

"Although there may not be many differences between those who own pets and those who do not, clearly owning a dog is associated with beneficial outcomes."

Study 2, 2017 [214]

"Owners reported deriving positive outcomes from dog walking, most notably, feelings of "happiness", but these were "contingent" on the perception that their dogs were enjoying the experience. Owner physical activity and social interaction were secondary bonuses but rarely motivating."

Study 3, 2018: [215]

> *"This literature review suggests that pet ownership can improve the quality of life in the elderly population through increased physical and mental health."*

Undecided about pet ownership

Study 2018 [216] – and a good example of why interpreting these studies is complex:

> *"Pet ownership was significantly associated with a higher likelihood of ever having had depression, with pet owners being 1.89 times more likely to have experienced depression."*

and

> *"The findings from this study could indicate a relationship between pet ownership and depression, but it is impossible to determine the directionality of that relationship. It is possible that owning a pet may put a person at an increased risk of developing depression, or individuals who are at risk, or who have already developed depression, may acquire a pet as a way of managing their depressive symptoms."*

Study 2018 [217]

> *"Dog owners ... fall asleep more easily than non-dog owners"*

but

> *"Associations with sleep were mixed, although dog owners had less trouble falling asleep than non-dog owners, with borderline statistical significance."*

Against pet-ownership

Now for the "cons." Herzog, 2017, [218] introduces a number of negative studies – and seems positively delighted to do so – so we use his introduction and a few from his list as an indicator:

> *"To provide a bit of balance to the abundance of overly rosy press reports on the healing power of pets, here are nine recent studies that found pets and therapy animals had little or no beneficial impact on human health and well-being."*

> *"Researchers at Purdue University conducted a year-long study of the impact of dog-walking. They assessed the effectiveness of e-mail reminders in motivating overweight and obese dog owners and non- owners to become more physically active and go for walks. The intervention worked; subjects that got the e-mails walked more than subjects in control groups who did not get the intervention. But, unfortunately, more dog walking did not translate into improved physical or mental health. Indeed, among the dog walkers, the number of "bad mental days" and "bad physical days" per month actually increased during the study. And dog-walking did not affect any of the health assessment measures."*

> *"Researchers from Mercer University investigated the impact of pet ownership and household income on life satisfaction among college students. They found having more money was related to increases in quality of life. Owning a pet, however, was not. In summarizing their findings, they wrote, "We found no evidence of a 'pet effect' as it relates to a general measure of satisfaction with life."*

"A research team headed by Dr. Carri Westgarth of the University of Liverpool examined whether owning or walking a dog reduced obesity and improved the fitness in 1,000 nine and ten year-old children. The researchers summarized their results clearly: "We found little evidence to support the idea that children who live with or walk with dogs are fitter or less likely to be obese than those who do not."

"In a 2016 article published in the journal Geriatrics, Nancy Needell and Nisha Mehta-Naik of the Weill Cornell Medical College analyzed all the published studies on the impact of pets on the incidence and severity of depression in elderly individuals. After carefully examining 11 studies, they concluded, "At present, there is insufficient evidence to back the claim in popular culture that pet ownership is helpful in preserving the mental health of older adults."

What about the impact of dogs in the workplace? Once again, mixed opinions well summarized by this statement from a 2016 article: [219]

"On the face of it, taking pets to work seems at best to be an idea guaranteed to polarize opinion. On the one hand, some people love dogs and cats, and will gain great satisfaction and peace of mind from having their pets close at hand or be able to interact with others' pets about the workplace. However, on the other hand, there are many people who simply loathe animals, or fear them, or are unable to go near them due to allergies. Having pets at work might work for some but might not work for others at all."

On a more light-hearted note, what type of dog or cat are you likely to select as a pet? Look at the conclusions of this study [220] – something we have all intuitively known.

"We show that in a significant proportion of human-pet pairs, sampled in pet beauty contests, the partners show much higher facial resemblances than can be expected by random pair formation."

Phil and his wife have a preference for boxers, and we are now trying to work out what that says about how they see themselves. ☺

So – positive or negative impact? We are inclined to think that whatever we write here, we will run against personal biases – assisted by confirmation bias run rampant.

r. The Brain and Martial Arts

The third topic area that some people have asked about in connection with the brain: If I do some form of martial arts, will it have a positive impact on my brain? The answer seems to be yes. Probably. Maybe. Let's look at some of the research studies; while recognizing that there is a wide range of martial arts, we focused our research on Tai Chi and Aikido as examples of non-violent martial arts.

Summing it up with regard to Tai Chi, a recent article [221] states the following:

"Tai chi's emphasis on rhythmic weight-shifting, symmetrical foot-stepping, controlled movements, and coordinated breathing can improve function and lower stress and anxiety levels"

and

"The martial arts' focus on meditation, relaxing, and breathing could decrease anxiety and depression"

Let's dig a little deeper. Here's an article [222] that suggests that Tai-Chi has a positive impact for "elders:"

> "The current study suggested the protective role of long-term Tai Chi exercise at slowing gray matter atrophy, improving the emotional stability and achieving successful aging for elders."

And, on a similar theme, Wu et al. [223] report:

> "Tai Chi as a mind-body exercise has positive effects on global cognitive and memory functions, and more consistent positive effects were found on memory function, especially verbal working memory."

Another study on the, albeit hesitatingly, positive side: [224]

> "These findings suggest that increased parasympathetic control of the heart and prefrontal activities may be associated with Tai Chi practice."

Wang et al. [225] basically say that it is too soon to tell if Tai Chi has a positive impact on the brain:

> "It is still premature to make any conclusive remarks on the effect of Tai Chi on psychosocial well-being."

A very recent study [226] looked at the differential impact of Tai-Chi and walking on a number of direct and peripheral cardiac measures e.g. blood pressure, pulse, heart rate etc. for people with hypertension. While clearly not studying neurological factors, what's good for the heart is probably good for the brain. However, they found no significant difference between the two exercise modes.

Finally, a recent article [227] that presents both a positive and neutral case, with respect to Tai-Chi:

> " ... the effects of Tai Chi on self-efficacy in various populations and found that Tai Chi appeared to have positive effects on self-efficacy in some populations. Fifteen research studies showed that Tai Chi had significant positive effects on self-efficacy, while 11 studies did not; only one study found a negative outcome at the follow-up. In addition, it is unclear which type, frequency, and duration of Tai Chi intervention most effectively enhanced self-efficacy."

What about Aikido? Szabolcs et al. [228] is a very recent paper that also claims to be a first:

> "These findings reveal relatively clearly for the very first time in the literature that aikido practice has acute, or immediate, psychological benefits akin to other martial arts and exercises."

Unfortunately for them, they are not the first in the literature. There have been a number of articles in the past decade or so, but certainly a lot less than Tai-Chi and they are much more difficult to find. There has been some focus on the use of Aikido with veterans, where the physical and social aspects of the art might have some appeal. But even then, they are exploratory without conclusive evidence of benefit to the brain.

So, what does all of that mean? There might be benefit to the brain with the practice of martial arts, but apparently not much more than the same amount of time spent on a brisk walk. If, however, learning a martial art is appealing in and of itself, there is probably some brain advantage – learning, per se, is good for the brain.

s. Anger and the Brain

There has been a lot of debate in the fields of therapy and psychology as to whether it is healthy to express anger or not. There is a lot of research to suggest that expressing anger compromises our health, indicating that it would be better not to be angry. Kitayama et al. [229], however, suggest that there may be another influence to consider. Since most of the research has been done in Western cultures – they found that in other cultures, for example the Japanese culture, expressing anger does not have the same deleterious effect. Their argument (and hypothesis) goes like this:

> " … in Asian cultural contexts, interdependence of the self is more strongly valued. The self is conceptualized as part of a hierarchically organized social group. In such settings, expression of anger is seen as socially disruptive and, as a consequence, there is a strong normative prohibition against it. An exception to the normative prohibition against anger expression comes from having power and dominance, such as being high in social status. Consistent with this view, Japanese adults with high (vs. low) social status expressed more anger and, further, this relationship was mediated by the amount of decision authority one had at work."

> "We suggest that if people express anger primarily when feeling dominant and privileged, the frequency of anger expression in this cultural context may serve as a reliable index of social privileges. We therefore hypothesized that anger expression would predict reduced biological health risk (BHR) in the Japanese cultural context. The sense of entitlement and power may likely relieve threats to the sense of the self as competent and in-control and, thus, the Japanese adults who display more anger may be likely to enjoy reduced BHR compared to those who show little anger."

So? What does this mean? Should you go around expressing your anger? Probably not. But this is a good example where we are continually discovering that a) we need to be careful about what we infer from even reasonably good science and b) that we need to be cautious when interpreting results across cultures.

[179] Levitin, D. J. (2015). The Organized Mind. Dutton.

[180] Eurich, T. (2017). Insight. Currency Books.

[181] California Task Force to Promote Self-Esteem and Personal & Social Responsibility (1966)

[182] Baumeister, R. F., Campbell, J. D., Krueger, J. I., & Vohs, K. D. (2003). Does high self-esteem cause better performance, interpersonal success, happiness, or healthier lifestyles? *Psychological Science in the Public Interest*, 1(1), 1–45.

[183] Fine, C. (2010). Delusions of Gender. W W Norton & Company.

[184] Saini, A. (2017). Inferior. Beacon Press.

[185] Rippon, G. (2019). The Gendered Brain. The Bodley Head.

[186] Fine, C., Joel, D., & Rippon, G. (2019). Eight Things You Need to Know About Sex, Gender, Brains, and Behavior:. *Scholar Feminist Online*, 15(2), 1–15.

[187] Gray, J. (1993). Men Are from Mars, Women Are from Venus:. Harper.

[188] Brizendine, L. (2006). The Female Brain (First). Broadway Books.

[189] Brizendine, L. (2010). The Male Brain: (First). Harmony.

[190] Baron-Cohen, S. (2003). The Essential Difference. Basic Books.

[191] Voskuhl, R., & Klein, S. (2019). Sex is a variable in the brain too. *Nature*, 568, 171.

[192] Holloway, R. L. (2016). In the trenches with the corpus callosum: Some redux of redux. *Journal of Neuroscience Research*, 95(1-2), 21–23. http://doi.org/10.1002/jnr.23818

[193] Ardekani, B. A., Figarsky, K., & Sidtis, J. J. (2013). Sexual Dimorphism in the Human Corpus Callosum: An MRI Study Using the OASIS Brain Database. *Cerebral Cortex*, 23(10), 2514–2520. http://doi.org/10.1093/cercor/bhs253

[194] Luders, E., Toga, A. W., & Thompson, P. M. (2014). Why size matters: Differences in brain volume account for apparent sex differences in callosal anatomy. *NeuroImage*, 84, 820–824. http://doi.org/10.1016/j.neuroimage.2013.09.040

[195] Zhang, M., Liu, T., Pelowski, M., Jia, H., & Yu, D. (2017). Social risky decision-making reveals gender differences in the TPJ: a hyperscanning study using functional near-infrared spectroscopy. *Brain Cognition*, 119, 54–63.

[196] Bryant, K., Grossi, G., & Kaiser, A. (2019). Feminist Interventions on the Sex/Gender Question in Neuroimaging Research. *Redboud Repository*, 1–26.

[197] Hyde, J. S., Bigler, R. S., Joel, D., Tate, C. C., & van Anders, S. M. (2019). The future of sex and gender in psychology: Five challenges to the gender binary. *American Psychologist*, 74(2), 171–193. http://doi.org/10.1037/amp0000307

[198] Martin, C. R., Osadchiy, V., Kalani, A., & Mayer, E. A. (2018). The Brain-Gut-Microbiome Axis. *Cellular and Molecular Gastroenterology and Hepatology*, 6(2), 133–148. http://doi.org/10.1016/j.jcmgh.2018.04.003

[199] Bhat, S., Ferraris, A., Gupta, D., Mozafarian, M., DeBari, V. A., Gushway-Henry, N., et al. (2015). Is There a Clinical Role For Smartphone Sleep Apps? Comparison of Sleep Cycle Detection by a Smartphone Application to Polysomnography. *Journal of Clinical Sleep Medicine*, 11(07), 709–715. http://doi.org/10.5664/jcsm.4840

[200] Shin, J. C., Kim, J., & Grigsby-Toussaint, D. (2017). Mobile Phone Interventions for Sleep Disorders and Sleep Quality: Systematic Review. *JMIR mHealth and uHealth*, 5(9), e131–18. http://doi.org/10.2196/mhealth.7244

[201] Khosla, S., Deak, M. C., Gault, D., Goldstein, C. A., Hwang, D., Kwon, Y., et al. (2018). Consumer Sleep Technology: An American Academy of Sleep Medicine Position Statement. *Journal of Clinical Sleep Medicine*, 14(05), 877–880. http://doi.org/10.5664/jcsm.7128

[202] Choi, Y. K., Demiris, G., Lin, S.-Y., Iribarren, S. J., Landis, C. A., Thompson, H. J., et al. (2018). Smartphone Applications to Support Sleep Self-Management: Review and Evaluation. *Journal of Clinical Sleep Medicine*, 14(10), 1783–1790. http://doi.org/10.5664/jcsm.7396

[203] Schlosser, M., Sparby, T., Vörös, S., Jones, R., & Marchant, N. L. (2019). Unpleasant meditation-related experiences in regular meditators: Prevalence, predictors, and conceptual considerations. *Plos One*, 14(5), e0216643–18. http://doi.org/10.1371/journal.pone.0216643

[204] Tunney, C., Cooney, P., Coyle, D., & O'Reilly, G. (2018). Comparing young people's experience of technology-delivered v.face-to-face mindfulness and relaxation: Two-armed qualitative focus group study. *British Journal of Psychiatry*, 210(4), 284–289. http://doi.org/10.1192/bjp.bp.115.172783

[205] Economides, M., Martman, J., Bell, M. J., & Sanderson, B. (2018). Improvements in Stress, Affect, and Irritability Following Brief Use of a Mindfulness-based Smartphone App: A Randomized Controlled Trial. *Mindfulness*, 9, 1584–1593. http://doi.org/10.1007/s12671-018-0905-4

[206] Mrazek, A. J., Mrazek, M. D., Cherolini, C. M., Cloughesy, J. N., Cynman, D. J., Gougis, L. J., et al. (2018). The Future of Mindfulness Training Is Digital, and The Future is Now. *Current Opinion in Psychology*, 1–17. http://doi.org/10.1016/j.copsyc.2018.11.012

[207] Flett, J. A. M., Hayne, H., Riordan, B. C., Thompson, L. M., & Conner, T. S. (2018). Mobile Mindfulness Meditation: a Randomised Controlled Trial of the Effect of Two Popular Apps on Mental Health. *Mindfulness*, 1–14. http://doi.org/10.1007/s12671-018-1050-9

[208] Markey, P. S., Jakesch, M., & Leder, H. (2019). Art looks different – Semantic and syntactic processing of paintings and associated neurophysiological brain responses. *Brain and Cognition*, 134, 58–66. http://doi.org/10.1016/j.bandc.2019.05.008

[209] Solso, R. E. (2003). The Psychology of Art and the Evolution of the Conscious Brain. MIT Press.

[210] Silvia, P. J., & Brown, E. M. (2007). Anger, disgust, and the negative aesthetic emotions: Expanding an appraisal model of aesthetic experience. *Psychology of Aesthetics, Creativity, and the Arts*, 1(2), 100–106.

[211] Krauss, L., Ott, C., Opwis, K., Meyer, A., & Gaab, J. (2019). Impact of contextualizing information on aesthetic experience and psychophysiological responses to art in a museum: A naturalistic randomized controlled trial. *Psychology of Aesthetics, Creativity, and the Arts*. Advance online publication. https://doi.org/10.1037/aca0000280

[212] Bao, K. J., & Schreer, G. (2016). Pets and Happiness: Examining the Association between Pet Ownership and Wellbeing. *Anthrozoös*, 29(2), 283–296. http://doi.org/10.1080/08927936.2016.1152721

[213] Bao, K. J., & Schreer, G. (2016). Op cit

[214] Westgarth, C., Christley, R., Marvin, G., & Perkins, E. (2017). I Walk My Dog Because It Makes Me Happy: A Qualitative Study to Understand Why Dogs Motivate Walking and Improved Health. *International Journal of Environmental Research and Public Health*, 14(8), 936–18. http://doi.org/10.3390/ijerph14080936

[215] Cook, M., & Busch, S. (2018). Health Benefits of Pet Ownership for Older Adults. *DePaul University Libraries*, 1–20.

[216] Mueller, M. K., Gee, N. R., & Bures, R. M. (2018). Human-animal interaction as a social determinant of health: descriptive findings from the health and retirement study, 1–7. http://doi.org/10.1186/s12889-018-5188-0

[217] Mein, G., & Grant, R. (2018). A cross-sectional exploratory analysis between pet ownership, sleep, exercise, health and neighbourhood perceptions: the Whitehall II cohort study, 1–9. http://doi.org/10.1186/s12877-018-0867-3

[218] Herzog, H. (2017). "Study Finds Dog-Walkers Have More Bad Mental Health Days!." *Animal Studies Repository*, 1–5.

[219] Linacre, S. (2016). Pets in the workplace: A shaggy dog story? *Human Resource Management International Digest*, 24(4), 17–19.

[220] Payne, C., & Jaffe, K. (2005). Self seeks like: Many humans choose their dog-pets following rules for assortive mating. *Journal of Ethology*, 23.

[221] Batcheller, L. J. (n.d.). Tai Chi May Improve Balance and Quality of Life. *Brain & Life*, 10.

[222] Liu, S., Li, L., Liu, Z., & Guo, X. (2019). Long-Term Tai Chi Experience Promotes Emotional Stability and Slows Gray Matter Atrophy for Elders. *Frontiers in Psychology*, 10, 1–11. http://doi.org/10.3389/fpsyg.2019.00091

[223] Wu, Y., Wang, Y., Burgess, E. O., & Wu, J. (2013). The effects of Tai Chi exercise on cognitive function in older adults: A meta-analysis. *Journal of Sport and Health Science*, 2(4), 193–203. http://doi.org/10.1016/j.jshs.2013.09.001

[224] Lu, Xi, Hui-Chan, C. H.-C., & Tsang, W. W.-N. (2016). Changes of heart rate variability and prefrontal oxygenation during Tai Chi practice versus arm ergometer cycling. *Journal of Physical Therapy Science*, 28, 3243–3248.

[225] Wang, W. C., Zhang, A. L., Rasmussen, B., Lin, L.-W., Dunning, T., Kang, S. W., et al. (2009). The Effect of Tai Chi on Psychosocial Well-being: A Systematic Review of Randomized Controlled Trials. *Journal of Acupuncture and Meridian Studies*, 2(3), 171–181. http://doi.org/10.1016/S2005-2901(09)60052-2

[226] Marsh, S. A., Winter, C. R., Paolone, V. J., & Headley, S. A. E. (2019). *Comparing the Changes in Blood Pressure After Acute Exposure to Tai Chi and Walking*. International Journal of Exercise Science (Vol. 12, pp. 77–87).

[227] Tong, Y., Chai, L., Lei, S., Liu, M., & Yang, L. (2018). Effects of Tai Chi on Self-Efficacy: A Systematic Review. *Evidence-Based Complementary and Alternative Medicine*, 2018(6), 1–21. http://doi.org/10.1155/2018/1701372

[228] Szabolcs, Z., Szabo, A., & Köteles, F. (2019). Acute Psychological Effects of Aikido Training. *Baltic Journal of Sport and Health Sciences*, 1(112), 42–49. http://doi.org/10.33607/bjshs.v112i1.778

[229] Kitayama, S., Park, J., Boylan, J. M., Miyamoto, Y., Levine, C. S., Markus, H. R., et al. (2015). Expression of Anger and Ill Health in Two Cultures. *Psychological Science*, 26(2), 211–220. http://doi.org/10.1177/0956797614561268

Appendix B: Bibliography

Lead Author	Title	Date	Category	Rating
Aamodt, S.	*Welcome to Your Brain*	2008	Brain	**
Ackerman, D.	*An Alchemy of Mind*	2005	Brain	**
Allen, D.	*Getting Things Done*	2002	Time Mgt	***
Amen, D. G.	*Magnificent Mind at Any Age*	2009	Brain	**
Amen, D. G.	*The Brain in Love*	2009	Brain	**
Anderson, R. J.	*Mastering Leadership*	2016	Leadership	***
Ariely, D.	*Perfectly Irrational*	2010	Brain	****
Badenoch, B.	*Being a Brain-Wise Therapist*	2008	Brain	**
Banaji, M. R.	*Blindspot*	2013	Brain	***
Baumeister, R. F.	*Losing Control*	1994	Brain	**
Baumeister, R. F.	*Willpower*	2011	Brain	****
Begley, S.	*Train your Mind, Change your Brain*	2008	Brain	***
Bennis, W. G.	*On Becoming a Leader*	2003	Leadership	*****
Benson, N. C.	*The Psychology Book*	2012	Psych	**
Benziger, I. K.	*The Art of Using Your Whole Brain*	1992	Brain	***
Benziger, K.	*Thriving in Mind*	2004	Brain	***
Berger, J.	*Invisible Influence*	2017	Brain	***
Bolton, R.	*Social Style/Management Style*	1984	Style	***
Borg, J.	*Persuasion*	2007	Brain	**
Brafman, O.	*Sway*	2008	Brain	***
Breuning, L. G.	*Meet Your Happy Chemicals*	2012	Brain	**
Bridges, W.	*Surviving Corporate Transition*	1988	Change	***
Bridges, W.	*Transitions*	2004	Change	****
Brizendine, L.	*The Female Brain*	2006	Brain	**
Brizendine, L.	*The Male Brain*	2011	Brain	**
Brooks, D.	*The Social Animal*	2011	Brain	****
Buettner, D.	*The Blue Zones of Happiness*	2017	Longevity	***
Buonomano, D.	*Brain Bugs*	2011	Brain	**
Burnett, D.	*Idiot Brain*	2017	Brain	***
Burton, R.	*On Being Certain*	2008	Brain	***
Burton, R.	*A Skeptics Guide to The Mind*	2013	Brain	**
Buzan, T.	*Mind Map Mastery*	2018	Tools	***
Cain, S.	*Quiet*	2013	Style	****
Caproni, P. J.	*The Practical Coach*	2000	Coach	***
Carter, R.	*Multiplicity*	2008	Brain	****

Chamorro-Premuzic, T.	Why Do So Many Incompetent Men Become Leaders?	2019	Leadership	***
Charan, R.	The Leadership Pipeline	2011	Leadership	***
Churchland, P. S.	Braintrust	2011	Brain	**
Churchland, P. S.	Touching a Nerve	2013	Brain	***
Cialdini, R. B.	Influence	2007	Brain	****
Cialdini, R. B.	Pre-Suasion:	2016	Brain	***
Collins, S.	Neuroscience for Learning and Development	2015	Brain	**
Cortman, C.	Your Mind: An Owner's Manual for a Better Life	2010	Brain	**
Cozolino, L. J.	The Neuroscience of Human Relationships	2007	Brain	***
Crenshaw, D.	The Myth of Multitasking	2008	Brain	***
Damasio, A.	Self Comes to Mind	2012	Brain	***
Damasio, A. R.	Descartes' Error	1998	Brain	***
Damasio, A. R.	The Feeling of What Happens	2000	Brain	***
Davidson, R. J.	The Emotional Life of Your Brain	2012	Brain	**
De Waal, F.	Are We Smart Enough to Know How Smart Animals Are?	2016	Brain	***
Dehaene, S.	Consciousness and the Brain	2014	Brain	**
DiSalvo, D.	What Makes your Brain Happy	2011	Brain	***
Doidge, N.	The Brain That Changes Itself	2007	Brain	***
Doidge, N.	The Brain's Way of Healing	2015	Brain	***
Duhigg, C.	The Power of Habit	2012	Brain	****
Eagleman, D.	The Brain	2015	Brain	***
Edelman, G. M.	A Universe of Consciousness	2001	Brain	**
Eurich, T.	Insight	2017	Brain	****
Ferdman, B. M.	Diversity at Work	2013	Diversity	***
Ferrucci, P.	What We May Be	2004	Style	***
Fields, R. D.	The Other Brain	2011	Brain	***
Fine, C.	Delusions of Gender	2010	Gender	***
Fine, C.	Testosterone Rex	2018	Gender	***
Finkelstein, S.	Why Smart Executives Fail	2004	Leadership	***
Fisher, H.	Anatomy of Love	1994	Brain	***
Fisher, H. E.	Why him? Why her?	2010	Brain	***
Flam, F.	The Score	2009	Brain	**
Fredrickson, B.	Positivity	2009	Brain	****
Gallwey, W. T.	The Inner Game of Tennis	1984	Brain	****
Gallwey, W. T.	The Inner Game of Work	2000	Brain	***

Gallwey, W. T.	The Inner Game of Stress	2009	Brain	***
Gardner, H	Leading Minds	1996	Brain	***
Gardner, H	Intelligence Reframed	2000	Brain	***
Gardner, H	Changing Minds	2006	Brain	***
Gardner, H	Multiple Intelligences	2006	Brain	***
Gazzaniga, M. S.	The Ethical Brain	2006	Brain	**
Gazzaniga, M. S.	Human	2009	Brain	**
Gediman, C. L.	Brainfit	2005	Brain	**
Gilbert, D. T.	Stumbling on Happiness	2006	Brain	****
Givens, D. B.	Love Signals	1984	Brain	**
Gladwell, M.	Blink	2005	Brain	****
Gladwell, M.	Outliers	2008	Brain	****
Gladwell, M.	Talking to Strangers	2019	Brain	***
Goldberg, E.	The New Executive Brain	2009	Brain	**
Goldstein, N. J.	Yes!	2007	Brain	***
Goleman, D.	Emotional intelligence	1995	Brain	***
Goleman, D.	Vital Lies, Simple Truths	1996	Brain	**
Goleman, D.	Primal Leadership	2004	Brain	***
Goleman, D.	Social Intelligence	2007	Brain	***
Gordon, Dr. E.	The Brain Revolution	2012	Brain	***
Gordon, E.	Integrative Neuroscience	2000	Brain	**
Goulston, M	Just Listen	2010	Style	**
Grawe, K.	Neuropsychotherapy	2007	Brain	**
Green, C. H.	The Trusted Advisor Fieldbook	2011	Coach	***
Greenfield, S.	Mind Change	2015	Brain	**
Greenspan, N. T.	The End of the Certain World	2005	General	***
Haidt, J.	The Happiness Hypothesis	2006	Brain	***
Hallowell, E. M.	Shine	2011	Brain	***
Hanna, H.	Stressaholic	2014	Brain	***
Hanson, R.	Buddha's brain	2009	Brain	**
Hanson, R.	Hardwiring Happiness	2013	Brain	***
Harari, Y. N.	Sapiens	2014	General	*****
Harari, Y. N.	Homo Deus	2018	General	*****
Harari, Y. N.	21 Lessons for the 21st Century	2019	General	***
Heath, C.	Made to Stick	2008	General	***
Heath, C.	Switch	2010	General	***
Hedges, K.	The Power of Presence	2012	Brain	***
Herrmann, N.	The Whole Brain Business Book	1996	Brain	**
Hesselbein, F.	Be, Know, Do	2004	Leadership	***

Hollender, J.	The Responsibility Revolution	2010	Leadership	***
Holmes, H.	Quirk	2011	Brain	***
Hood, B. M.	The Self Illusion	2012	Brain	***
Horstman, J.	The Scientific American: Day in the Life of Your Brain	2009	Brain	**
Howard, P. J.	The Owner's Manual for the Brain	2006	Brain	***
Hudson, F. M.	Life Launch	1995	General	***
Hudson, F. M.	The Adult Years	1999	General	***
Ibarra, H.	Working Identity	2003	Style	**
Iyengar, S.	The Art of Choosing	2011	Brain	***
Johansen, R.	Leaders Make the Future	2012	Leadership	****
Johansen, R.	The New Leadership Literacies	2017	Leadership	****
Kabat-Zinn, J.	Full Catastrophe Living	2013	Brain	***
Kahneman, D.	Thinking, Fast and Slow	2011	Brain	*****
Kaipa, P.	From Smart to Wise	2013	Leadership	***
Kaiser, R. B.	The Perils of Accentuating the Positive	2009	Style	***
Kofman, F.	Conscious Business	2006	Leadership	***
Lakoff, G.	Don't think of an elephant!	2006	Brain	**
Langer, E. J.	Mindfulness	1989	Brain	***
Langer, E. J.	Counterclockwise	2009	Brain	***
LeDoux, J.	Synaptic Self	2003	Brain	***
LeDoux, J. E.	The Emotional Brain	1998	Brain	***
Lehmiller, J. J.	Tell Me What You Want	2018	Brain	**
Lehrer, J.	Proust was a Neuroscientist	2008	Brain	***
Lehrer, J.	How we Decide	2009	Brain	***
Lehrer, J.	Imagine	2012	Brain	***
Lencioni, P	The 5 Dysfunctions of a Team	2002	Team	***
Lencioni, P	Overcoming the 5 Dysfunctions of a Team	2005	Team	***
Levitin, D. J.	The Organized Mind	2014	Brain	*****
Lieberman, D. Z.	The Molecule of More	2018	Brain	***
Lieberman, M. D.	Social	2014	Brain	****
Linden, D. J.	The Compass of Pleasure	2012	Brain	***
Livermore, D. A.	Cultural intelligence	2009	Leadership	***
Livermore, D. A.	The Cultural Intelligence Difference	2011	Leadership	***
Lyubomirsky, S.	The How of Happiness	2007	Brain	***
Maister, D. H.	The Trusted Advisor	2001	Coach	****
McGonigal, K.	The Willpower Instinct	2012	Brain	****
McKay, S.	Demystifying the Female Brain	2018	Brain	***

Medina, J.	Brain Rules for Baby	2011	Brain	****
Merrill, D. W.	Personal Styles and Effective Performance	1999	Style	***
Millman, D.	Way of the Peaceful Warrior	2006	Self-help	****
Minto, B.	The Pyramid Principle	2002	Leadership	****
Mlodinow, L.	Subliminal	2012	Brain	***
Nagoski, E.	Come as you are	2015	Brain	***
Nanus, B.	Visionary Leadership	1992	Leadership	****
Nataraja, S.	The Blissful Brain	2009	Brain	***
Nisbett, R. E.	The Geography of Thought	2003	Brain	***
Nørretranders, T.	The User Illusion	1999	Brain	**
Nørretranders, T.	The Generous Man	2005	Brain	**
Paul, B.	Neuropsychology for Coaches	2012	Brain	**
Pearson, C.	The Transforming Leader	2012	Leadership	***
Peters, T.	Neuroleadership	2012	Brain	**
Pfeffer, J.	What Were They Thinking?	2007	Leadership	***
Pfeffer, J.	Leadership BS	2015	Leadership	***
Pink, D. H.	A Whole New World	2006	Brain	***
Pink, D. H.	Drive	2009	Brain	***
Pink, D. H.	To Sell Is Human	2012	Brain	***
Pink, D. H.	When	2018	Brain	***
Pinker, S.	How the Mind Works	1997	Brain	***
Pinker, S.	The Stuff of Thought	2008	Brain	***
Pinker, S.	Enlightenment Now	2018	General	****
Ratey, J. J.	A User's Guide to the Brain	2002	Brain	***
Ratey, J. J	Spark	2008	Brain	***
Restak, R., M. D.	The Secret Life of the Brain	2001	Brain	**
Review, H. B	Leadership Presence	2018	Leadership	***
Rieger, T.	Breaking the Fear Barrier	2011	Leadership	***
Rippon, G.	The Gendered Brain	2019	Gender	****
Rippon, G.	Gender and Our Brains	2019	Gender	****
Rock, D.	Quiet Leadership	2007	Brain	***
Rock, D.	Your Brain at Work	2009	Brain	***
Saini, A.	Inferior	2018	Gender	***
Sapolsky, R. M.	The Trouble with Testosterone	1998	Brain	***
Sapolsky, R. M.	A Primate's Memoir	2002	Brain	***
Sapolsky, R. M.	Why Zebras Don't Get Ulcers	2004	Brain	***
Satel, S. L.	Brainwashed	2013	Brain	**

Scarlett, H.	*Neuroscience for Organizational Change*	2016	Brain	***
Schutz, W.	*The Human Element*	1994	Self-Help	***
Schwartz, J.	*Brain Lock*	1997	Brain	***
Schwartz, J.	*You Are Not Your Brain*	2011	Brain	***
Schwartz, J. M.	*The Mind and the Brain*	2003	Brain	***
Seligman, M. E.	*Learned Optimism*	2006	Brain	***
Seligman, M. E.	*Flourish*	2012	Brain	***
Siegel, D. J	*The Mindful Therapist*	2010	Brain	**
Snyder, R. A.	*The Social Cognitive Neuroscience of Leading Organizational Change*	2016	Brain	**
Steinbrecher, S.	*Heart-Centered Leadership*	2003	Leadership	***
Sukel, K.	*Dirty Minds*	2012	Brain	**
Sukel, K.	*This Is Your Brain on Sex*	2013	Brain	**
Swaab, D. F.	*We are our Brains*	2014	Brain	***
Swart, T.	*Neuroscience for Leadership*	2015	Brain	***
Syed, M.	*Bounce*	2011	Brain	***
Tavris, C.	*Mistakes Were Made (But Not by Me)*	2007	Brain	****
Thaler, R. H.	*Nudge*	2009	Brain	****
Underhill, P.	*Why We Buy*	1999	Brain	***
Vaillant, G. E.	*Adaptation to Life*	1997	Longevity	***
Vaillant, G. E.	*Aging Well*	2002	Longevity	****
Van Der Kolk, B.	*The Body Keeps the Score*	2015	Brain	****
Van, M. L.	*The Brain Advantage*	2009	Brain	***
Vedantam, S.	*The Hidden Brain*	2009	Brain	**
Wilson, T. D.	*Strangers to Ourselves*	2004	Brain	***
Wilson, T. D.	*Redirect*	2011	Brain	***
Zak, P. J.	*The Moral Molecule*	2013	Brain	***
Zenger, J. H.	*The Extraordinary Leader*	2002	Leadership	****

Appendix C: Other Useful Items

1. Oxford Happiness Questionnaire
2. Worldviews
3. Connor Davidson Resilience Scale (Adapted)
4. Personal Descriptors
5. Workplace Social Courage Scale (Original 49 items)
6. Executive Presence

1. Oxford Happiness Questionnaire

INSTRUCTIONS. Below are a number of statements about happiness. Indicate how much you agree or disagree with each by entering a number alongside it according to the following code:

1=strongly disagree;   2=moderately disagree;   3=slightly disagree;
4=slightly agree;   5=moderately agree;   6=strongly agree.

You will need to read the statements carefully because some are phrased positively and others negatively. Don't take too long over individual questions; there are no 'right' or 'wrong' answers and no trick questions. The first answer that comes into your head is probably the right one for you. If you find some of the questions difficult, please give the answer that is true for you in general or for most of the time.

1. I don't feel particularly pleased with the way I am (_) …
2. I am intensely interested in other people …
3. I feel that life is very rewarding…
4. I have very warm feelings towards almost everyone…
5. I rarely wake up feeling rested (_) …
6. I am not particularly optimistic about the future (_) …
7. I find most things amusing …
8. I am always committed and involved …
9. Life is good …
10. I do not think that the world is a good place (_) …
11. I laugh a lot …
12. I am well satisfied about everything in my life …
13. I don't think I look attractive (_) …
14. There is a gap between what I would like to do and what I have done (_) …
15. I am very happy …
16. I find beauty in some things …
17. I always have a cheerful effect on others …
18. I can fit in everything I want to …
19. I feel that I am not especially in control of my life (_) …
20. I feel able to take anything on …
21. I feel fully mentally alert …
22. I often experience joy and elation …
23. I do not find it easy to make decisions (_) …
24. I do not have a particular sense of meaning and purpose in my life (_) …
25. I feel I have a great deal of energy …
26. I usually have a good influence on events …
27. I do not have fun with other people (_) …
28. I don't feel particularly healthy (_) …
29. I do not have particularly happy memories of the past (_) …

Notes. Items marked (_) should be scored in reverse.

The sum of the item scores is an overall measure of happiness, with high scores indicating greater happiness.

2. Worldviews

Koltko-Rivera's model which outlines a comprehensive set of dimensions for a describing or establishing worldview.

Group	Dimension	Option	Brief explanation Do you believe that ...
Human Nature	Moral Orientation	Good	... humanity is fundamentally good?
		Evil	... humanity is fundamentally evil?
	Mutability	Changeable	... human nature is changeable?
		Permanent	... human nature is fixed?
	Complexity	Complex	... human nature is complex?
		Simple	... human nature is simple?
Will	Agency	Volition	... human beings have free will?
		Determinism	... behavior is determined in one way or another?
	Determining Factors	Biological determinism	... genetic factors primarily determine behavior?
		Environmental determinism	... social factors primarily determine behavior?
	Intrapsychic	Rational–conscious	... behavior is rational and conscious?
		Irrational–unconscious	... behavior is irrational and nonconscious?
Cognition	Knowledge	Authority	... knowledge is given to us by authority figures?
		Tradition	... knowledge is given to us through tradition?
		Senses	... knowledge is obtained from our own experience?
		Rationality	... knowledge is obtained through rational processes?
		Science	... knowledge is obtained through scientific research?
		Intuition	... knowledge is obtained through a sixth sense?
		Divination	... knowledge is obtained through spirituality?
		Revelation	... knowledge is revealed by a greater entity?
		Nullity	... there are no reliable sources of knowledge?
	Consciousness	Ego primacy	... the highest state of human consciousness is within ourselves?
		Ego transcendence	... the highest state of human consciousness is driven by external factors such as peak experiences?
Behavior	Time Orientation	Past	... the most important facet of your life is the past – you highly value tradition and stability?

		Present	... the most important facet of your life is the here and now i.e. the present moment?
		Future	... the most important facet of your life is the future - you emphasize future rewards and planning?
	Activity Direction	Inward	... inward focused activities (e.g. affect, personality and spirituality) are most important.?
		Outward	... externally focused activities (e.g. achievement and possessions) are most important.?
	Activity Satisfaction	Movement	... your overall behavioral aim is improvement or change?
		Stasis	... your overall behavioral aim is enjoyment of the present?
	Moral Source	Human source	... that society is the source of moral guidance?
		Transcendent source	... moral guidance transcends human society?
	Moral Standard	Absolute morality	... morality is absolute?
		Relative morality	... morality depends on time, culture and situation?
	Moral Relevance	Relevant	... society's moral guidelines are relevant to you?
		Irrelevant	... society's moral guidelines are not relevant to you?
	Control Location	Action	... one's own actions determine life's outcomes?
		Personality	... personal charm or style determines life's outcomes?
		Luck	... personal magic determines life's outcomes?
		Chance	... chance (right place and time) determines life's outcomes?
		Fate	... personal destiny determines life's outcomes?
		Society	... favoritism or prejudice determine life's outcomes?
		Divinity	... a greater entity determines life's outcomes?
	Control Disposition	Positive	... the impacts of the above forces are generally positive?
		Negative	... the impacts of the above forces are generally negative?
		Neutral	... the impacts of the above forces are generally neutral?
	Action Efficacy	Direct	... personal or group impact is effective in creating change in the world?
		Thaumaturgic	... change in the world is created by external forces e.g. ritual, sacrament or prayer?

		Impotent	… there is no way to take effective action to create change in the world?
Interpersonal	Otherness [1]	Tolerable	… those that are different should be punished, changed or exterminated?
		Intolerable	… those that are different should be embraced?
	Relation to Authority	Linear	…it is best and most natural for society to have clearly defined and authoritative, top-down leadership?
		Lateral	…it is best and most natural for society to have an egalitarian and fluid leadership style?
	Relation to Group	Individualism	… the individual's agenda takes priority over the group's needs?
		Collectivism	… the group's agenda takes priority over the individual's needs?
	Relation to Humanity [1]	Superior	… the rights and prerogatives of one's own group have priority over other human groups?
		Egalitarian	… the rights and prerogatives of one's own group are essentially equivalent to other human groups?
		Inferior	… one's own group deserves less rights and prerogatives than other human groups?
	Relation to Biosphere	Anthropocentrism	… the rights and prerogatives of human beings have priority over non-human species?
		Vivicentrism	… humans and non-human species share equivalent rights?
	Sexuality	Procreation	… the primary purpose of interpersonal sexual activity is procreation?
		Pleasure	… the primary purpose of interpersonal sexual activity is pleasure?
		Relationship	… the primary purpose of interpersonal sexual activity is to strengthen emotional bonds between partners?
		Sacral	… the primary purpose of interpersonal sexual activity is to experience a spiritual dimension?
	Connection	Dependent	… people need to conform to the norms and pressures of the group to which they belong?
		Independent	… people may act independently from the norms and pressures of the group to which they belong?
		Interdependent	… people need to act in balance between group norms and pressures and individual needs?

	Interpersonal Justice	Just	… outcomes of interactions between families and small groups are inherently just?
		Unjust	… outcomes of interactions between families and small groups are inherently unjust?
		Random	… outcomes of interactions between families and small groups are unpredictable?
	Sociopolitical Justice	Just	… outcomes of interactions between society and large groups are inherently just?
		Unjust	… outcomes of interactions between society and large groups are inherently unjust?
		Random	… outcomes of interactions between society and large groups are unpredictable?
	Interaction	Competition	… by default, our group's orientation to other similar groups should be competitive?
		Cooperation	… by default, our group's orientation to other similar groups should be cooperative?
		Disengagement	… by default, our group's orientation to other similar groups should be to disengage?
	Correction	Rehabilitation	… society's attitude to people who have transgressed important social standards should be rehabilitative?
		Retribution	… society's attitude to people who have transgressed important social standards should be retribution?
Truth [1]	Scope	Universal	… certain truths are applicable always and everywhere?
		Relative	… truth varies in its accuracy and applicability by situation?
	Possession	Full	… our group has all that is important to have a to have a full understanding of the truth?
		Partial	… our group knows that there are important aspects of the truth that we do not yet have?
	Availability	Exclusive	… that only our group has the full truth?
		Inclusive	… other groups, that might be very different from us, have aspects of the truth too?
World and Life	Ontology	Spiritualism	… a spiritual approach is a legitimate explanation for metaphysical matters?
		Materialism	… nothing exists except demonstrable matter and energy?
	Cosmos	Random	… the universe and life came about by chance, without purpose?

		Planful	... the universe and life are the result of some transcendent plan or purpose?
	Unity	Many	... reality is a collection of many different and conflicting entities and concepts?
		One	... reality is a manifestation of a singular reality in which paradoxes and conflicts are transcended?
	Deity	Deism	... God is an external impersonal force?
		Theism	... God/s/Goddess/es exist as a personal being or beings?
		Agnosticism	... one either does not, or in principle, cannot know about the existence of a deity?
		Atheism	... there is/are no deity/deities?
	Nature-Consciousness	Nature conscious	... consciousness exits within nonhuman natural phenomena (e.g rocks, trees, earth)?
		Nature nonconscious	... nonhuman natural phenomena are not conscious?
	Humanity-Nature	Subjugation	... people are at the mercy of nature?
		Harmony	... people are a part of nature and should work with and within it?
		Mastery	... it is a human prerogative to subdue nature?
	World Justice	Just	... the world as a whole (except sociopolitics) functions in a just manner?
		Unjust	... the world as a whole is unjust?
		Random	... the world as a whole, functions randomly?
	Well-Being	Science–logic source	... our well-being comes from adherence to a set of empirically, scientifically observed principles?
		Transcendent source	... our well-being comes from adherence to a set of principles that derive from something beyond science?
	Explanation	Formism	... the cause behind events in the world can be explained by class or category membership?
		Mechanism	... the cause behind events in the world can be explained on the basis of cause-and-effect?
		Organicism	... the cause behind events in the world can be explained by organic processes?
		Contextualism	... the cause behind events in the world can be explained on the basis of context?
	Worth of Life	Optimism	... life is worthwhile; social and individual fulfillment are possible?

		Resignation	... life is inevitably headed for deterioration?
	Purpose of Life	Nihilism	... there is no purpose to life?
		Survival	... survival and reproduction exist for their own sake?
		Pleasure	... life is about pleasure and happiness?
		Belonging	... life is about belonging to one or more others?
		Recognition	... life is about being recognized by one or more others?
		Power	... life is about having power and control over others?
		Achievement	... life is about personal achievement?
		Self-actualization	... life is about personal self-actualization?
		Self-transcendence	... life is about being in service to one or more others?

One way of using this table to become more self-aware is to 'allocate' 100% to each of the dimensions and to distribute them across the defined options (or more if there are others that seem more meaningful to you).

3. Connor Davidson Resilience Scale (Adapted)

After each statement, circle the statement that best describes you:

1. I am able to adapt to change

Very much like me	Like me	Neutral	Unlike me	Very much unlike me
5	4	3	2	1

2. I develop close and secure relationships

Very much like me	Like me	Neutral	Unlike me	Very much unlike me
5	4	3	2	1

3. Sometimes fate, luck or God can help

Very much like me	Like me	Neutral	Unlike me	Very much unlike me
5	4	3	2	1

4. I know that I can deal with whatever comes along

Very much like me	Like me	Neutral	Unlike me	Very much unlike me
5	4	3	2	1

5. My past successes give me confidence for new challenges

Very much like me	Like me	Neutral	Unlike me	Very much unlike me
5	4	3	2	1

6. I can always see the humorous side of things

Very much like me	Like me	Neutral	Unlike me	Very much unlike me
5	4	3	2	1

7. I know that coping with stress strengthens me

Very much like me	Like me	Neutral	Unlike me	Very much unlike me
5	4	3	2	1

8. I tend to bounce back after illness or hardship

Very much like me	Like me	Neutral	Unlike me	Very much unlike me
5	4	3	2	1

9. I know that things always happen for a reason

Very much like me	Like me	Neutral	Unlike me	Very much unlike me
5	4	3	2	1

10. I give my best effort, no matter what

Very much like me	Like me	Neutral	Unlike me	Very much unlike me
5	4	3	2	1

11. I know that I can achieve my goals

Very much like me	Like me	Neutral	Unlike me	Very much unlike me
5	4	3	2	1

12. Even when things look hopeless, I never give up

Very much like me	Like me	Neutral	Unlike me	Very much unlike me
5	4	3	2	1

13. I always know where to turn to when I need help

Very much like me	Like me	Neutral	Unlike me	Very much unlike me
5	4	3	2	1

14. Under pressure, I can always focus and think clearly

Very much like me	Like me	Neutral	Unlike me	Very much unlike me
5	4	3	2	1

15. I prefer to take the lead in problem solving

Very much like me	Like me	Neutral	Unlike me	Very much unlike me
5	4	3	2	1

16. I am not easily discouraged by failure

Very much like me	Like me	Neutral	Unlike me	Very much unlike me
5	4	3	2	1

17. I think of myself as a strong person

Very much like me	Like me	Neutral	Unlike me	Very much unlike me
5	4	3	2	1

18. I am willing and able to make unpopular or difficult decisions

Very much like me	Like me	Neutral	Unlike me	Very much unlike me
5	4	3	2	1

19. I can handle unpleasant feelings

Very much like me	Like me	Neutral	Unlike me	Very much unlike me
5	4	3	2	1

20. If I have a hunch, I have to act on it

Very much like me	Like me	Neutral	Unlike me	Very much unlike me
5	4	3	2	1

21. I have a strong sense of purpose

Very much like me	Like me	Neutral	Unlike me	Very much unlike me
1	2	3	4	5

22. I am in control of my life

Very much like me	Like me	Neutral	Unlike me	Very much unlike me
5	4	3	2	1

23. I like challenges

Very much like me	Like me	Neutral	Unlike me	Very much unlike me
1	2	3	4	5

24. I work to attain my goals

Very much like me	Like me	Neutral	Unlike me	Very much unlike me
5	4	3	2	1

25. I take pride in my achievements

Very much like me	Like me	Neutral	Unlike me	Very much unlike me
1	2	3	4	5

4. Personal Descriptors

Place an X next to any words that you see show up in your work or your life in general.

Charm		
Charisma	Fascination	Pleasing others
Grace	Magnetism	Wow factor
Allurement	Delightfulness	Draw in others
Attraction	That special something	Put under a spell
Attractiveness	Star quality	Sweep off feet
Chemistry	Bewitch	Win Over Others
Desirability	Captivating	
Vulnerable/Sensitive		
Delicate	Responsive	Accessible
Pained	Susceptible	Defenseless
Tender	Tense	Exposed
Easily	Touchy	Wide open
Conscious	Tricky	Unsafe
Emotional	Unstable	Weak
Hypersensitive	Acute	Naked
Keen	Feeling	Thin skinned
Nervous	Knowing	Unguarded
Perceptive	Seeing	Unprotected
Precise	Understanding	Receptive
Easily Affected		
Danger/Violence		
Bad	Crazy	Forceful
Deadly	Cruel	Forcible
Fat	Fierce	Frantic
Nasty	Homicidal	Furious
Risky	Hysterical	Great
Serious	Murderous	Headstrong
Terrible	Passionate	Hotheaded
Threatening	Potent	Impassioned
Treacherous	Powerful	Maddened
Ugly	Savage	Maniacal
Unstable	Uncontrollable	Mighty
Dangersome	Vicious	Rough
Formidable	Agitated	Strong
Hot	Bloodthirsty	Unrestrained
Impending	Coercive	Urgent

Loaded	Distraught	Vehement
Malignant	Disturbed	Wild
Menacing	Enraged	Fiery
Brutal		

Beauty/Other worldly

Allure	Inappropriate	Rare
Artistry	Incompatible	Remarkable
Delicacy	Precocity	Significant
Elegance	Pizzazz	Singular
Grace	Sorcery	Mythological
Refinement	Spell	Magnetize
Exquisiteness	Witchery	Possess
Fairness	Symmetry	Send
Fascination	Demonic	Slay
Glamor	Mad	Loveliness
Psychic	Take	Polish
Supernatural powers	Transport	Exotic
Alien	Vamp	Incongruous
Gifted	Voodoo	Unusual
Regal	Wile	Conflicting
Odd	Special	Separate
Phenomenal	Strange	

Off-beat/Quirky

Amazing	Uncommon	Unfamiliar
Astonishing	Unconventional	Unparalleled
Awesome	Unexpected	Bizarre
Unique	Idiosyncratic	Curious
Weird	Odd	Exceptional
Abnormal	Off the wall	Extraordinary
Atypical	Peculiar	Incredible
Awe inspiring	Strange	Memorable
Brainy	Noteworthy	Gifted
Unusual	Talented	Wacky
Phenomenal	Rare	Inconceivable
Far out	Remarkable	Out of the ordinary
Freakish	Singular	Outstanding
Kinky	Special	Prodigious
Refreshing	Something else	Way out
Surprising		

Heart

Character	Sympathy	Bold

Feeling	Temperament	Courageous
Love	Tenderness	Daring
Nature	Understanding	Epic
Soul	Fearless	Affection
Mind	Noble	Benevolence
Valiant	Compassion	Spirit
Classic	Concern	Boldness
Inflated	Disposition	Bravery
Intrepid	Good hearted	Dauntless
Lion hearted	Nurturing	Fortitude
Stand tall	Watch over	Gallantry
Unafraid	Humanity	Pluck
Sensitivity	Purpose	Valorous
Sentiment	Heroic	

Power

Capability	Force	Prestige
Influencer	Intensity	Privilege
Skill	Potential	Strength
Talent	Dynamism	Weight
Aptitude	Might	Authorization
Bent	Muscle	Birthright
Competency	Potency	Command
Vigor	Domination	Effectiveness
Vim	Omnipotence	Endowment
Authority	Regency	Faculty
Clout	Superiority	Gift
Supremacy	Virtue	Jurisdiction
Sway	Energy	Leadership

Intelligence

Agility	Subtlety	Brightness
Brilliance	Understanding	Cleverness
Intellect	Wit	Discernment
Judgement	IQ	Mind
Perception	Acuity	Smarts
Quickness	Alertness	The Right Stuff
Savvy	Aptitude	What it takes
Skill	Brainpower	Sense

Sex

Hot	Charm	Animal
Inviting	Drawing power	Provocative
Glamor	Wanton	Racy

Sexiness		Coquette		Seductive	
It		Cruiser		Sensual	
Animal magnetism		Heartbreaker		Sensuous	
Confidence		Operator		Arousing	
Enchantment		Philanderer		Come hither	
Lure		Player		Flirtatious	
Magnetism		Seducer		Provoking	
Presence		Siren		Risque	
Pull		Tease		Slinky	
Seductiveness		Vixen		Spicy	
Sexual magnetism		Lustful		Steamy	
Star power		Passionate		Suggestive	
Erotic		Fierce		Titillating	
Intimate		Intense		Voluptuous	
Stormy		Allure		Reproductive	
Charisma					

5. Workplace Social Courage Scale (Original 49 items)

1	If I thought a question was dumb, I would still ask it if I didn't understand something at work
2	If I thought I may fail at a task at work, I would still volunteer to do it
3	Despite making my coworker angry, I would tell him/her what they need to hear
4	Although it would make me look bad, I would admit to my mistakes at work
5	Although my coworker may disagree, I would stand up to him/her when they are being unfair
6	If I was not confident in my abilities at work, I still wouldn't make excuses for my shortcomings
7	I would not tolerate when a coworker is rude to someone even if I make him/her upset
8	Although it may show how little I know about the topic, I would still volunteer for workshops and other learning opportunities at work
9	Even if my coworkers could think less of me, I'd lead a project with a chance of failure
10	If I failed at a task, I would still show to my coworkers that I tried my best
11	Despite looking bad in the end, I would take control of a risky project
12	Although it may damage our friendship, I would tell my superior when a coworker is doing something incorrectly
13	If a coworker asked me a question about my job that I didn't know, I would tell him/her that I am unsure
14	Although my coworker may become offended, I would suggest to him/her better ways to do things
15	Although it draws attention to my faults, I would own up to my mistakes when I mess up at work
16	Even if a coworker didn't ask for it, I would give him/her negative feedback
17	Although my ideas may sound dumb, I share them with my coworkers
18	Although my supervisor may get offended, I would question their orders if I disagreed with them
19	Even if it would make a bad impression on my coworkers, I would do what I should at work
20	I would give coworkers my opinion even if it is an unpopular one
21	Although it makes me seem like a "goodie–goodie" I would publicly acknowledge someone for doing a good job
22	Despite making my coworker angry, I would tell him/her my thoughts about him/her
23	Although it makes me look incompetent, I would tell my coworkers when I've made a mistake
24	I would tell a coworker my beliefs about our workplace although (s)he disagrees with my thoughts

25	Despite appearing dumb in front of an audience, I would volunteer to give a presentation at work
26	Despite upsetting my coworker, I would let him/her know when they've made me mad.
27	Although my coworkers may notice my mistakes and judge me for them, I would let them look over my work
28	I would do what I think is best for the organization, although my coworkers may make fun of me for it
29	Although my actions would be seen as impolite, I would criticize a coworker when (s)he has done a poor job
30	Although it makes my coworkers angry, I would do what is expected at work
31	Although it could make matters worse, I would try to "make up" with a coworker that does not like me
32	Despite my subordinate disliking me, I would tell him/her when they're doing something against company policy
33	Despite my coworkers thinking I'm an overachiever, I would perform to the best of my abilities at work
34	Even if my supervisor wouldn't like me as much, I would tell him/her when I think they are being unreasonable
35	Despite my coworkers thinking I'm just trying to look good I would do extra things at work
36	I would be stern to a coworker to get a point across, even if they'd think differently of me
37	Even if it may damage our relationship, I would confront a subordinate who had been disrupting their workgroup
38	I would let my coworkers know when I am concerned about something even if they'd think I am too negative
39	Although my coworkers would think I am a "suck-up" would do more than what my boss expects me to do
40	I would go against the norms of my coworkers if they were against company policy, even if they might think I'm weird for it
41	Despite making other employees angry, I would do everything that I could to make my customers happy
42	Although my coworker might become annoyed, I would correct him/her if they were being unsafe
43	Even if my subordinate would become unhappy with me, I would point out and correct them on a task s(he) did incorrectly
44	Although it may completely ruin our friendship, I would give a coworker an honest performance appraisal
45	I would do everything I can at work despite my coworkers getting mad at me for making them look bad
46	I would privately tell a coworker if I thought they were doing their job incorrectly, even if s(he) may get angry at me

47	I would follow company policy even if all my coworkers were breaking it and may think I'm different for not doing so
48	I would discreetly tell my coworker when (s)he has messed up even if they think it'd be rude to tell them
49	I would tell a subordinate when they're not meeting my standards even if s(he) may dislike me for it

6. Executive Presence

On a scale of 1 to 10, I see myself as always:

- ➤ … projecting mature self-confidence
- ➤ … making tough choices or decisions in a timely manner
- ➤ … remaining calm
- ➤ … leveraging humor to defuse difficult situations
- ➤ … interacting in a manner which fully engages the other stakeholders
- ➤ … instructing as and when needed
- ➤ … stimulating and motivating
- ➤ … remaining silent if appropriate
- ➤ … holding my own with other talented members of a team
- ➤ … holding my own with other strong-willed members of a team
- ➤ … demonstrating wisdom
- ➤ … showing compassion
- ➤ … making sense of a wide variety of situations
- ➤ … giving credit where credit was due
- ➤ … influencing others
- ➤ … focusing on others
- ➤ … having an even demeanor even in the face of other people's emotional responses
- ➤ … having outstanding listening skills
- ➤ … having an upright and positive posture
- ➤ … having an appropriate energy level
- ➤ … having an acute sense of knowing when to enter a conversation and when not to
- ➤ … taking control of difficult and unpredictable situations
- ➤ … having body language that shows comfort in all situations
- ➤ … having empathy
- ➤ … being appropriately succinct, focused and on-point
- ➤ … being unruffled, unflappable and unharried
- ➤ … being appropriately dressed and groomed
- ➤ … being organized
- ➤ … being unrushed and on time
- ➤ … being appropriately deferential
- ➤ … being sure-footed in my approach
- ➤ … being authentic
- ➤ … being appropriately open and vulnerable
- ➤ … having powerful speaking and presentation skills
- ➤ … being able to read an audience
- ➤ … knowing what I am talking about – or admitting otherwise

Index

Made in USA - Kendallville, IN
1185918_9781733830737
10.26.2020 1339